A Nation of Emigrants

A Nation of Emigrants

HOW MEXICO MANAGES
ITS MIGRATION

David Fitzgerald

UNIVERSITY OF CALIFORNIA PRESS
Berkeley   Los Angeles   London

University of California Press, one of the most distinguished university presses in the United States, enriches lives around the world by advancing scholarship in the humanities, social sciences, and natural sciences. Its activities are supported by the UC Press Foundation and by philanthropic contributions from individuals and institutions. For more information, visit www.ucpress.edu.

University of California Press
Berkeley and Los Angeles, California

University of California Press, Ltd.
London, England

Library of Congress Cataloging-in-Publication Data

Fitzgerald, David, 1972–
    A nation of emigrants : how Mexico manages its migration / David Fitzgerald.
        p.   cm.
    Includes bibliographical references and index.
    ISBN 978-0-520-25704-7 (cloth : alk. paper)—ISBN 978-0-520-25705-4 (pbk. : alk. paper)
    1. Return migration—Mexico.   2. Mexico—Emigration and immigration—Government policy.   3. Mexico—Emigration and immigration—Religious aspects—Catholic Church.   4. Mexicans—United States.   I. Title.

    JV7402.F57   2009
    325.72—dc22   2008013445

Manufactured in the United States of America

18   17   16   15   14   13   12   11   10   09
10   9   8   7   6   5   4   3   2   1

This book is printed on Natures Book, which contains 50% postconsumer waste and meets the minimum requirements of ANSI/NISO z39.48–1992 (R 1997) (*Permanence of Paper*).

For Gabriela

Contents

Illustrations

Acknowledgments

This study was generously supported by fellowships and grants from the Social Science Research Council, Fulbright/García-Robles program, UCLA Mellon Program in Latin American Sociology, UC Institute for Labor and Employment, UC MEXUS, UCLA Latin American Center, UC Office of the President, and UCLA Global Fellows Program. Earlier versions of chapters 2 and 4 were published as "Inside the Sending State: The Politics of Mexican Emigration Control" in *International Migration Review* 40(2): 259–93, 2006, and "Colonies of the Little Motherland: Membership, Space, and Time in Mexican Migrant Hometown Associations" in *Comparative Studies in Society and History* 50(1), 2008.

Of the many colleagues who shared their ideas during this project, I would especially like to thank Roger Waldinger, Frank Bean, Ödül Bozkurt, Rogers Brubaker, Wayne Cornelius, David Cook-Martín, Tomás Jiménez, and Christian Joppke. During the research phase, Jorge Durand at the Universidad de Guadalajara offered an institutional home and collaboration with the Mexican Migration Project. Many friends in Jalisco gave richly of their hospitality, particularly Martina Aguirre, Jesús Valle, Don Luis González, Netzahualcoyotl González, Eduardo León Guzmán, José María Lozano Jiménez, Sr. Cura Gerardo Orozco, Sr. Cura Pedro Vásquez Villalobos, and the staff of the Arandas *ayuntamiento*, the Agua Negra *delegación*, the archbishopric of Guadalajara, the state of Jalisco archives, and *El Informador*. Sergio Avalos Beleche and Sahara Lou Grande Ferrer provided research assistance and many happy months of camaraderie. A postdoctoral fellowship at UC San Diego's Center for Comparative Immigration Studies enabled me to complete the manuscript. I am also grateful for the sage council of Richard Alba, Chiara Capoferro, Peter Evans, Jon Fox, Vikki Katz, Tamara Kay, David Lopez, Mara Loveman, Fernando Lozano Ascencio, Jenna Nobles, Shannon O'Neil, Eric Van Young, and Andreas Wimmer. Angela Garcia and Jessica Sisco assisted with the preparation of the manuscript. Naomi Schneider at the University of California Press helped move this project to fruition, as she has for so many before.

I will always be deeply indebted to my father, Dean, from whom I learned my love of history, and to my mother, Dona, with whom I shared my first passport. Sara Jane Shapira in many ways set me on this circuitous path beginning on the shores of the Mediterranean. I am fortunate to have accompanied Valeria Fitzgerald for a year and a half in Mexico as she told a larger audience many of the same stories found here. Her support for this project never wavered. Finally, I thank Gabriela Godines Fitzgerald, who learned to crawl and then ride her tricycle at my side as I researched and wrote this book. I will cherish her spirit and stamina on the road long after these pages have faded.

Introduction

In January 1954, armed Mexican police clashed with thousands of rioting Mexican workers trying to enter California at Calexico. A news photographer focused his lens on a man in a sombrero straddling the borderline. As the migrant's friends tugged him north, Mexican police tried to drag him back into Mexico.[1] Negotiations between Washington and Mexico City had collapsed in the latest round of the bracero accords, which since World War II had provided for the legal importation of hundreds of thousands of contracted workers to fill labor shortages in U.S. agriculture. An even larger number of illegal migrants followed the braceros north. With an abundant supply of unauthorized labor, the U.S. government had little incentive to improve braceros' low wages and poor working conditions. Aware of their weak bargaining position, Mexican officials tried to squeeze the supply of both legal and illegal migrants by sealing their northern border. Although official U.S. policy was to deter illegal immigration, the U.S. Border Patrol often turned a blind eye to unauthorized crossers or enforced the letter of the law while violating its spirit: During harvest season, U.S. agents who caught unauthorized Mexican immigrants brought them back to an official crossing point, pushed them twenty-four inches into Mexican territory, and then pulled them back into the United States. Now "legalized," the workers were handed over to employers waiting to truck them to the fields.[2]

Fifty years later, the scene on the two-thousand-mile U.S.-Mexican border has changed dramatically. On the U.S. side, flying drones with infrared cameras monitor the desert below. The National Guard and ten thousand border agents monitoring the walls and fences of a fortified border turn back more than a million unauthorized migrants a year.[3] On the Mexican side, rather than pulling back prospective crossers, the Mexican border police hand out booklets to thousands of its citizens trekking north, warning migrants of the dangers of illegally entering the United States but also providing them with practical tips about how to cross safely and avoid apprehension in U.S. cities.

These changes in how the United States and Mexico manage the movement of people across their shared border are a window into understanding the relationships between a government, a citizenry, and a territory during a period of intensive globalization. Scholars and pundits have focused their attention on immigrant destination countries, raising questions about how newcomers stitch together, alter, or tear the national fabric. Do immigrants assimilate? How do they affect the economy? Do they take more from the government in social services than they pay in taxes? Can the police control them? These same questions are equally relevant in the countries of origin of the world's 191 million emigrants.[4] What do governments do when a large part of the population simply gets up and walks away? How do they extract the resources of millions of citizens who are gone? How does international mobility change the social contract between citizens and their government? Are new forms of globalization transforming the nation-state?

This book helps answer the second set of questions by showing how Mexico has tried to manage the emigration of as much as a tenth of its population. Emigration has been a demographic hemorrhage for some interests, while for others it is an escape valve relieving the pressures of too many poor people. Emigrants have been called both traitors to the motherland and national heroes sustaining their families with remittances, agents of modernization who will transform the Mexican mentality and carriers of gringo cultural pathologies. I explore how politicians and bureaucrats at different levels of government have tried to regulate emigrants' exit and return, control them while they are abroad, and deal with the effects of their absence. My goal is to show how emigration is implicated in nation-state building, the multifaceted process of administering, educating, and policing the population; creating a sense of common belonging; accumulating more wealth and prestige for the home country; and managing relations with other countries. Countless studies have examined these qualities of nation-state building from the perspective of countries of destination, but the perspective of countries of origin has been relatively ignored.

Analysts of globalization are keenly interested in explaining how international flows of people, ideas, goods, and services transform the nation-state. Globalists, those who see major transformations, argue that nation-states lose control over their sovereignty when they do not effectively regulate immigrants coming into their country. Centralized governments either lack the capacity to control immigration or have shifted the place of policy making upward to authorities such as the European Union or downward to local authorities. A group of scholars working in the growing field of transnational studies makes similar arguments, which tend to pay more attention to these processes from the point of view of countries of emigration. Only the most radical claim the demise of the nation-state, but this scholarship takes as its departure the ability of migrants to use modern communication and transportation technologies to create lives that span international borders. Nation-states still matter in these accounts, but those with high levels of emigration have become "deterritorialized" as governments reach out to citizens abroad and membership in the nation is no longer claimed by virtue of residence in the country.[5]

Some commentators and activists in the United States seeking to restrict immigration from Mexico see an insidious plot on the part of the

Mexican government to trespass on U.S. sovereignty by reaching out to its citizens in the United States. As one pundit wrote of former president Vicente Fox's claim to speak on behalf of Mexicans on both sides of the border: "Where the Fox Plan is unusual, and where Americans should take heed, is in its discussion of emigration and the role of the Mexican government in the lives of Mexicans abroad. That proposed role is interventionist in a way that can only be achieved by encroaching on the sovereignty of any country that plays host to very many Mexicans [the United States]."[6] Although restrictionists and many scholars of globalization may have polar political orientations, they share the view that international migration, and sending-country policies in particular, are weakening the nation-state system. What the cold language of academia calls "deterritorialization" becomes "our sovereignty under attack!" in hot policy debates over immigration.

These stories miss how the resilience of the international system of sovereign states fundamentally shapes the relationships between migrants and their countries of origin. Despite all the flows of migrants across borders, and the many people who feel as if they live in two places at once, international boundaries still limit a government's ability to manage its mobile populations using traditional techniques and bargains. Many emigrants have severed ties to their homeland altogether rather than maintain the simultaneous ties to two or more countries that the literature of transnationalism celebrates. The governments of migrant-sending countries such as Mexico have to figure out not only how to attract the emigrants willing to maintain homeland ties, but also how to deal with the effects of losing all contact with much of their population. Emigrants are in another state's grip, so governments of countries of emigration must develop creative ways to manage citizens abroad, preserve their national loyalty, and extract their resources. Their tools are primarily symbolic, though the consequences are real, because sending-country governments cannot use the implicit threat of force against citizens abroad, as they can against those who stay home. The limits of sovereignty have prompted governments to model their stance toward emigrants on the policies of an institution that has also struggled with the question of emigration and membership: the Catholic Church. The unintended consequence of this modeling has been a radical revision of the contract between the nation-state and its citizens abroad, from coercive membership to ties that are much more optional, based on rights over obligations, and supportive of multiple national memberships.

MEXICAN MIGRATION

The Mexican experience offers several advantages for understanding the interplay between emigration and nation-state building. Migration between Mexico and the United States is "the largest sustained flow of migrant workers in the contemporary world."[7] The most unusual feature of Mexican migration is the concentration of more than 98 percent of Mexico's mi-

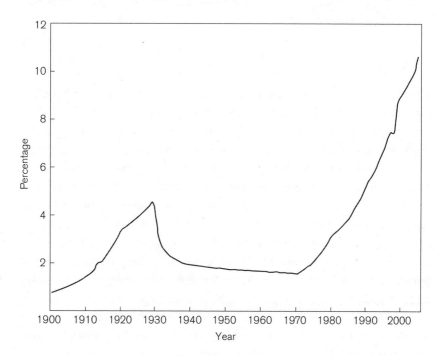

Figure 1. Mexican emigrants to the United States as a percentage of the Mexican population, 1900–2005. Calculated from U.S. and Mexican census data taken from the Mexican Migration Project NATLHIST file 2002 (http://mmp.opr.princeton.edu) and CONAPO 2006.

grants in one destination country: the United States. Mexicans' exposure to their northern neighbor takes place on a massive scale. Twenty-five percent of the Mexican adult population has visited or lived in the United States, and 60 percent has a relative living there. Roughly 11 million Mexicans, representing 11 percent of Mexico's population, lived in the United States in 2005. An estimated 400,000 more Mexicans join the net U.S. population each year. Another 16.8 million people of Mexican origin were born in the United States.[8] Mass emigration has continued for more than a century and shows no signs of abating. Such a long emigration has spawned a wide range of official responses, from putting troops on the border to stop citizens from leaving to negotiating agreements so more Mexicans can exit through legal channels. Mexico's long history of strong migratory and economic ties to the United States reveals with particular intensity the challenges and opportunities for governance in an age of globalization.

Revisiting Arandas

The forces of globalization often seem to roar through the atmosphere like the jet stream. They are powerful but abstract and hard to see well from the ground. Los Altos de Jalisco, the highlands rising above Guadalajara, juts into these winds. Here globalization sweeps down among the fields of blue agave and rocky red earth to carry its people away to Los Angeles and Chicago. The region's prominence in the study of Mexican migration began with the pioneering work of the University of California agricultural economist Paul Taylor, one of the leading scholars of Mexican immigration to the United States in the 1920s and 1930s. When Taylor turned to study the source of those migrants, he picked the county (*municipio*) of Arandas in Los Altos "as generally representative of the larger region."[9] Jalisco and the neighboring states of Guanajuato and Michoacán have consistently been the top three sources of Mexican migrants for a hundred years.[10] In Arandas and the surrounding region the abstractions of emigration and nation-state building come alive.

The two greatest waves of Mexican emigration arose in the 1920s, during the time of Taylor's research, and at the turn of the twenty-first century. I revisited Arandas and the Altos region for eighteen months be-

tween 2002 and 2004 to compare responses to the contemporary and earliest periods of mass emigration. My approach draws on the sociologist
Jeff Haydu's observation that revisiting a site that has been studied previ-
ously is a way to compare historical periods as "sequences of problem
solving" for different historical actors in similar structural positions.[11]
While comparing how the challenges of emigration have been met at
different periods in the same place, I explain why different solutions were
chosen during each period and how the menu of contemporary policy options is constrained by earlier decisions. To understand these historical sequences, in addition to relying on Taylor's published work and unpublished notes, I conducted archival research at the municipal and provincial
level in Jalisco. At the national level, I consulted all Mexican laws of migration, nationality, and population.

Studies of international migration are replete with legalistic or abstract
discussions based on analysis of national-level policies alone. My approach
of linking macro-level processes of nation-state building with their articu-
lation in local practices yields a deeper understanding of "everyday forms
of state formation."[12] I examine how local officials subverted orders issued
in Mexico City and effectively created their own policies. Investigating the
activities of various agencies at different levels of government is a practical
strategy for breaking "the state" down into its components. I conducted
and recorded eighty-five in-depth interviews with government officials,
politicians, teachers, priests, employers, and returned migrants in Arandas,
Guadalajara, and migrants from Arandas living in Orange County, California. A survey of 297 randomly selected household heads in the city of
Arandas and the nearby village of Agua Negra, and twenty household
heads in the satellite communities of Arandenses in Chicago and Orange
County, assessed broader currents of public opinion about migration in
these communities.[13] To establish rigorous measures of how typical of Mexican migrant source communities Arandas and its migrants are, I surveyed
the same 317 households using the methodology and questionnaire of the
Mexican Migration Project (MMP), which has surveyed more than a hundred Mexican migrant source communities since 1982.[14] My aim is not to
determine whether emigration on balance is "good" or "bad" for Mexico or
sending countries generally. Neither do I seek to describe all the social

effects of migration on the sending country. Rather, my goal is to uncover what institutional actors in Mexico have done to manage emigration and its effects in specific domains of state and nation building and analyze how that has transformed citizenship on the ground in an age of globalization.

From Los Altos to Los Angeles

In Taylor's day, Arandas was an isolated county seat (*cabecera*) of seventy-five hundred in a municipio of twenty-eight thousand bearing the same name. Horses and twenty-six motor vehicles shared the cobblestone streets leading past whitewashed adobe houses and the church built in 1780 in honor of the Virgin of Guadalupe. During the Sunday *serenata*, men and women flirted with each other by walking around the plaza in segregated, concentric circles as the municipal band played *alteño* melodies. Seven decades later, stereos hammering out songs of the Detroit rap artist Eminem rattle the boutiques and Internet cafés of a cabecera grown to forty thousand. The weekend serenade has become an informal parade of young men in vehicles with shining chrome circling young women on foot. The music is even louder and the cars shinier during the January patron saint fiesta. Long after the elders honoring the return of the migrants have gone to bed, drivers of pickups with California plates rev their engines in the plaza, sending up clouds of smoke before releasing the brakes and surging through the narrow streets.

Twenty-two miles northeast, in the village of Agua Negra, suburban-style homes financed with dollars are deserted until the patron saint fiesta in February, when migrants return from the United States and other parts of Mexico.[15] A *jaripeo* (rodeo) held on the land of a former bracero draws practically the entire population with its live *banda* music, bull riding, and a soccer game in the ring where a bull runs loose among the players. Without the infusion of remittances by migrants who renew their hometown ties during the fiesta, Agua Negra (pop. 462) would wither even further. The ruins of Rancho La Ordeña across the hollow are a visual reminder of a darker fate. La Ordeña numbered twenty-five large families in the 1940s before its residents moved to Agua Negra, other Mexican cities, and the United States. The owners of the ranch now live in Virginia and have hired a family from a neighboring county to take care of the *casa grande* and its remaining cows. Taylor-era houses of rough fieldstone covered with adobe are crumbling back into the earth from which they were formed. Several years ago, the last native resident fell and hit his head while drinking alone in the doorway of his house. His dead body lay in the sun for three days before a passerby found him. Facing extremely high levels of migration and a fragile economy, Agua Negrans wonder aloud if their village will eventually disappear like La Ordeña.

As Taylor observed when he selected Arandas for a case study in 1931, no single community can be typical in every way, but the county's emigration story closely follows the national narrative. The pioneer Arandense migrants left around 1905 to work seasonally on railroad tracks from Kansas to California. A contractor from the Santa Fe Railroad visited Arandas in 1913 and recruited three or four workers to return with him, but most Arandenses learned about work opportunities in the United States by word of mouth. Migrants from the county joined a stream of workers from the central plateau heading north on the railroad that had connected Mexico City to El Paso via northeastern Los Altos in 1884. The rate of emigration quickened during the 1910–20 revolution as the Mexican economy deteriorated and the U.S. entrance into World War I created greater labor demand. The economic depression in the United States in 1921 prompted return migration to Arandas, but as the U.S. economy improved, migration reached new highs. Illegal migration began as early as the 1920s, when Arandenses paid coyotes four to eight pesos to cross the Rio Grande. Emigration reached its early apex during the 1926–29 Cristero War between Catholic rebels and the federal government.[16] Residents asked family members in the United States to stay away for their own safety and to continue to send remittances to support household economies destroyed by the conflict. As the Cristero War ended, the onset of the Great Depression in the United States generated intense pressure for Mexicans to repatriate. Among the wave of returnees in the 1930s was Luisa, now Agua Negra's oldest surviving migrant, who was born in Chicago in 1924 to parents fleeing the Mexican Revolution.

During World War II, hundreds of Arandenses participated in the bracero program. As in the rest of Mexico, undocumented emigration

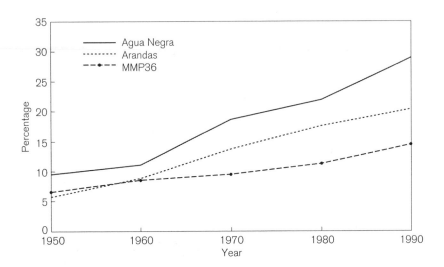

Figure 2.   Percentage of adult population with U.S. migration experience in Arandas, Agua Negra, and the MMP36, 1950–90. Source: MMP COMMUN File, MMP 2003 Los Altos Survey, available at http://mmp.opr.princeton.edu. The MM36 is the mean of the thirty-six communities surveyed by the Mexican Migration Project from 1998 to 2002, weighted by population.

accelerated during the program and continued after its demise in 1964. The 1986 U.S. Immigration Reform and Control Act (IRCA) benefited many Arandenses who were able to legalize their status and bring their families with them to the United States. Whole families of Arandense migrants are increasingly likely to settle permanently. More than three-quarters of Arandense migrants now live in California or Illinois, with the largest concentrations in greater Los Angeles and greater Chicago. The rest are scattered throughout the United States.

In 1931, Taylor found that Arandenses were generally representative of Mexicans in the United States, with the exception of their predominantly Spanish ancestry and light skin.[17] Contemporary Arandense migrants share most characteristics of migrants from the thirty-six communities located throughout Mexico surveyed by the MMP from 1998 to 2002 (the MMP36).[18] The "median" Arandense migrant is an undocumented, married, thirty-six-year-old man with an elementary school education.

Emigration levels are relatively high in the county of Arandas. By 1990, 30 percent of adult Agua Negrans and 20 percent of adult Arandenses had lived in the United States, compared to only 15 percent in the MMP36. But unlike most counties in the central west, Arandas experienced rapid economic growth from a tequila boom. For most of its history, farmers in Arandas struggled to produce corn and beans from small private plots of rocky soil in a wrinkled terrain where seasonal rains drowned crops one year and droughts scorched them the next. Fortunately for Arandenses, the red earth that is so poor for most crops is exceptionally rich for growing the *weber azul* agave, known as "Blue Gold" for the wealth it brings those who distill its juices into tequila. Returned migrants invested their U.S. earnings in several distilleries in the 1970s. The richest and most politically powerful man in Arandas is a returned migrant who started his first business with US$4,000 he earned working on U.S. railroads as a seventeen-year-old in 1948. He later founded Tequila Cazadores, the fifth highest selling brand of tequila in the world.[19] A tequila boom in the late 1990s made fortunes as the price of agave rose more than 2,000 percent in a single year. Agave became so valuable that farmers would wake up in the morning to find that an entire field of the sixty-pound plants had been looted overnight. A glut later forced the price of agave back down, but Arandas is still a model of the economic success that can be achieved by using remittance investment to add value locally to agricultural products.[20] The county now ranks in the top quarter of Mexican counties in its overall level of development.[21]

Many migrants believe Arandas is becoming more prosperous, and they are willing to invest there even as they continue to migrate. Ten percent of households in Arandas receive remittances from the United States, compared to 7.7 percent of the households in Jalisco and 4.4 percent in Mexico as a whole. The median annual remittance of US$2,500 in the county of Arandas is twice as high as in Jalisco and Mexico as a whole.[22] Remittances have fueled a construction boom. Developers estimate they sell at least half of their property and housing to migrants, whom they target with advertising campaigns on an Arandense Internet site and at the county fair during the January patron saint fiesta. "Welcome paisano. We have the ideal house for your family," beckons a banner advertising red-tiled, three-bedroom homes for US$30,000. As elsewhere in Mexico, communities with vibrant economies attract more remittances.[23] Arandas is not like the many source communities that have experienced such high levels of migration against a backdrop of failed economic development that they become little but nurseries for future migrants and nursing homes for returnees.[24]

Local authorities are both excited and preoccupied by a migration that has brought wealth and cultural changes to Arandas. The municipal government has tried to get its hands on the dollars and potential political power of its "absent children" by creating a directory of migrants, sending official delegations to visit them in the United States and throwing banquets for returnees. Police try to control the disruptive behavior of young men returning from U.S. cities. Teachers complain that young migrants and the second generation lose their Spanish and come back Americanized. In past years, officials have tried to figure out how to conscript absent youth into the army. Emigration's challenges and opportunities extend to the Catholic Church. Local priests concerned with migration's contribution to divorce, vices, and lack of religiosity hold special masses for returnees and take patron saint images on tours of U.S. satellite communities. In places like Agua Negra, the vicar keeps careful track of the mobile faithful, whose tithes are a critical portion of his budget. Migrants in the United States actively participate in many of these secular and religious projects, but they do so through hometown associations of their own making that negotiate with local authorities and allow migrants to choose the kinds of ties they want. Revisiting the region seven decades after Taylor shows how attempts to manage migration have unfolded on the ground with unintended consequences for the relationship between Mexico and its migrants.

A CHART FOR THE WATERS AHEAD

In this book I explain the different ways the Mexican government has reacted to the challenges and opportunities of emigration and how those responses have changed the social contract between emigrants and their home country. In chapter 1 I describe how the familiar problems and possibilities that international migration creates for countries of immigration are also faced by countries of origin. Some scholars of globalization have taken governments' difficulty in controlling migration as further evidence that the nation-state is declining as a way of organizing politics. Others argue that the nation-state is stronger than ever. Against both of these perspectives, I argue that mass emigration cracks apart the triple rings of government, people, and territory that are fused in the nation-state. Those cracks appear precisely because the international principle of a state's exclusive sovereignty over its territory is so robust despite the large flows of people between countries.

In chapter 2 I analyze the Mexican government's changing stance toward emigration over the past century at the federal, state, and local levels. The immigration policies of the United States and Mexico's demographic transformations have primarily shaped Mexico's responses. Mexican policies have influenced migration patterns, but these effects were caused not so much by federal strategies to control emigration as by local policies and the unintended consequences of Mexican state building in other domains.

How the Mexican Catholic Church, like the nation-state with which it shares many organizational features, has confronted the challenges of emigration is the subject of chapter 3. Like the state, the Church saw its early policies of dissuading emigration fail, prompting the Church to focus on the management of emigrants already on the move rather than controlling emigration before it happens. The state has adopted the Church's organizational strategies for administering migrants and its model of voluntaristic ties with a mobile membership.

In chapter 4 I show how domestic hometown associations (HTAs) of internal migrants who moved to large Mexican cities in the 1940s were the source of contemporary HTAs based in the United States that institutionalize ties between the Mexican government and its emigrants. The domestic HTAs, originally inspired by the Church, are remarkably similar to the transborder HTAs as channels for migrant participation in Arandas's economy and politics. The Mexican government at all levels uses HTAs in the United States to make symbolic appeals to hometown ties and to tap migrants' economic resources and political support, but migrants participate voluntarily only when it serves their own interests.

Rather than focus on the conventional preoccupation with the cultural *assimilation of immigrants*, in chapter 5 I examine the cultural *dissimilation of emigrants*. Teachers, police, and employers in Arandas worry about migrants becoming different from those who stay behind. They generally emphasize the negative cultural effects of migration while praising its economic effects. That ambivalence suggests a further limitation on attempts by political entrepreneurs to extend claims of belonging to include members outside the territory. In the conclusion I develop the concept of "citizenship à la carte" and a political sociology of emigration that explains how exit, absence, and return influence the organization and development of the nation-state in Mexico and beyond.

ONE The Politics of Absence

One of the most critical issues in contemporary politics is whether the nation-state—the organizational fusion of a territory, a government, and a people—can control the forces of globalization that threaten to overwhelm it. Nowhere is this question more important than in the study of international migration. This chapter places Mexico's handling of emigration in the context of broader historical debates around the world about the effects of globalization on each country's ability to shape its political life. Although the contemporary system of nation-states is often taken for granted as the normal way of organizing politics, that system is only one of several historical alternatives, including tribes and empires, and there is no reason to believe that history is dead. New ways of organizing politics are emerging in response to international migration and other features of globalization. Most attention to the challenges and opportunities that international migration creates for building state and nation focuses on immigration, but emigration also implies perils and promises for countries of migrant origin. Many scholars look at the effects of international migration and conclude that the nation-state is becoming "deterritorialized" and that its sovereignty is in decline. Against this view, I argue that for countries of mass emigration such as Mexico, it is precisely the continuing strength of the sovereignty of states that is driving a reconfiguration of the relationship between a government, a territory, and a people. One consequence of this particular form of the nation-state is a new kind of social contract between emigrants and their countries of origin.

INTERNATIONAL MIGRATION AND THE NATION-STATE

Humans have organized their politics in many ways. The nation-state appears to have destroyed its historical competitors. Unlike empires, which encompass a swath of communities whose only commonality is living under the boot of the same ruler, nation-states are imagined as containers of a single people. Unlike tribes—political communities principally defined by kinship rather than geography—nation-states are defined by their control over carefully marked pieces of land. The nation-state is both an organization of citizens (a nation) and a government over a territory (a state). Nation-states are based on the principle of sovereignty, the exclusive authority to make and coercively enforce the law within a specific territory.[1] In a world so divided, certain people are in the club, while others are excluded from it. Some enjoy the rights that membership bestows, while others are denied them.

International migrants upset the neat distinctions between insiders and outsiders. Immigrants are subject to the laws of the host country by virtue of their presence in its territory, but they are not (yet) considered members. By virtue of their absence, emigrants are not directly subject to the laws of their country of origin, but they may still be considered part of the legal and cultural nation. The presence of foreigners and the absence of citizens crack apart the fusion of polity, society, and territory that constitutes the nation-state as a specific form of political organization.[2] Emigration and immigration challenge the fundamental organization of the nation-state and many of its functions. At the same time, international migration also promises new opportunities.

Perils and Promises of Immigration

Most attention to these issues has focused solely on countries of immigration. One of the reasons immigration debates are so emotionally charged is that immigration is deeply implicated in nation building. Governments often select immigrants based on a particular vision of who belongs to the nation or can at least be assimilated over time. In the United States, the 1924 quota law aimed to increase the numbers of northern Europeans and exclude altogether the most despised racial groups. Bans on the entry of groups such as the Chinese were the rule among most major countries of immigration prior to World War II. The sociologist Christian Joppke[3] notes that singling out particular groups for negative discrimination has become internationally disreputable, but positive discrimination in favor of particular groups is still practiced widely. Spain has given immigration preferences to citizens of Latin American countries because Latin Americans' shared language, religion, and historical ties presumably make them easier to integrate into Spanish society than immigrants from North Africa. Israel exists as the result of an explicit project of Jewish nationalism, attracting Jews from around the world in a demographic race against the Palestinians. Ostensibly a country without immigration, Japan recruits second- and third-generation ethnic Japanese, primarily from Brazil, who fill Japan's labor needs without upsetting the myth of a homogeneous society. Other countries have used immigration to reengineer their racial demography. Across Latin America in the nineteenth and early twentieth centuries governments encouraged the immigration of Europeans to "whiten" their national population. Countries such as Argentina successfully reduced the indigenous and African proportions of their population by importing Spaniards and Italians. Other countries, such as Mexico, largely failed, despite their best efforts, to attract significant European immigration for the same purpose.[4]

While immigration can be a tool for nation building, it can also complicate that effort by introducing diverse languages, religions, and ethnic identities. The extent to which this is seen as a challenge depends on how much social difference is accepted within the nation. The least accommodating pole is social exclusion, typified in the Persian Gulf, where most immigrants are perpetual foreigners excluded from legal membership as well as a part in the imagined nation. Assimilationism that actively seeks to integrate foreigners into a single cultural nation, along the lines of the classic French republican model, lies in the middle of the continuum. At the opposite extreme lies state-sponsored multiculturalism, practiced by the Netherlands in the 1980s, that recognizes and even encourages substantial cultural differences within the host nation.[5]

Immigration policy is driven by many other reasons of state, not the least of which is strengthening the economy by responding to employers' demands for foreign labor. Western European states recruited millions of Turks, Yugoslavs, and North Africans through their postwar guest-worker programs. Countries such as Canada and Australia systematically try to attract highly skilled immigrants through their "point systems." Rich welfare states with rapidly aging populations have considered welcoming the immigration of younger workers to generate the resources necessary to support retirees. Immigration is also a tool of foreign policy. During the cold war, the United States gave admission preferences to immigrants from communist countries in an attempt to embarrass communist governments by showing that their citizens were voting with their feet. Attracting these refugees enhanced the ideological power of the United States on the world stage.[6]

Immigration creates challenges to as well as opportunities for state building. Much of the debate about whom to select revolves around the problem of educating immigrants' children and providing them with welfare services once they settle. Numerous studies have tried to assess whether immigrants pay more in taxes than they receive in government benefits. The answers to these accounting exercises vary widely by context and researcher. The National Research Council concluded that in the

United States during the mid-1990s, the federal welfare system tended to take more money from immigrants than it paid in benefits, while local and state governments tended to pay out more in benefits than they received from immigrants' taxes.[7] Immigration also introduces problems in such areas of state building as policing. Law enforcement is especially difficult among undocumented immigrants, who by definition are less accessible than legal residents to standard systems of surveillance and control. A large undocumented population is such a challenge to police that many local agencies in the United States, such as the Los Angeles Police Department since 1979, have drafted policies against routinely checking immigration status for fear that unauthorized migrants will become less willing to cooperate with police on other matters.[8]

Governments and publics in destination countries are often ambivalent about immigration because it entails both costs and benefits. Policy analysts try to calculate the sum of these costs and benefits for countries of immigration, usually in a particular area such as the economic impacts of immigration but sometimes taking into account political goals such as cultural homogeneity or accepting refugees for moral reasons. Both the policy- and theory-driven research fill a vast library that is the basis for understanding the links between immigration and nation-state building.

Perils and Promises of Emigration

This study explores the neglected half of the same political question: the link between emigration and nation-state building.[9] Like their counterparts in countries of destination, political actors in countries of origin are ambivalent about international migration. According to the United Nations, the percentage of countries with policies aimed at lowering emigration rose from 13 percent in 1976 to 24 percent in 2003.[10] Emigration creates challenges and opportunities for administering the population, accumulating wealth, strengthening military power, and managing foreign relations. When it comes to nation building, emigration creates challenges mostly for national prestige and reproducing the cultural community. Governments' ability to manage the problems and promises of emigration varies with its phase. Emigration encompasses departure, absence, and return. An individual migrant may move through those phases in a linear progression or cycle through them repeatedly, never standing still long enough to be captured by static categories. Even in death, the bodies of thousands of emigrants are still in motion as repatriated remains in airline cargo holds below the seats of returnees in the cabin above.[11]

Emigration policies aim to control exit and return, while emigrant policies manage relations with citizens already abroad.[12] Departing emigrants and returnees stepping back onto the state's soil are directly subject to its authority. Governments trying to administer emigrants abroad face a greater challenge. They must rely on the coercive intervention of the government of the destination country or on the voluntary cooperation of emigrants, or they must take action against the family or property that emigrants left behind. The literature on migrant transnationalism has usefully drawn attention to emigrant policies, but it often goes to such great lengths to establish that migrants retain home-country ties that it ignores the absence of people who are gone forever. A comprehensive political sociology of emigration includes policies directed at the entire spectrum of exit, long-distance ties, disengagement with the homeland, and return.

Emigration's challenge for statecraft begins with the practical problem of administering a population that is gone. Identification cards such as passports are one of the main tools that states use to control migration and "embrace" individuals for purposes of conscripting, policing, taxing, and rationing the social benefits of citizenship. These documents are part of a system of knowledge and power enabling the administration of a population—a system that Michel Foucault calls "governmentality." The system becomes possible through the all-seeing gaze of the state's "panoptic" eye. Missing in Foucault's account is the agency of the people who are monitored and disciplined and the degree to which specific techniques of governmentality are effective.[13] Citizens do not always sit still for the state to watch them. In many developing countries, the state has a cataractous eye that cannot see well enough even to count its citizens, a condition made all the more difficult when citizens move internationally.[14] Emigrants can take advantage of their foreign residence to avoid the controls of the sending state and agitate for revolution in the homeland. History records many such émigré groups, from Irish Fenian rebels in nineteenth-century America to Iranian followers of Ayatollah Khomeini in France in the 1970s.[15]

The political scientist James Scott has addressed some of the deficiencies of a Foucauldian account in his work *Seeing Like a State*, in which he describes how governments try to make their populations "legible" by arranging people and their physical environment in an ordered way that simplifies social control. By attending to developing states with limited capacities, Scott also sheds light on the ways that various kinds of "premodern" mobility pose a challenge for governmentality. "Nomads and pastoralists (such as Berbers and Bedouins), hunter-gatherers, Gypsies, vagrants, homeless people, itinerants, runaway slaves, and serfs have always been a thorn in the side of states," he argues.[16] I build on Scott's insight by discussing relationships between source-country governments and labor migrants that elude the state's fumbling embrace. The classical accounts of nation-state formation emphasize the development of the earliest and strongest modern states, whose practices became models adopted throughout the globe, first by colonization, then by the diffusion of international standards.[17] Once the first nation-states were consolidated in the nineteenth century, their populations had good reason to accept the state's penetration and embrace, because in return they received policing and military protections and negotiated access to an unprecedented level of material and political resources. The same cannot be said of twentieth-century labor migrants from poor countries. Millions of citizens have been motivated to elude their state's embrace by stepping out of the space that it controls, in part because the incentives offered by home state membership are comparatively meager. Labor migrants complicate statecraft because they have little incentive to submit themselves to the administration of a state that provides limited rewards in return.

Emigration implies a loss of resources, at least in the short run. Mercantilists, who believe that states should hoard their people like any other factor of production or war making, fear that losing population not only weakens the source economy, but also strengthens the economy of rival destination countries. The problem is aggravated when emigrants' very bodies are a valuable military resource.[18] For these reasons, most European states tried to restrict population exit during the seventeenth through early nineteenth centuries, especially if it was directed outside their colonies. The political scientist Aristide Zolberg relates that migration was punishable by execution in Prussia under Frederick William I (1713–40). Other tools of dissuasion included bans on labor recruitment by foreigners, restrictions on receiving remittances, prohibiting emigrants from taking their property with them, and stripping them of their nationality.[19]

Despite the general decline of mercantilism and the rise of market economies thriving on greater labor mobility, many countries continue to discourage the exit of citizens with military service obligations or special skills. Investments in human capital made through public education and medical care are wasted if emigrants permanently leave and sever their home-country ties. The specter of brain drain preoccupies many countries, particularly poor ones where highly educated workers are scarce. Extreme examples are Jamaica and West Africa; more than three-quarters of Jamaicans with university degrees live abroad, and more than a quarter of university-educated West Africans have left for the thirty rich member states of the Organization for Economic Cooperation and Development. Editorialists blame the global North for "looting doctors and nurses from developing countries."[20]

Emigration incurs an ideological as well as a material cost because it undermines national prestige. Nationalists complain that emigrants have turned their backs on their country by leaving. Fidel Castro has famously called Cuban emigrants *gusanos* (worms). Even when emigrants are viewed sympathetically, the humiliations they suffer abroad can be interpreted as the dishonoring of the nation they represent. These problems are exacerbated when citizens migrate to countries with a legacy of unfriendly relations with the homeland. The world-systems approach to international migration theory emphasizes that colonialism and other foreign interventions generate migration streams in the opposite direction: Algerians migrate to France, Indians to Britain, and Filipinos to the United States. As immigrant activists in Britain put it, "We are here because you were there."[21] There are differences in the mechanisms that generate postcolonial migration and the migration between Mexico and the United States, but they are all cases of migration born of sharply asymmetrical relationships. Mexicans have gone to the United States not only because it is a rich neighbor, but also because the United States conquered half of Mexico in the nineteenth century, militarily intervened through the early twentieth century, and continues to invest heavily in the Mexican economy. Emigration publicly highlights the source country's weakness vis-à-vis the destination country by underscoring the push and pull factors that drive migration. Avoiding the associated loss of national prestige is an "ideal interest" that can motivate states to control emigration.[22]

Long-term emigration also creates a challenge for governments worried about the denationalization of their population abroad. The sociologist Michael Mann describes the modern state as a "caging device" that constrains social relations within a state's territory and institutions.[23] How does a state create a sense of shared nationhood when much of the population it claims lives in another state's cage? The sociologist Abdelmalek Sayad summarizes the problem of emigrant denationalization for a source country such as Algeria: "Its emigrant nationals . . . are *absent*, outside its territory, its sovereignty, its authority and, more generally, beyond the action of the integrating mechanisms and identificatory processes typical of any society. They are, in short, outside its common culture (and, correlatively, in the territory and under the sovereignty and authority and, more generally, subject to the integrating action and culture of some other nation)."[24]

Return migration, even if temporary, carries risks for nationalists when migrants introduce noxious ideas and practices associated with the foreign nemesis. Cross-border contamination reduces the cultural similarities and ability to communicate with each other that unify a national population.[25] Consistent evidence from around the world suggests that many nonmigrants consider these cultural imports to be pathological.[26] Creating cultural homogeneity and national loyalty is especially difficult in contexts of mass emigration because nationalization is not only the result of a deliberate project using public education and patriotic rituals as its instruments; nationalization is also the unintended outcome of other government efforts directed at such goals as universal conscription and providing social welfare for all. Citizens come to think of themselves as forming part of the same collectivity because the nation-state shapes everyday lives to be relatively confined within its institutional and territorial boundaries. While they can be transgressed by various processes of regional exchange and globalization, the boundaries of countries continue to shape the language that people speak, where they live and work, whom they marry, and how they identify themselves.[27] Once citizens are outside the "normal" cage of the state, a government cannot rely on the diffuse effects of its sundry policies to sustain its citizens' sense of national belonging. Source-country governments are forced to adopt an explicitly nationalist project to uphold the absent population's loyalties and cultural practices.

Emigration is not all bad news. Despite the challenges that emigration poses for administering the population outside the state's borders, the loss of human resources and national prestige, and the problem of reproducing the national cultural community, emigration may also supply important benefits for enhancing state power. Human beings are a resource for the state, but too many of them create a burden when rapid population growth coincides with increased expectations of social services. In such settings, emigration becomes an escape valve that releases unemployment pressures and demands on the state to provide relief. The British government "shoveled out paupers" to the United States and Australia during the nineteenth century.[28] Morocco, the Philippines, and Mexico have made the export of labor a deliberate policy, at least in part because their governments cannot meet their citizens' expectations of work and living conditions at home.[29]

Positive economic and political incentives offer more reasons to encourage emigration. Promoting the temporary education and training of citizens abroad is a way for states to upgrade their population's human capital by transferring skills, technology, and "modern" attitudes from more economically developed countries. In the most hopeful scenarios, what began as "brain drain" can become "brain gain." Migrants abroad can become, in the words of Chinese president Jiang Zemin in 1999, "our mine of resources."[30] Most important, emigrants are a source of remittances. The World Bank estimated that in 2005, workers from the developing world remitted $167 billion to their home countries, representing

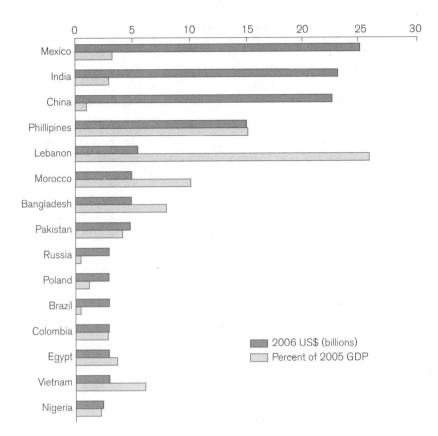

Figure 3. Top fifteen remittance-receiving countries, 2006. Source: "Migrants' Remittances," *Economist*, November 23, 2006, based on World Bank figures, 2006 forecast.

twice the level of international aid. There is a running debate in policy circles about whether remittances stimulate development in the home country or create a debilitating dependence. Survey data across a wide variety of settings show that most remittances are used for household expenses and real estate rather than productive investments. Skeptics conclude that remittances aggravate economic inequality and raise consumptive expectations beyond a level that can be sustained through local employment; the result is further emigration. A more sanguine camp argues that under certain conditions, remittances can be economically productive; in India and

China, for example, remittances are major sources of direct investment. In general, remittances supplement the incomes of micro-entrepreneurs and small-scale farmers who would otherwise be forced to migrate. Even when remittances are spent on household consumption, they have multiplier effects that indirectly create jobs for workers who produce the goods and provide the services that households consume. At the macroeconomic level, remittances are a source of foreign exchange that stabilizes national currencies and balances current accounts. Regardless of whether remittances are harmful or beneficial, source-country governments are anxious to get their hands on them to meet their needs today.[31]

Sending states try to turn emigrants into a political asset when they encourage expatriates to form ethnic lobbies in their destination country. Countries around the world take the American Jewish lobby in the United States as their model of what emigrants or coethnics abroad can achieve. An emigrant lobby makes sense only under two conditions: Emigrants must establish themselves in countries that permit immigrant political participation, and the destination country must have some political or economic leverage of use to the home country. The United States generally fulfills both of these conditions, and most research on emigrant lobbies has focused on the U.S. case. Since the 1990s, many Latin American countries with large populations in the United States have actively tried to form emigrant lobbies. The political scientist Rodolfo de la Garza has argued that such lobbies are rarely effective because Latin American emigrants and their U.S.-born offspring usually have negative attitudes toward the government of their country of origin. Nevertheless, the dream of emigrant lobbies in Washington continues to entice policy makers in El Salvador, the Dominican Republic, Colombia, and Mexico.[32] In the Mediterranean, Cyprus has embraced Greek Cypriots living in the United Kingdom for the same reason, and Turkey extended the possibility of dual citizenship in 1995 partly in the hopes that Turks living in Western Europe would become more integrated into their host countries and push the European Union to admit Turkey.[33]

Like immigration, then, emigration is a tool for increasing the state's power in some ways, while it complicates that project in others. It has mixed effects on economic growth and political stability and mostly negative effects on conscription and state-led nationalizing. When a significant portion of the population emigrates, the weight of absentees in nation-state building increases. And when source-country governments respond by trying to embrace the national membership spilling over into another state's territory, their policies threaten to crack apart the triple rings of government, people, and territory that are fused in the ideal-typical nation-state. An analysis of the state's ties with emigrants and its ability to control migration flows across its borders sheds light on raging debates across the social sciences about whether or not political power is being reconfigured to supersede the system of sovereign nation-states that has anchored global politics since the seventeenth century. In the words of the political scientists David Held and Anthony McGrew, "Today, questions arise as to whether we are living through another political transformation which might be as important as the creation of the nation-state. Is the exclusive link between territory and political power being broken by globalization?"[34]

LOSING CONTROL?

Analysts awed by the rapid pace of social change at the turn of the millennium argue that "globalization breaks the territorial principle, the nexus between power and place."[35] These "globalists" offer evidence to show that the nation-state container has sprung a leak: Transnational corporations move their assets all over the world to force concessions from national governments eager to tax corporate revenues but fearful of driving away the geese that lay the golden eggs; international treaties and transnational norms progressively constrain the authority of states to act as they please within their borders; committing "crimes against humanity" such as genocide, even against one's own citizens, has become grounds for legitimate intervention by other states. The European Union is the premier example of the upward shifting of sovereignty to a supranational scale in areas as diverse as banking, environmental regulation, and immigration policies, all of which were formerly the exclusive domain of the nation-state. The EU allows free migration within its boundaries for nationals of member states and has increasingly influenced their individual immigration and asylum policies toward nationals from non-EU countries.[36] The sociologist Yasemin Soysal argues that immigrants enjoy universal rights of personhood that minimize the importance of national citizenship for enjoying human and civil rights, and even the welfare benefits of social rights.[37] Based on research conducted around the world, migration experts such as Douglas Massey and his colleagues call international migration inevitable, and in a 2004 survey of eleven countries, Wayne Cornelius and his colleagues highlight the growing gap between the intent of immigration control policies and their failures in practice.[38] Surveying all these changes, the social theorist Saskia Sassen concludes that national governments are "losing control" over the flows of goods, ideas, and people across their borders.[39]

Scholars of migrant transnationalism share the globalists' goal of understanding broken linkages between territory and polity. Transnationalists call for a reconceptualization of such terms as *community, citizenship,* and *nation-state.* For them, deterritorialization signifies the uncoupling of residence in a territory from membership in a community and the displacement of culture from geography. Numerous observers argue that international migrants and the governments of their countries of origin are primary agents of deterritorialization. According to this perspective, countries of emigration are becoming "deterritorialized nation-states" as citizens abroad are incorporated by their homelands.[40] In short, globalists and transnationalists contend that the undermining of the nation-state's sovereignty, the decline in its capacity to control flows across its border, and the deterritorialization of the nation-state through emigration reveal dramatic transformations in the territoriality of political power.

Skeptics of globalization argue that the exclusive link between territory and political power is actually at its historical apex. The international system defined by the territoriality and autonomy of each nation-state is conventionally dated to the 1648 Treaty of Westphalia, which ended Europe's Thirty Years War. But the Westphalian system was not fully institutionalized until the 1990s, following the end of European colonialism and the collapse of the Soviet empire. The political map of the world looked more like the Westphalian ideal type at that time than ever before. The supranational institutions of the EU are the exceptions that prove the national rule everywhere else. Organizations such as the United Nations and the World Trade Organization are formed by sovereign states, which are voluntary signatories to the treaties that then constrain their policies. To be sure, transnational corporations operate across the borders of nation-states, but the vast majority of them are headquartered in a handful of rich countries that continue to exercise significant authority over their operations. The political and economic power of these same states undergirds the institutions governing international trade. When it comes to international migration and territoriality, there is much talk about states losing control over their borders, but in general states are establishing a semblance of control for the first time. Unlike the open immigration of the nineteenth century, when practically anyone could walk off the ship in New York or Buenos Aires, immigration since World War I has become restricted by an unprecedented system of fences, passports, visas, and government databases.[41]

As far as emigration is concerned, the major flaw in the notion of a *deterritorialized* world is its assumption that political life was entirely territorialized at an earlier point. There is nothing new about states recognizing the legal nationality of large numbers of citizens abroad. Major European countries of emigration in the nineteenth and twentieth centuries vigorously maintained legal claims on their overseas nationals.[42] At the level of cultural nationhood, the imagined inclusion of coethnics in the diaspora traces back even further, to the Jews and Greeks of antiquity. Making the comparative points of reference more explicit clarifies changes in the relationships among a group of citizens, a government, and a place. The reference point may be an ideal type such as the Westphalian system, historical practices in a particular migration circuit, or the world-historical stage.

Consider the idea of a deterritorialized nation. Historically, definitions of legal nationality and cultural nationhood based on birth in a state's territory have been particularly important in Latin America and the Caribbean. These formations are a legacy of the extreme ethnoracial heterogeneity of populations living within countries whose borders were based on the arbitrary administrative divisions of colonialism. Within Latin America and the Caribbean, some countries' recent claims to include large numbers of emigrants in the imagined nation represents a shift away from a primarily territorial definition of nationhood.[43] In Haiti, the government began making the novel claim in the 1990s that the nation includes a "tenth department" of Haitians living abroad, in addition to members of the nine geographic departments within Haiti. It is fascinating to discover changes in claims about a nation's composition, with all of its attendant political consequences, while still recognizing antecedents in other settings. The contemporary Haitian case evokes the late nineteenth-century notion of Polonia, the corporate body of Poles in the United States, which claimed to be the "fourth province of Poland."[44]

Drawing on theoretical debates in cultural geography and sociology, Neil Brenner argues that while the concept of deterritorialization usefully draws attention to historical changes in the implication of territory in organizing political life, its suggestion of the demise of territoriality eliminates an understanding of how the territoriality of the state is being reconfigured rather than eliminated.[45] The international relations theorist John Ruggie advances the concept of "unbundled territoriality" to describe how rulers deal with the transterritorial aspects of the relationships between states by voluntarily withdrawing some of their exclusive territorial claims. He points to territorial unbundling in such arrangements as the legal fiction that embassies are islands of extraterritorial sovereignty within a sovereign nation-state; for example, the French embassy in London is governed by French law as if it were a small piece of France inside the United Kingdom. The existence of sovereign embassies does not imply that the nation-state has become deterritorialized. On the contrary, embassies uphold the territoriality of the nation-state system more generally by carving out carefully defined exceptions to the general rule of sovereignty over a broad geographic area.[46]

Attempts by sending states to embrace their emigrants unbundle the territoriality of those polities by including members abroad as critical actors in the sending state's political, legal, and economic arenas. Yet the inclusion of emigrants is only partial because of the ongoing endurance of legal territorial sovereignty. Sending states cannot act toward emigrants as they would toward resident citizens because the former are within the borders of another state. Efforts at emigrant inclusion such as extending the right to vote in absentia have created a distinct form of extraterritorial citizenship precisely because the territoriality of the nation-state system prevents the functioning of "normal" residential citizenship. The demographic weight of the absent population and its control over economic and political resources coveted at home turn extraterritorial citizenship from a trivial curiosity into a cornerstone of that particular nation-state. The ensuing attempts to manage the perils and promises of emigration reveal important changes, but also the limits to change, in how governments exercise power over citizens and territories.

A NEW SOCIAL CONTRACT

National citizenship is often compared to a marriage between a citizen and his or her state, and historically the state has been a jealous spouse. The nation-state is based on the principle that each nation (that is, each people) has one state, and each individual belongs to only one nation. During the mass transatlantic migrations of the nineteenth century, changing citizenship, much less holding dual citizenship, was a major source of tension between European states that kept claims on their overseas citizens and New World states bent on assimilating them. Most European governments cited the doctrine of "perpetual allegiance" when they refused to recognize New World naturalizations: Once an Englishman, always an Englishman. One of the proximate causes of the War of 1812 was British impressment into its navy of British subjects who had become naturalized U.S. citizens. The United States did not resolve this issue with many European source countries until the series of bilateral Bancroft treaties in the 1860s and 1870s. The U.S. experience was hardly exceptional. The Italian government vehemently protested Brazil's 1891 Constitution that automatically naturalized resident foreigners, and Rome even tried to cut off emigration in response. The principle of exclusive nationality was codified in the 1930 Hague Convention concerning Certain Questions relating to the Conflict of Nationality and reaffirmed in international agreements such as the 1963 Convention on Reduction of Cases of Multiple Nationality.

Germany's constitutional court in 1974 called multiple nationality "an evil that should be avoided or eliminated in the interests of states as well as in the interests of the affected citizen. . . . States seek to achieve exclusivity of their respective nationalities in order to set clear boundaries for their sovereignty over persons."[47]

Nonetheless, acceptance of dual nationality has increased in recent years, to the point that eighty-nine countries allowed some form of it in 2000.[48] The 1997 European Convention on Nationality takes a much more permissive view of dual nationality than earlier European accords. Some countries of immigration, such as France, Canada, and the United Kingdom, openly accept dual nationality; others, such as the United States and Germany, increasingly tolerate it despite formal reservations. Several secular trends are driving the growing legitimacy of dual nationality. Governments assign nationality based on *jus sanguinis* (the principle of descent) and/or *jus soli* (the principle of birth in the territory), so that a child born in a jus soli country to immigrant parents from a jus sanguinis country carries both nationalities. As nationality regimes increasingly adopt elements of both sanguinis and soli, the opportunities for overlapping nationalities increase. International regimes against gender discrimination have reduced rules that force women to take the nationality of their husband and pass nationality to children only via the father, so international marriages are now more likely to result in mixed-status families. The decline in the number of wars between states has also made the prospect of dual loyalty seem less threatening than it did until the end of World War II. Finally, the acceptance of dual nationality has become a policy tool of countries of emigration trying to maintain claims on emigrants and their economic and political resources in host countries.[49]

In Mexico, one way the state is restructuring its ties to emigrants in the United States is by promoting a dual nationalism of affection toward both countries rather than promoting exclusive devotion to Mexico. Historically, the law in Mexico has been just as hostile to dual nationality as it has been in most countries; naturalizing abroad was grounds for losing Mexican citizenship or nationality beginning in 1857. In 1998, the law of "non-forfeiture" (*no pérdida*) of nationality went into effect, protecting native

Mexicans from mandatory denationalization for becoming nationals of another country, though they can still voluntarily expatriate. In effect, it is a dual nationality law.[50] The novelty in promoting legal dual nationality extends to promoting a sort of cultural and political dual affiliation in which Mexican migrants are encouraged to become Americans while maintaining their *mexicanidad* (Mexicanness). President Ernesto Zedillo in 1995 privately told a group of U.S. Latino leaders in Texas that the goal of dual nationality was "to develop a close relationship between his government and Mexican Americans, one in which they could be called upon to lobby U.S. policy-makers on economic and political issues involving the United States and Mexico."[51]

Carlos González Gutiérrez, one of the founders of Mexico's Program for Mexican Communities Abroad, has argued that the integration of Mexicans into U.S. society is desirable for the same reason: "In the policies of state, the objective is to influence the way first-generation immigrants and their children (the majority of whom are United States–born) assimilate into American society. The idea is not to obstruct or stop their assimilation, because this is not possible; the purpose is rather to foster in Mexican Americans a pluralistic sense of belonging to the Mexican nation, without failing to recognize that the majority are Americans by choice."[52] In this claim, the "assimilation" of Mexicans into another culture does not strip them of their mexicanidad. The interests of the Mexican state are best served by allowing Mexicans in the United States to adopt not only the legal category of dual nationality, but also the practices and self-identification of dual nationalism. To be an effective ethnic lobby, emigrants must integrate into the U.S. political community. Emigrants are also better able to protect their human and social rights as U.S. citizens than as Mexicans living under the tattered umbrella of consular protection. The promotion of duality for both of these reasons represents a new development in Mexican attempts to embrace emigrants.

Like Turkey, the Dominican Republic, Brazil, and El Salvador, Mexico is just one of many countries of mass emigration that have recently allowed dual nationality. In Latin America, only four countries accepted dual nationality before 1991, but six more recognized it in the following six years.[53] Of course, many countries have recognized some form of dual nationality for generations. As early as 1912, the Italian government accepted the reality of mobile Italians' plural ties as a practical concession to maintain some kind of state-emigrant relationship, but it did not encourage emigrants to adopt dual ties. The novelty of contemporary emigrant citizenship lies in the strengthening of emigrant rights in particular countries, the global scale of the acceptance of dual nationality, and source-country governments' *active* promotion of dual nationality.

A second way that the tie between emigrants and their home state is changing is the institutionalization of a more voluntaristic relationship between the two. The state has renegotiated the social contract with emigrants by following the membership model of the Catholic Church. Like the state, the Church in a given country is both a membership organization and an organization with administrative authority over a specific territory. As such, Church and state share many of the dilemmas posed by emigration. Foucault has observed that the modern state, like the Church, exercises the "pastoral power" of wielding "power over a flock rather than over a land."[54] One of the defining features of the modern state is the monopolization of power in a specific territory, but Foucault's emphasis on the flock resonates with state and Church efforts to control even those members of the flock who stray beyond the territory. The concept of pastoral power also points to the ways that both Church and state concern themselves with the discipline and ideological education of the population in areas such as sexuality, the family, and work. Strong parallels emerge between the challenges of governmentality for state and Church because of their shared interest in administering people, rather than places alone, and their totalizing projects of pastoral care.

The Church went through the transition from coercive to voluntary relations with its members in the nineteenth century, when it was disestablished as the religion of state in Mexico as part of a broader process of secularizing government throughout much of Europe and its former colonies. To borrow from Michael Mann's distinction among different types of power, the modern Church wields "ideological power" through its dominance over systems of meaning, morals, and ritual. It no longer exercises significant "political power" in the sense of the regulation over territories that states brandish.[55] The Church has learned to rely on the ideological power of religion and pleas for contributions rather than forced tithing. Consequently, it has been better equipped than the state to deal with members who leave a particular jurisdiction. The state, which stripped the Church of its secular powers over many bloody decades, has now adopted the Church's basic model of membership to embrace the emigrants whom both organizations covet. At the local level in migrant-sending communities, Church and state authorities attempt to manage the cultural effects of emigration through similar expressions of pastoral power. Both institutions have become loose collaborators in their attempts to embrace emigrants, and they deploy a similar set of administrative techniques and nationalist symbols toward that end. The ongoing salience of territorial sovereignty has forced these institutions to find creative ways to embrace emigrants outside the territory. The result has been a much more voluntaristic and limited form of citizenship tying emigrants to Mexico, whereby the government passes a transborder collection plate seeking remittances in exchange for the mostly ideological rewards of proclaiming emigrants heroic absent sons and daughters.

Policies in Mexico and other migrant-sending countries are converging toward this more voluntaristic and pluralistic model of emigrant citizenship. State strategies negotiated with emigrants that take advantage of their international mobility have created a citizenship à la carte, based on voluntary membership, a choice of multiple political affiliations, and an emphasis on rights over obligations.[56] These shifts have not been driven by the impending demise of the nation-state system, as some globalist and transnationalist scholars have argued. Rather, new forms of citizenship and strategies for embracing emigrants are the product of an international system that limits the reach of states outside their territory to the politics of symbolism and soft cultural nationalism.

TWO Inside the Sending State

At a Fourth of July party held at the U.S. consul's house in Guadalajara, several U.S. Foreign Service officers who decide whether to issue Mexicans visas asked me about my research. "Mexico's emigration policy?" one laughed incredulously. "They don't have one!" The officer's perception is common in both countries. Yet the Mexican government has always had an emigration policy. Almost forgotten today is that Mexico City generally tried to restrict emigration to the United States prior to World War II and select particular kinds of workers to participate in the 1942–64 bracero program. Its laissez-faire attitude toward emigration in the 1970s and 1980s was itself a policy following a demographic interest in releasing the pressures of rapid population growth. The overt efforts of President Vicente Fox (2000–2006) to negotiate a bilateral migration accord with the United States were simply the latest in a series of evolving policies.

To be sure, Mexican authorities have struggled to manage population movements in practice. The transformation of emigrant citizenship in the 1990s grew out of the government's difficulty in shaping the major characteristics of its emigration throughout the twentieth century. This chapter uncovers a largely forgotten history of how the Mexican government tried to control the flow of workers to the United States. To what extent did Mexican policy affect the size of flows, types of migrants, and remittance levels? What constrains the Mexican government's ability to affect those outcomes? Understanding the early failures of emigration policy helps explain why subsequent policies have focused on embracing emigrants rather than controlling their departure.

The standard explanation for the end of serious emigration controls in most parts of the world is drawn from the European experience. Mercantilist European governments subscribed to the theory that economic assets such as land, capital, and workers are finite resources; countries that acquire these assets and turn them into traded goods are successful at the expense of competing countries. Such states tried to control exit during much of the eighteenth and nineteenth centuries because they saw a large population as a source of economic and political strength. As these states moved toward capitalist economies, they discovered the value of allowing greater labor mobility that responded to local supply and demand. Major European governments began dropping emigration restrictions in what Zolberg calls "the Exit Revolution."[1] Political liberalism, emphasizing individual rights and freedom from state intervention, has an elective affinity with capitalism, and the right of citizens to leave their country eventually was enshrined in prominent legal expressions of liberal philosophy such as the 1948 Universal Declaration of Human Rights. The fall of the Iron Curtain in 1989–90, which allowed citizens to emigrate from the former Soviet bloc, is further evidence of the importance of a liberal polity and capitalist economy in explaining the end of exit control. In the conventional account, the external constraints of global political liberalism reduce the ability of countries to exercise their sovereign right to regulate emigration. Preventing citizens from leaving has become internationally unacceptable.

The Mexican experience provides a counterpoint to the standard story of the end of exit controls. In broad strokes, Mexican policies have shifted from failed efforts to control emigration until the early 1970s to policies of managing emigrants already in the United States since the 1990s. The Mexican government effectively stopped trying to control emigration in 1974, when its economic model was still geared toward national economic self-sufficiency. The transition to a neoliberal, export-oriented economy did not happen until the 1980s. A change in economic policies cannot explain the change in emigration policy, because the economic transition in the 1980s *followed* the laissez-faire emigration policy of the 1970s. Likewise, an ascendant liberal political ideology does not explain the shift toward laissez-faire emigration policies in the 1970s, because the formal Mexican liberalism proclaiming a right to exit dates back to the 1857 and 1917 Constitutions. Formal liberalism coexisted with authoritarian regimes that subjected the right to exit to qualifications and contradictory, expedient interpretations. The Mexican political system did not fundamentally open until the 1990s, when the groundwork was laid for the consolidation of democracy with the 2000 election of Vicente Fox, the first opposition candidate elected after seventy-one years of one-party rule.

If changes in the political economy and ideological limits on the sovereign right to control emigration do not explain the end of exit controls in Mexico, what does? This chapter shows that the Mexican federal government's efforts to control the volume and selection of emigrants have been constrained from within and without. Looking "inside the state," to use the sociologist Kitty Calavita's term, shows that county governments defied restrictive federal policy by using emigration as an escape valve to alleviate local political and economic crises. Conflicts within the Mexican state have not been about whether there should be any emigration at all, but rather what kinds of people should be allowed to leave, under what conditions, and how to control internal and international labor migrations at the same time. The unintended consequences of other government projects and systemic corruption further blocked the implementation of federal policies. From without, the U.S. government periodically permitted, or even stimulated, illegal migration. United States policies exercising sovereignty over immigration matters usually undermined Mexican emigration policy.

By the 1970s, Mexico's stunning population growth had removed the demographic and economic rationale for exit control, and it abandoned the effort altogether. The massive size of the emigrant population and a trend toward permanent U.S. settlement in the 1980s and 1990s created the foundation for a new emigrant policy, which promotes remittances, dual nationality, integrating emigrants into Mexican party politics symbolically while limiting their real political influence, and a Mexican ethnic lobby in Washington. While these policies were developed among migrants and political actors within Mexico, the underlying conditions for them were created by the often unintended consequences of U.S. policies and U.S. employers' insatiable demands for Mexican workers.

"BLEEDING MEXICO WHITE," 1900–1925

From the beginning of mass Mexican migration to the United States at the turn of the twentieth century, Mexican officials and intellectuals raised concerns about the demographic, economic, and ideological effects of emigration. In a series of Mexico City newspaper articles, the consular functionary Enrique Santibáñez called the presence of almost half a million native Mexicans in the United States "a veritable hemorrhage suffered by the country." A study published by the Secretariat of the Interior claimed emigration was "bleeding Mexico white."[2] These losses came on the heels of the demographic disaster of the revolution, which had reduced the country's population by 6 percent between 1910 and 1921. Mexico's leaders believed that its population was insufficient to achieve its full economic potential, particularly in the vast northern provinces. They blamed the 1848 loss of the northern half of Mexico to the United States on the weak Mexican population base in Texas and California prior to the war. Their ideal solution was massive European immigration to colonize sparsely populated areas. Unfortunately for Mexico, the United States and Argentina proved to be more attractive destinations for Europeans. Only half a percent of late nineteenth-century transatlantic European immigrants settled in Mexico. Preventing further emigration of Mexicans to the United States thus became central to elite understandings of national demographic h~ ˙

Ideological objections to emigration complemented ec demographic calculations. The Mexican government souȿ populace splintered by ethnicity and class around the common foreign menace of the United States, a country that had intervened militarily in Mexico as recently as the 1914 occupation of Veracruz and the 1916–17 "punitive expedition" into northern Mexico in pursuit of the revolutionary leader Pancho Villa. Rumors of war between Mexico and the United States circulated as late as 1926.[4] State-led nationalism was threatened by an emigration to the northern nemesis that stripped many Mexicans of their cultural nationality in a process that Mexican president Plutarco Elías Calles (1924–28) disparagingly called *desmexicanización*.[5]

Attempts to dissuade emigration began as early as 1904, when Mexican federal and state authorities ordered county governments to stop issuing travel documents used by U.S.-bound workers. The secretariat complained to county governments that many of the migrants were "people from the low class." Allowing them to migrate would "make the condition of our needy compatriots [in the United States] more precarious, with the danger that the most severe and unfavorable comments about the economic and political situation of Mexico will continue to be made."[6] Mexican elites interpreted the humiliations of emigrants in the United States as humiliations not only of individuals, but of Mexico herself. To make matters worse, federal and local authorities feared that masses of unemployed migrants waiting to cross the border "could eventually turn dangerous" and that emigration was creating labor shortages in the states of Jalisco, Michoacán, and Guanajuato. In repeated orders to county and state governments, the Secretariat of the Interior attempted to avoid these problems by controlling emigration six hundred miles from the border in the source communities.[7]

How to stop emigration was another question. The Secretariat of the Interior noted in a 1910 letter to governors that the propaganda pamphlets distributed by state governments were ineffective at deterring illiterate peasants. Source-state governors repeatedly asked the secretariat to restrict or prohibit emigration to protect their supply of labor. Federal officials usually argued that constitutionally they could dissuade exit, but not prevent it.[8] The Constitution leaves room for situational interpretations, however. Article 11 of the 1857 Constitution, which was in effect until 1917, established freedom of exit and travel within the country, subject to administrative restrictions in criminal and civil matters.[9] The 1917 Constitution restricted exit further through its reference to a secondary body of migration law and Article 123, which specified that county authorities must ensure that migrating workers left with signed contracts detailing wages and hours and including the provision that employers cover repatriation costs.[10]

The 1917 Mexican ban on *leaving without* a contract, combined with the 1885–1952 U.S. ban on *entering with* a contract, meant that Mexican labor migration to the United States was illegal according to the laws of at least one of the countries.[11] From 1917 to 1921, the United States allowed in seventy thousand contracted workers as a unilateral emergency measure to fill labor shortages during World War I. In violation of Mexican law, the contracts were not approved by U.S. consular authorities in Mexico prior to the workers' departure. The United States made another exception to the ban on admitting contracted immigrant workers beginning with the 1942 bracero program, but from 1921 to 1942, U.S. policy meant that Mexico could not enforce its own contract laws aimed at protecting emigrants.[12]

The 1910–20 Mexican Revolution sent hundreds of thousands fleeing north and made emigration control even more tenuous.[13] The state effectively ceased to exist in many parts of the country during the early years of the revolution. Even during its denouement, the multiple agencies of the federal government charged with implementing emigration policy developed contradictory initiatives. Confusion reigned within the Mexican government about whether the Secretariat of the Interior, Foreign Relations, or Commerce and Labor was responsible for enforcing the labor contracts and preventing abuses by U.S. employers. Yet the Mexican federal government did not try to block the exit of contracted workers, largely because the presidency and Secretariat of Foreign Relations did not want to antagonize the United States during a moment of extreme Mexican vulnerability. At the same time, the government of President Venustiano Carranza (1917–20) was disturbed by the U.S. military's conscription of Mexican nationals during World War I. It accelerated a campaign in 1918 to convince potential migrants that Mexico City was taking strong measures to prevent the exit of uncontracted workers. In practice, this was the bluff of a weak government without a coherent policy. Complying with a directive from the Department of Labor to subsidize rail passage for unemployed workers traveling within Mexico to find jobs, federal railroads brought hundreds of unemployed workers to the northern border. Many of them immediately crossed into the United States without a contract, in violation of the Secretariat of the Interior's policy.[14]

Following the end of World War I, the Carranza government feared the prospect of massive deportations of Mexican workers no longer needed by the United States. Carranza selectively financed repatriations as a preemptive measure to avoid the national humiliation of seeing thousands of Mexican citizens deported by the United States, underlining how potential U.S. actions could shape Mexican policy even before Washington acted. Mexico City sponsored fifty thousand repatriations at a cost of US$1 million during the 1921–22 U.S. depression. Such expenses prompted the federal government to suspend its program in 1923 and once again rely on periodic public warnings not to leave and a 1925 ban on selling railway tickets in the interior to laborers heading to the United States.[15] A 1926 migration law gave authority to the Secretariat of the Interior "to use *la fuerza pública* [law enforcement] to prevent the departure of individuals who have not complied with the requirements of the law"; specifically, migrants were required to carry labor contracts approved by the county president in their place of residence. To enforce this law and fine violators, emigration control officers were deployed along the border, in trains, and in major cities of the interior.[16]

Emigration policies varied by region during the revolutionary period. The governors of the sparsely populated northern states of Sonora and Chihuahua ordered migration offices in the border cities of Ciudad Juárez and Nogales to deny workers exit permits and to prevent the operation of *enganchadores* (labor recruiters from U.S. companies). In 1918, the border state of Tamaulipas raised its international bridge fees to discourage emigration, which was sucking labor away from regional industries. The following year, the government of Jalisco restricted the issuance of passports to appease local industrialists and farmers complaining of worker shortages. It asked county presidents to select the emigrants most in need of state repatriation aid and financed the return of 1,178 Jaliscienses. Given that Jalisco was heavily populated, claims of labor shortages seem to have been cover for employers' reluctance to pay higher wages to attract laborers from a sufficient pool.[17] The historian John Martinez claimed that during this period "the fact is that Mexico did not really desire to stop the emigration," but multiple interests operated within the state, and its agents simply did not have the capacity to enforce formal directives.[18]

THE CRISTERO RUPTURE, 1926–1929

Civil war opened another major cleavage between the Secretariat of the Interior's emigration policy and actual practices of local governments. The federal government's effort to weaken the Catholic Church as an institutional competitor exploded into armed conflict with Catholic Cristero rebels between 1926 and 1929. A less intense, second war sputtered through the mid-1930s. Most of the fighting took place in the central west states of Jalisco, Michoacán, Guanajuato, and Zacatecas—states that already contributed 60 percent of Mexican emigrants to the United States.[19] Despite federal efforts to restrict emigration, from the perspective of local government in war-torn areas encouraging emigration was a political escape valve.

The experience of Arandas in the Altos de Jalisco region during the Cristero War illustrates the contradictions of emigration control practices among different levels and agencies of government. During three different periods, the federal army throughout Los Altos forcibly concentrated peasants into towns as part of its counterinsurgency strategy. Patrols executed men traveling in the countryside without a pass on the presumption that they were rebels. Tens of thousands of peasants were forced to leave their crops and cattle behind. In some cases, owners destroyed their own livelihood to deny the federal troops food; Cristeros and federal soldiers ruined the rest. Concentrating the population in towns stripped the rebels of their cover in the countryside, but it also created volatile social conditions throughout Los Altos. Local governments with limited resources were forced to deal with the influx of impoverished peasants. In Arandas, the local government converted public buildings into shelters. In crowded conditions without proper sanitation, a thousand cases of smallpox broke out in April 1927. Motivated to "avoid violence due to the scarcity of food," the county president of Arandas formed an aid committee composed of local elites that donated food to the peasants.[20]

The fastest way to ease the crisis was simply to encourage people to leave the region. Several thousand Arandenses joined an estimated 200,000 internal migrants and nearly 340,000 U.S.-bound emigrants on the move between 1926 and 1931.[21] During the 1920s and early 1930s, the county government of Arandas issued hundreds of *salvoconductos* (safe conduct passes allowing the bearer to pass government checkpoints). The passes were issued to men—and, less frequently, their families—seeking work in the United States or other parts of Mexico. The documents gave the bearer's name, birthplace, a physical description, and certification that the bearer "has been an honorable and hardworking person, who is heading for the cities on the northern border with the United States, for the purpose of seeking work for his family." Although local governments effectively controlled the issuance of documents that were used for both domestic and international travel, the federal government had long complained about this practice, noting that according to federal law, only migration inspectors, county presidents in border towns, and governors in the interior had the authority to issue passports for travel to the United States.[22] The 1926 migration law created a new passport regime controlled by the Secretariat of the Interior within Mexico and the Secretariat of Foreign Relations abroad. In practice, however, county governments continued to issue their own documents for travel to northern border states, thus resisting federal attempts to prevent U.S.-bound emigrants from ever leaving the Mexican heartland.

Different ministries and levels of government promoted competing policies. On the one hand, the government of Arandas sought to encourage emigration. This required the cooperation of the federal army, which had imposed martial law and checked safe conduct passes on the roads. The army offered Cristeros amnesty and a safe conduct pass to the United States if they surrendered. Some Cristeros accepted those terms and joined the Church hierarchy and parish priests in exile in the United States.[23] At the same time, the Secretariat of the Interior continued its propaganda campaign against emigration and enganchadores. The agencies of the federal government that were focused on crushing the Cristeros indirectly undermined the Secretariat of the Interior's emigration strategy. In an attempt to provide better cooperation between federal agencies, the 1930 Law of Migration established an Advisory Council of Migration led by the chief of the Secretariat of the Interior's Department of Migration and including representatives from the federal secretariats of Foreign Relations; Communications and Public Works; Treasury; Industry, Commerce, and Labor; Agriculture and Development; Public Health; and National Statistics. The council was charged with developing policies to control the flow of workers, provide consular protection in the United States, and study the push factors causing emigration.[24] But their efforts at coordination came too late. In war-torn areas, local governments, economic elites, and the army eagerly opened the economic and political escape valve at a critical moment, when emigration soared to relative levels not seen again until the 1980s.

A second Cristero War in the mid-1930s pitted Catholic rebels against agrarian reformers and a federal government intent on monopolizing education at the expense of the Church.[25] County presidents again ignored repeated federal instructions to "make intense propaganda" to dissuade emigration, which the federal government continued to insist was a source of labor shortages and a problem because of the lack of protections for workers abroad.[26] In practice, local authorities provided hundreds of travel documents for emigrants. Paul Taylor found that the Arandas oligarchy representing ranching and commercial interests actively encouraged emigration to prevent a concentration of landless laborers who might turn into *agrarista* radicals demanding the redistribution of land. Arandas and southern Los Altos were a bastion against the agrarian reform, unlike many high emigration areas, where agrarianist radicals were active and often included returned migrants.[27] Elites wrote letters of recommendation to county presidents for workers seeking travel documents. Acquiring an international passport required the signature of "three persons of recognized honorability" in the applicant's place of residence. Given low literacy rates, the requirement effectively meant a recommendation from three elites.[28] Some elites provided loans to finance emigrants' journey north, though one leading merchant told Taylor he refused to lend money to departing Arandenses because he opposed emigration's effects on Mexico: "Every Mexican who goes likes the United States better than Mexico. . . . After 100 years, it will be good-bye to Mexico. I am afraid they will like America better than Mexico. We are making 'war' [nationalist propaganda] so they won't become Americanized. They will not like the Mexican flag; they have not love of country, and that is a great danger to Mexico." While this merchant feared that emigrants were traitors to the motherland, the material incentives to make loans usually trumped other interests. As Taylor observed, "The paucity of large employers of labor, the ample supplies of laborers produced locally by a prolific people, the remunerative rates on interest, with the knowledge that if one person did not lend, another would, eliminated any possible reluctance to assist emigration."[29]

Once again, policies with greater priority undermined the Secretariat of the Interior's emigration strategy; the federal executive gave precedence to achieving control over the Church, remaking the nation through "socialist education," and redistributing land. In Arandas, the simple threat of federal land reform (which never happened on a significant scale in the region) prompted the oligarchy controlling the Arandas government and economy to undermine official emigration policies by encouraging the exit of potential agraristas.[30] Agrarian reform was supposed to reduce the emigration of landless peasants, yet in regions where the policy was enacted, it often spurred even more migration to the United States. Faced with limited government support or sources of credit, peasants went to the United States to work and save enough money to invest in farm equipment, seeds, and fertilizer for their newly acquired land back home.[31] The unintended consequences of the agrarian reform and fight against the Catholic Church shaped migration patterns more than emigration policy itself.

MASS REPATRIATION, 1930–1941

At the same time as it was being undermined from within, Mexico's emigration policy was hit by an avalanche from without. Encouraging repatriation had been federal policy on and off since the Porfirian era

(1877–1911),[32] but the government's ability to control the flow of repatriates and design effective reintegration programs was limited by Mexico's weak position relative to the United States. With the onset of the Great Depression, U.S. officials at all levels of government began using multiple forms of suasion, including high-profile deportation raids, to repatriate an estimated four hundred thousand Mexicans between 1929 and 1939. Trying to make the best of a difficult situation, Mexican authorities cast repatriation as the calling home of the nation's sons by a state dedicated to protecting all its workers. The Mexican government cooperated with U.S. authorities and paid for the transportation home of thousands of returnees.[33] But an influx of four hundred thousand repatriates threatened greater social and political unrest than smaller, earlier repatriations. The quasi-governmental National Repatriation Committee in 1932 distributed posters to county governments urging the public to help pay for the expenses of return and resettlement: "Help our own, not only offering them food and clothing, but also . . . incorporating them once again into the bosom of the motherland. Their fraternal blood, full of vigor and learning, impregnated with civilization and modern virtues, will generously repay the support of the people."[34]

In private correspondence to county governments, the National Repatriation Committee dropped its flowery language and appealed for donations to avoid "the danger of seeing our cities filled with ever greater groups of people without work." Through their contributions, local authorities could address the "problem of [job] displacement that is beginning to develop, which the public does not yet realize, but that is already obvious in our statistics," and "stave off this evil before it assumes the character of social disorder."[35] The key to resolving this problem, in the federal government's view, was the distribution of labor across Mexico's territory. According to the six-year plan of president Lázaro Cárdenas (1934–40), returnees would establish colonies, mostly in sparsely populated northern states. The colonies would be close enough to existing settlements that returnees would share modern farming methods with the natives, but without being so close that returnees would revert to "backward" ways of living.[36] Government officials and academics (who were often one and the same) such as Manuel Gamio, the father of Mexican anthropology, had long dreamed that repatriates would be engines of economic, cultural, and political modernization based on their exposure to the United States. Instead, most repatriates returned to heavily populated states of origin such as Jalisco, where they did little to transform local agriculture. The colonies withered from insufficient planning and a lack of resources.[37] If the Mexican government had not adequately integrated smaller streams of repatriates in the early 1920s, it could hardly do better when faced with nearly half a million returnees in a single decade. In this case, Mexican capacity to respond to repatriations was constrained by push factors in the United States that were out of Mexican control.

THE BRACERO (DIS)AGREEMENTS, 1942–1964

As late as 1941, the Secretariat of the Interior had warned county presidents that workers who attempted to enter the United States "would only swell the ranks of the prison populations already serving sentences for violating migration laws."[38] The policy changed within a matter of months when the U.S. and Mexican governments in 1942 negotiated a series of agreements that would expire in 1964, providing 4.6 million bracero contracts for temporary agricultural work in the United States. (American authorities made five million apprehensions of unauthorized migrants during the same period.) The immediate cause of the shift in Mexican policy was a sudden improvement in its bargaining position with the United States brought on by the wartime alliance with the Allied powers and increased U.S. demand for agricultural workers. These circumstances allowed the Mexican government to negotiate a favorable agreement supervised by both countries to ensure adequate wages and working conditions. In theory, Mexico would exchange a pool of unemployed laborers for a source of remittances and modernizing influences.[39] From a longer historical perspective, the unintended consequences of consolidated state building caused the shift to promoting mass, temporary emigration. Nationalist arguments against emigration as a betrayal of the motherland in its moment of crisis lost resonance as the economy grew, the postrevolutionary state was consolidated, and the threat of armed U.S. intervention faded. Most important, an increase in life expectancy prompted by state-led development began to create pockets of excess population.[40]

As the bracero program continued following the end of World War II, disagreements simmered between Washington and Mexico City over U.S. government supervision of wages and working conditions. The quality of the contracts declined and abuses of workers multiplied, prompting the Mexican federal government to try to negotiate better contracts. Through the mid-1950s, the Mexican government continued a cycle of promoting bracero emigration one week and then suddenly trying to stop *all* emigration, depending on the vicissitudes of the guest-worker negotiations. Unfortunately for the government, the escape valve is only a metaphor, and humans do not respond as quickly and compliantly as a mechanical device. For example, the Mexican federal government urgently called for more braceros from the counties in May 1948. When the government abrogated the agreements only nine days later, it demanded that county presidents warn bracero aspirants of the "grave harm" they risked by emigrating without contracts.[41] The bilateral dispute erupted again in October 1948. Mexican officials pressured the U.S. government to make concessions by refusing to allow any workers to cross into the United States. Under pressure from employers, U.S. immigration officials opened the gates at El Paso, allowing an estimated four thousand illegal entrants across in three days. Mexico responded by abrogating the agreement, which was not renegotiated until August 1949. Similarly, when the U.S. government adopted a policy of unilateral contracts in January 1954, the governor of Jalisco ordered county presidents to prevent emigrants from leaving and warned that citizens who disobeyed would be punished.[42] As Mexican troops clashed with thousands of rioting workers attempting to cross the border illegally, U.S. immigration officials welcomed successful crossers and sent them on to the fields.[43]

By turning a blind eye when convenient, U.S. immigration practice, which often directly contradicted U.S. law, once again undercut Mexico City's stance on emigration. Mexican authorities attempted to restrict illegal migration while powerful elements within the U.S. government encouraged it. Mexico remained at a structural disadvantage in the negotiations. The United States had the option of replacing Mexicans with workers from other areas, such as the Caribbean, whereas Mexican labor emigration was exclusively dependent on the United States. Given the asymmetries in their relationship and a proven inability to stop emigrants from leaving, the Mexican government had few means of forcing U.S. concessions.

Subversions from Within

The Mexican federal government's attempts to control the numbers of emigrants, their wages, and their working conditions were thus weakened by the policies of the United States. At the same time, the government's attempts to control the types of emigrants were subverted by internal actors. Establishing the types of workers eligible to participate in the bracero program was negotiated within the Mexican government and the official party's labor and peasant unions. Authorities at all levels argued that excessive emigration, particularly when workers abandoned their jobs, was detrimental to the economy of major sending states. The labor sector of the ruling Institutional Revolutionary Party opposed the bracero program, fearing that it would reduce the number of industrial workers from which it derived its strength. Industrialists and large farmers complained of labor shortages, and leaders of the *ejido* agricultural sector (based on a corporatist land tenure arrangement) worried that the emigration of ejido members would sap productivity. National interest groups did little to oppose the program actively, however—most likely because significant shortages were localized.[44]

Some provincial and local leaders controlled emigration more successfully. The governors of Jalisco, Guanajuato, and Michoacán banned the contracting of braceros between 1943 and 1944.[45] The governor of Jalisco praised the ban, which would prevent "the immoderate flow of Jalisciense braceros, with the purpose of protecting the productive activities of the State, as it has become increasingly noticeable that in agricultural work, in skilled work, and in the factories, there is a growing scarcity of human resources that would guarantee the filling of local demand."[46] County officials in the state of México and state officials in Coahuila and Baja California adopted similar policies, citing laws written in the 1930s giving the government authority to restrict emigration when there was a shortage of workers. Governments also regulated labor they needed for their own projects. The state of Oaxaca demanded a 100-peso fee from braceros to release them from their obligations to perform community work such as building roads and public buildings: In Janos, Chihuahua, local authorities refused to apply for a bracero quota despite bitter local protests because they needed workers for infrastructure projects.[47] The Bureau of Migratory Farm Labor Affairs allocated bracero quotas to the governors of selected states, who then divided the quota among their counties. In principle, bracero quotas were allotted based on local unemployment rates. In practice, the percentage of the state's quota given to a county tended to remain stable once established unless politicians intervened on the behalf of their clients.[48]

The Inter-Governmental Commission on Emigrant Worker Affairs ordered county presidents to prepare registries of applicants. Eligibility was restricted to unemployed men ages twenty to forty who were physically fit for agricultural labor. Ejido members, peasants active in the current agricultural cycle, public employees, employees of private companies, skilled workers, and those who had not completed their military service were banned from participating. According to rules in effect for most of the program, the first stage of selecting braceros was a county lottery for eligible workers. Winners then traveled to contracting centers in selected cities. Jalisco authorities in 1952 specified that the county lottery was necessary only if there were more eligible aspirants than the county quota. That year, Arandas officials reported that the lottery was unnecessary because exactly one hundred aspirants had applied for the one hundred available slots![49]

In the three main traditional sending states of Michoacán, Jalisco, and Guanajuato, there were generally twenty aspirants per contract awarded. In practice, bribery was the usual way to get a bracero contract. A 1957 report estimated that bracero bribery was a US$7.2 million business.[50] None of the twelve former braceros interviewed in Arandas in 2003 was selected through the formal county lottery system. "Only a few got lucky [in the lottery], and a lot of us wanted to go," explained a seventy-two-year-old bracero who had five contracts from 1956 to 1962. He obtained his contracts by giving "a little gift" to friends in the Secretariat of the Interior in

Mexico City. On at least one of their trips, nine of the twelve had paid a domestic coyote between 200 and 400 pesos to enroll them with corrupt government officials in Mexico City or at the contracting centers in the northern cities of Monterrey, Nuevo León, and Empalme, Sonora. Participating in the formal program involved corruption as well. A sixty-five-year-old bracero contracted in 1958 and 1959 said that obtaining the required letter of good conduct from the county president was difficult for someone living in the countryside: "Well, there were little problems, because sometimes [county officials] didn't know you. But working through friends, through someone you knew in the county president's office, they gave you a letter. Because sometimes [the officials] didn't want to give you a letter just because you went and asked for one. It was more like, 'You're my friend and you help me, so here's a little donation.'"

Aspirants saw little reason to wait for the next lottery when bribery might be necessary in any case and services were available from coyotes (the same term used for their international smuggling counterparts). An eighty-one-year-old who had nine contracts from 1954 to 1964 said he never bothered with the lottery because there was no guarantee of being selected: "I heard so-and-so was signing people up, so I contacted him. . . . With a coyote we didn't lose time." In Arandas, even the official rolls of hundreds of men applying to become braceros listed carpenters, blacksmiths, bakers, shoemakers, barbers, and other skilled workers who were formally ineligible regardless of their employment status. When asked about the requirements for bracero aspirants, a former county president during the 1950s said, "We didn't ask them anything. . . . They asked to be put on the list, and we put them on. There was no investigation of whether they were eligible or not." A commissar of the only ejido in the county of Arandas estimated that the majority of *ejidatarios* were braceros during the period even though the federal government restricted both the domestic and international migration of ejido members. Federal officials estimated that 20 percent of braceros had land despite the prohibition on their exit.[51] In short, most restrictions on eligibility were meaningless in practice.

The federal government announced periodic campaigns against corruption and passed a 1950 law detailing prison terms and fines for coyotes and enganchadores. On the orders of the Secretariat of the Interior, county officials or designated leaders accompanied contingents of braceros selected in the county lottery to the contracting centers to ensure that only legitimate braceros were contracted.[52] While efforts to squelch informal practices failed overall, the federal and state governments appear to have made an effort to crack down on corruption if only to better control the distribution of workers *within* Mexico.

Domestic migration policy had long adopted many of the methods of international emigration policy. In 1907, the states of Querétaro and Zacatecas banned the hiring of "their" workers by recruiters from other Mexican states. In the 1920s, the federal Department of Labor paid for hundreds of surplus domestic migrants seeking work around Tampico, Veracruz, to return to their hometowns in a sort of internal repatriation. The department ordered county presidents on the other side of the country from Veracruz to "use all the means at your disposal to deter the emigration of workers to the port." Attempts to control regional labor markets accelerated in the 1930s, when the Cárdenas government sharply increased state control over the economy. The Department of Labor created a formal program in 1935 to match workers with jobs county by county.[53] The attempted matching of workers and jobs reached its apogee in 1953 with the creation of a federal Labor Exchange Office. Cooperation with the Labor Exchange appears to have been spotty. The government of Arandas informed the exchange in 1953 that there was "neither need nor excess of workers," implying that labor supply and demand were neatly matched. Yet that same year, official Arandas records showed 507 unemployed workers meeting bracero requirements, the highest annual number recorded in the extant archives from 1942 to 1964.[54] Potential braceros preferred to work in the United States for higher wages than to migrate internally, and local officials had no incentive to send them elsewhere in Mexico, where wages were lower.

The federal government worked with governors, county presidents, and agribusiness in northern states to create a more effective plan to regulate internal labor markets. During the 1950s, braceros in several areas were required to work in domestic agriculture before being contracted as U.S. braceros. The bracero program paradoxically reversed the historical

problem faced by northern Mexican employers, who for years had recruited migrants from the Mexican interior only to see them lured over the
border by even higher wages.[55] In the border state of Tamaulipas, the federal Secretariat of the Interior authorized the creation of a commission in
1956 "to deter the continuation of economic losses in the region." The commission told county presidents in the sending regions that bracero aspirants bound for the contracting center in Monterrey first had to pick cotton for a minimum of twenty days in Tamaulipas. After that, they would
be issued a certificate giving them priority in the bracero queue.[56] In effect,
this was an internal bracero program tightly linked to the international
program. The northern states of Sonora, Baja California, and Chihuahua
established similar schemes in the 1950s and 1960s. In 1955, twenty thousand braceros worked in Sonora and thirty thousand in Tamaulipas. Aspirants were required to pick between one and two metric tons of cotton
in Sonora before receiving U.S. contracts. Laws against transporting
bracero hopefuls without contracts were used to prevent workers from
leaving the cotton fields before they had picked their quota.[57]

As always, there were creative ways to get around government regulations. A sixty-three-year-old Arandense veteran of four bracero contracts in the late 1950s told of sneaking away from the Sonoran cotton
fields one year for a family emergency and being refused a ride by passing trucks. Drivers feared they would be fined if police caught them with
ineligible braceros aboard. The Arandense finally stowed away on a
truck whose driver stopped to buy a snack. In the fields, where the cotton
quota was determined by weight, savvy workers filled sacks with more
dirt than cotton so they could get on with the business of heading north.
As the same bracero veteran described the trick, "We put a big handful of
dirt in the sack . . . no less than a kilo, eh? And we threw it in, *cabrón* [son
of a bitch]. . . . Then we gave the sack a few kicks so the dirt would go to
the bottom." Some coyotes bribed officials at the contracting centers to
allow aspirants to avoid the picking requirement in the first place.

Given the failure of previous Mexican policies managing emigration,
the moderate success of the internal bracero program is impressive.
Northern states took advantage of their location as areas of transit and recruitment to redirect part of the U.S.-bound flow. The federal government

cooperated with northern farmers because the internal bracero program was an efficient way to solve simultaneously the problems of temporary regional labor shortages and a structural national labor surplus. Yet the requirement that braceros first work in Mexican agriculture was successful only to the extent that it coincided with migrants' willingness to work outside their home region. Where migrants considered the obligation onerous, they evaded it through private exchanges with officials who were building clientelistic networks or simply fattening their purses. The bribe, in other words, is one more way that actors within the state apparatus undermine formal policy.

THE NATIONAL ESCAPE VALVE, 1965–PRESENT

Through the early 1970s, the Mexican government unsuccessfully attempted to revive the bracero agreements that ended in 1964. The U.S. government saw little reason to resume the program so long as undocumented immigrants met U.S. labor demand. Both governments tacitly accepted massive illegal migration. Based on the experience of the Mexican government, emigration appeared practically impossible to regulate. The rapidly increasing Mexican population, which rose from 19.7 million in 1940 to 48.2 million in 1970, meant that serious emigration restriction was no longer needed in any case. The demographic deficit had been resolved so well that population growth was becoming a new problem. Whereas the 1947 Law of Population outlined the government's attempt to increase population through natural growth, immigration, and repatriation, its 1974 reform noted that population increases were a growing strain on the economy and state services such as education. The federal government began a massive and ultimately successful campaign to reduce fertility. As part of this effort to slow demographic growth, official policy shifted from taking "measures to prevent and avoid emigration" and fining workers who emigrated without a contract in 1947 to "restrict[ing] the emigration of nationals when the national interest demands it" and removing the penalties for leaving without a contract in 1974. In October 1974, President Luis Echeverría informed President Gerald Ford that

Mexico no longer sought a renewal of the bracero program.[58] The policy of laissez-faire continued through the 1980s, when a series of economic crises sent growing numbers of mostly unauthorized migrants north. Without enough jobs being created each year for adolescents entering the labor force, Mexican authorities had little incentive to stem the flow. Emigration became an economic escape valve at a national level that had the added benefit of relieving pressure on the political system.

Embracing the Absent Children

Mexico's policies toward emigrants already abroad changed dramatically in the early 1990s. Underlying migration patterns had changed, in large part because of the 1986 U.S. Immigration Reform and Control Act (IRCA), which accelerated a trend toward permanent settlement by legalizing 2.3 million Mexicans. The newly legalized then sponsored the immigration of their family members. As U.S. border enforcement intensified, unauthorized migrants already in the United States returned home to Mexico less often to avoid the higher prices charged by coyotes and the physical dangers of an illegal crossing back into the United States. A pattern of circular, mostly male migration gave way to permanent migration of whole families.[59] Emigrants and their resources became less accessible within Mexico, prompting the Mexican government to reach out to them more aggressively.

Mexican partisan politics spilling over into the Mexican population in the United States was the proximate cause of the policy reorientation. For the first time since the 1920s, the ruling party and competitive opposition parties vied for the favor of the Mexican population in the United States. Cuauhtémoc Cárdenas, the center-left opposition candidate for president in 1988 who later founded the Party of the Democratic Revolution (PRD), drew large crowds of Mexican migrants while campaigning in California and Chicago. Cárdenas appealed to Mexican citizens to influence the vote of their family members in Mexico and promised emigrants dual nationality and the right to vote from abroad. His supporters formed a number of U.S.-based organizations, such as the Mexican Unity Group and the Organization of Mexicans for Democracy (OMD). At the PRD's first national

Figure 4. Campaign poster for the Party of the Democratic Revolution, 2000.

congress in Mexico City in 1990, the leader of the OMD and two southern California *cardenistas* were appointed as California delegates to the PRD's national assembly.[60] Emigrant rights groups, many of which were affiliated with the PRD, formed to demand the absentee ballot, a right for which the groundwork was laid in 1996 legislation but which was not approved until 2005.[61] The PRD's discourse and iconography emphasize a united Mexican nation that transcends the territorial borders of the United States and Mexico—not because Mexicans are trying to reconquer the Southwest or because they are one-worlders, but simply because they seek partisan advantage by including Mexicans abroad as political allies. A 2000 campaign poster printed by the party's offices in Los Angeles shows a map of the United States and Mexico without a border line between them and demands U.S. amnesty for unauthorized immigrants, absentee voting rights in Mexico, and congressional representation for Mexicans abroad.

The ruling Institutional Revolutionary Party (PRI) responded quickly to counter the PRD's overtures to migrants. Most points of the Mexican political spectrum now agree, at least publicly, that Mexicans outside the country should be included somehow in Mexican political life. In his 1995–2000 National Development Plan, PRI President Ernesto Zedillo declared, "The Mexican nation extends beyond the territory contained within its borders."[62] These were not irredentist claims, but rather discursive moves seeking the political and economic resources of Mexicans in the United States. Since 1989, the Paisano program has tried to ease the return of vacationing migrants by cracking down on police who extort money from returnees.[63] Mexican consulates began to pay more attention to legal protection for Mexican nationals in the United States, particularly the fifty or so Mexican nationals on death row, and the human rights of unauthorized border crossers. The Mexican Congress further attempted to integrate nationals abroad by changing the Constitution in 1997 to allow Mexicans who naturalize abroad and the children of Mexicans born abroad to claim Mexican nationality. People with dual *nationality* can buy property along the coast and border, which are restricted zones for foreigners, but strictly speaking they do not have dual *citizenship*. Most important, they cannot vote in Mexican elections.[64]

The Mexican government also institutionalized ties with emigrants through the Program for Mexican Communities Abroad (PCME) established by the Secretariat of Foreign Relations. Since 1990, the PCME has sought to preserve the cultural nationality of Mexicans in the United States by promoting patriotic events such as parades celebrating independence on September 16 and the study of Mexican history and the Spanish language. The PCME built on existing efforts by migrants and local priests to organize based on their Mexican hometowns, as discussed in detail in chapter 4. The PCME creates formal ties between the clubs and the Mexican government at the federal, state, and county levels. These relationships are the basis for matching-funds programs such as Tres por Uno ("3×1"), in which migrants and Mexican government agencies jointly develop infrastructure projects in migrants' hometowns. By 2005, the program was spending US$80 million a year, with a quarter of the funding coming directly from migrants. Migrants have had a strong hand in designing these programs and have avoided participating in projects that simply take their money without asking for their input into how the funds are spent.[65]

The major emigrant initiatives survived the change in administration from the PRI to the National Action Party in 2000. One of President Fox's first official acts in 2000 was to inaugurate a Presidential Office for Communities Abroad directed by Juan Hernández, a dual national professor of literature born in Texas. The cabinet-level position was abolished in 2002 after conflicts arose between Hernández and Secretary of Foreign Relations Jorge Castañeda over how to conduct foreign policy, as both cabinet agencies were empowered to do. In 2003, the PCME and the presidential office were folded in to the new Institute for Mexicans Abroad (IME), which includes an advisory council of 105 Mexican community leaders and ten Latino organizations in the United States, ten special advisors, and representatives of each of the thirty-two state governments in Mexico.[66]

Since the end of the bracero program Mexican emigration policy has accepted both legal and illegal labor emigration as inevitable while using mostly symbolic incentives to retain the most highly educated. Fox took office extolling migrants as "heroes" but encouraging them to return to jobs in Mexico they could find by dialing a toll-free jobs hotline, Chambatel. In 2003, applicants from both in and outside Mexico filled only 26,510 jobs using the phone service and its Internet equivalent, Chambanet.[67] Many migrants saw these heirs to the 1930s labor exchanges as empty political posturing, and the presidential discourse of repatriation has faded. Officials were moderately concerned that 30 percent of Mexico's scientific and engineering graduates and 10 percent of its university-educated population was living abroad in 1990. In response, the National Science and Technology Council began a "brain repatriation" program to bring back Mexicans who had completed advanced degrees abroad and to retain recent PhDs already working in Mexico. Despite these efforts, the percentage of Mexicans with a university education who migrated rose to 15 percent in 2000. Among member nations of the Organization for Economic Cooperation and Development (OECD) Mexico is the fourth largest source country of university-educated migrants.[68]

Emigration control is implemented now by the Grupo Beta police force, which first formed in Tijuana in 1990 and later expanded across the northern and southern borders. In 2000, the seventy-five Grupo Beta agents stationed on the two-thousand-mile U.S. border arrested around a hundred coyotes a month for violating the ban on human smuggling in the 1996 amendments to the General Law of Population. A debate within the Mexican government arose in June 2001 over whether Grupo Beta could forcibly prevent emigrants from crossing in the most dangerous areas. The government ultimately decided that migrants could not constitutionally be prevented from leaving, and in August 2001, Grupo Beta gave up its control functions altogether to focus on protecting undocumented migrants from bandits, conducting rescue operations, and supplying information about how to cross safely.[69] The National Migration Institute of the Secretariat of the Interior has developed a multimedia campaign asking citizens to report coyotes to a toll-free telephone number and to avoid crossing into the United States in dangerous wilderness areas where hundreds of migrants die every year. In 2005 it began distributing more than a million copies of an educational booklet for undocumented migrants with detailed tips on how to avoid the major risks of undocumented crossings: carry water, follow power lines north, always keep the coyote in sight, etc. A disclaimer on the back of the booklet summarizes the federal government's current stance toward illegal migration: "This consular protection guide does not promote the crossing of the border by Mexicans without the legal documentation required by the government of the United States. Its objective is to publicize the risks that [such crossings] imply, and to inform about the rights of migrants regardless of their legal residence."[70]

In the Mexican Constitution the right to exit has always been subject to situational interpretations and tempered by qualifications, including the authorization to use coercion in the 1926 migration law. The 1974 General Law of Population still in effect requires departing labor migrants to pres-

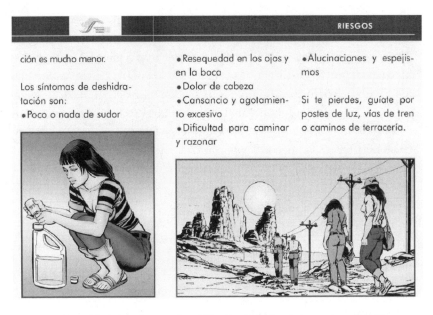

RIESGOS

ción es mucho menor.

Los síntomas de deshidra-
tación son:
• Poco o nada de sudor

• Resequedad en los ojos y
en la boca
• Dolor de cabeza
• Cansancio y agotamien-
to excesivo
• Dificultad para caminar
y razonar

• Alucinaciones y espejis-
mos

Si te pierdes, guíate por
postes de luz, vías de tren
o caminos de terracería.

Figure 5.   Detail from the Secretariat of Foreign Relations' 2005 migrant guide.

ent themselves to Mexican migration authorities, show a work contract authorized by the destination country consulate, and provide proof that they meet the entry requirements of the destination country.[71] Clearly, undocumented migrants hiking across the Arizona desert do not meet these criteria, and there are no longer penalties for violating this article in the General Law of Population. The argument for a constitutional right of exit is a convenient way of legitimating the federal government's minimal efforts to restrict unauthorized emigration.

The efforts of the Fox (2000–2006) administration to negotiate a new guest-worker program and amnesty for undocumented Mexicans in the United States marked the first active promotion of emigration since the bracero era. During a visit to Washington, DC, in September 2001, Foreign Minister Jorge Castañeda famously said that Mexico would accept nothing less than "the whole enchilada" of legalization, a guest-worker program, and Mexico's exemption from visa quotas. Movement toward an agreement foundered following the September 11 attacks days later, though it's not clear that a bilateral agreement was as close as it appeared.[72] Regardless, the political scientist Marc Rosenblum reports that a fundamental philosophical shift has taken place in the Secretariat of Foreign Relations away from the "policy of no policy" to a more active stance. Mexican officials do not want to repeat their lack of involvement in U.S. legislation like IRCA, whose debate they did not participate in for fear that Mexican intervention in sovereign U.S. policy making would legitimate U.S. intervention in Mexican politics.[73] President Felipe Calderón (elected in 2006) has downplayed his predecessor's vocal expectations of a bilateral migration accord but is clearly interested in the same goal of legalized flows.

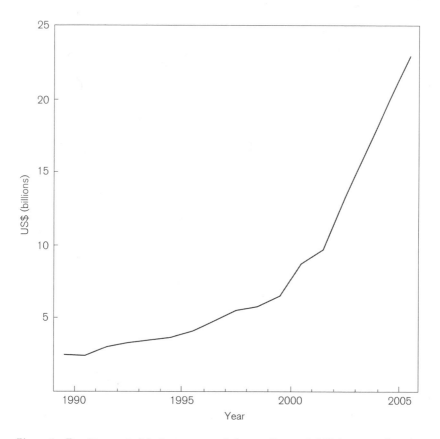

Figure 6.   Remittances to Mexico, 1990–2006. Source: Banco de México, www.banxico .org.mx/SieInternet/consultarDirectorioInternetAction.do?accion=consultarCuadro &idCuadro=CE81&locale=es.

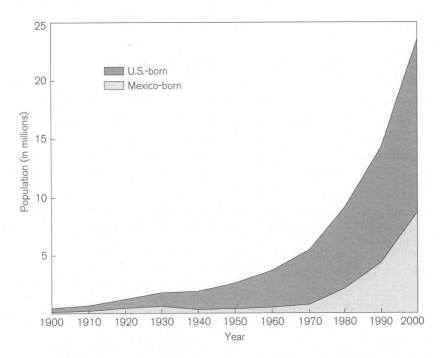

Figure 7. "Mexicans" in the United States by place of birth, 1900–2000. Source: "Población de origen mexicano residente en Estados Unidos, 1900–2007," http://conapo.gob.mx/mig_int/s2008/material/03_05_01xls.

There are two major explanations for the new policy of actively encouraging both temporary and permanent emigration. First, the dramatic growth of the Mexican population in the United States has yielded remittances that reached US$20 billion in 2005, the second largest source of foreign income after oil. More Mexicans in the United States means more remittances for Mexico. Second, a policy of close political and economic alignment with the United States since the 1994 North American Free Trade Agreement has weakened nationalistic arguments against migrating to the northern colossus and provided an opportunity to try to couple migration with bilateral issues such as trade and investment policy. The growth in the population of U.S.-born Mexicans and naturalized citizens has fueled what are probably illusory hopes that Mexicans might become a powerful ethnic lobby in the United States that would support the policy preferences of the Mexican government in these negotiations.

Back to Provincia

The creeping centralization of emigration policy over the twentieth century started to reverse itself in the 1990s. The state of Zacatecas, which has the highest international emigration rate in Mexico, is in the vanguard of policies incorporating emigrants into its political and economic life. Since 2003, Zacatecanos living abroad may even run in Zacatecas congressional and county elections.[74] Ties between provincial governments and emigrants have been a vehicle for spreading Mexican partisan politics to the Mexican population in the United States through visits by gubernatorial candidates and incumbents seeking emigrants' political support. That has prompted the party in control of the federal government to respond with its own programs to avoid being left out of the transborder game. Noting Zacatecano success, the Secretariat of Foreign Relations has encouraged all states to create their own emigrant affairs offices and participate in the National Coordination of State Offices of Attention to Migrants. Coordination between the state offices and the Secretariat of Foreign Relations has been subject to tensions within the secretariat over the extent to which provincial-level offices should be allowed to carry out foreign policy functions that the federal government has tried to monopolize over the past century, but the state-level organizations have had the blessings of Presidents Zedillo and Fox.[75]

Provincial governments are developing new mechanisms to channel remittances away from family consumption to business investment and infrastructural development. Beginning in 1998, Jalisco's FIDERAZA program used seed money from the state of Jalisco, two banks, and a quarter of 1 percent of transactions through the Raza Express remittance service to fund projects in areas of high emigration. By 2000, FIDERAZA had spent only 5.6 million pesos on five productive projects, such as establishing dairy collection centers and buying sewing machines for a workshop, and fourteen social benefit projects, including building schools and homes for the elderly poor. The program was not very successful in part because migrants wanted to design their own ventures rather than invest in projects prefabricated by bureaucrats. A new governor in 2001 replaced FIDERAZA with Por mi Jalisco (For my Jalisco). The program helps emigrants develop business plans and loans them start-up capital to invest in communities with the highest emigration rates. Four projects were operating in 2004: a factory manufacturing piñatas from recycled cardboard, a tequila distillery, a plastics recycling facility, and a sheep farm. The state government estimates that the projects attracted US$6 million in investment and will generate two hundred jobs directly and thousands more indirectly.

Although there are no bilateral guest-worker programs between the United States and Mexico, individual Mexican states effectively help to administer the U.S. government's H2B program for temporary, unskilled, nonagricultural workers. For example, since 2001, the government of Jalisco has recruited workers and helped them to apply through U.S. consulates to fill positions, mostly as golf course landscapers. In 2004, 136 H2B visas were issued with the office's assistance. The alternative is to leave the program to what one state official called "a mafia" of H2B veterans who arrange the paperwork for newcomers for an exorbitant fee. In response to a new breed of enganchador charging US$1,500 to US$4,000 in recruitment fees, the government of Zacatecas went a step further in 2001 by negotiating a pilot program with the U.S. consulate in Monterrey that recruits temporary workers under the direction of the Zacatecas government. Although these guest-worker programs operate independently of the Mexican federal government, they are a window into the sort of large-scale, truly bilateral programs that are the federal government's goal.[76]

For most of the twentieth century, the Mexican federal government attempted to control what types of people emigrated, where they came from, when they left, and the conditions of their return. The instruments of emigration control included propaganda campaigns, refusal to issue travel documents to certain occupational and geographic categories of workers, material incentives to repatriate, requirements that emigrants first work in domestic agriculture, and even coercion at the border and on train routes.

The federal government has attempted to monopolize the "legitimate means of movement" and strip local governments of this competence.[77] From 1904 to the 1950s, the federal government repeatedly ordered county authorities in sending areas to stop issuing their own international travel documents.[78] The early modeling of international passport policy on the example of more developed states occurred at a moment when the

Mexican state simply did not have the administrative capacity to enforce its own regulations. By 2003, the federal government had successfully monopolized this competence and was expediting passports through a decentralized network of 114 county liaison offices of the Secretariat of Foreign Relations, whereby county and federal authorities share the costs of providing services to local residents. Although county authorities continue to issue their own letters of recommendation to migrants, who are often unclear about the bureaucratic requirements in both countries, these letters are of little value because U.S. consular officials say they do not pay attention to them. The fact that international migration now takes place in a system of states that recognizes only passports issued by the central governments of other states has contributed to the centralization of Mexican emigration policy.

While formal exit control policy has become increasingly centralized, substantive exit control has practically ended for a variety of reasons. Through the 1930s, the fractured state lacked the capacity to enforce the policy dictates of the central authorities. This was especially true in the crucial period of the 1920s, when massive emigration took root in the source communities of the central west. When it served their interests, local officials encouraged emigration to the United States even as the federal government tried to deter it. When local and state governments saw emigration draining local labor supply and thus driving wages higher, they tried to restrict emigration by pressuring the federal government. Policies of local governments in Mexico are less autonomous from the interests of economic elites than are the policies of the federal government,[79] leading to a patchwork of emigration control practices reflecting the interests of local elites. The most successful local and provincial governments to manage the labor drain were in northern states, which were able to tie international migration to internal migration by requiring braceros to fill the domestic labor demands of large-scale agriculture. The corporatist state attempted to manage the local supply and demand of labor by distributing workers within Mexico first and then exporting sectoral excesses to the United States. From the perspective of local governments, however, the distribution of labor in other parts of Mexico was someone else's problem, and they ignored or subverted federal policies.

Within the Mexican federal government, the pursuit of disparate goals of state building had unintended consequences on emigration policy. The attempt to crush the secular power of the Catholic Church indirectly caused local army commanders and county authorities to promote emigration as an escape valve during the Cristero War. In some areas, such as Arandas, even the 1930s agrarian reform that theoretically gave peasants a stake in staying provided a further impetus for the local oligarchy to encourage their exit.[80] Government policies that concentrated economic development in major cities and supported large-scale, export-oriented agriculture in northern states at the expense of small-scale agriculture in the central west aggravated an excess of unemployed rural labor.[81] Government improvement of infrastructure, sanitation, and health systems created a sharp decline in mortality, leading to a population boom. With more farmers in 1960 than in 1910, emigration provided an outlet for the country's overall surplus population.[82] Different features of state building thus worked at cross-purposes with efforts to restrict emigration.

Emigration policy options for Mexico have been restricted sharply by the policies of the United States, with which Mexico has historically had a relationship of "asymmetric interdependency."[83] Mexican bans on the emigration of laborers *without* contracts in 1917 were difficult to implement because the United States already had banned the immigration of laborers *with* contracts in 1885. During the bracero program, the U.S. government periodically opened its borders as a tactic to undercut Mexico's bargaining position in its effort to secure better conditions for contracted workers. Mexico opposed illegal migration, while the U.S. Immigration and Naturalization Service often tacitly allowed it. In the 1970s, the U.S. government generally turned a blind eye to border control, having found that jobs would be filled by undocumented migrants without the bother or expense of maintaining a bilateral program. Mexico's diplomatic claims that international migration should be addressed as a bilateral issue historically have been rebuffed by the response that U.S. immigration policy is an issue of national sovereignty to be determined by the U.S. government alone. Bilateral talks that appeared to be moving toward some sort of legalization and guest-worker program in 2001, prior to the events of September 11, incorporated much of the language and many of

the positions of the Mexican proposal. However, the success of such policies is determined much more by domestic political processes in the
United States than by the bilateral relationship. The openings and restrictions of immigration policies have been the result of the relative strength
at a given juncture of what Zolberg calls coalitions of "strange bedfel-
lows."[84] On the one hand, Latino and civil rights groups work with businesses seeking access to a legal source of cheap labor to create more open
immigration policies, while on the other hand, cultural conservatives, the
post-9/11 security lobby, and some unions opposed to guest-worker programs work together to restrict immigration.

There is little that the Mexican government can realistically do now to
shape the flows of U.S.-bound migrants. Social processes such as cultural
expectations of migration, structural reliance on migrant remittances, and
a migration industry of smugglers further restrict the Mexican government's room for maneuver in managing migration. Social networks linking specific source and destination localities are especially important for
circumventing state controls because they are conduits for experienced
migrants to provide beginners with the money and information needed
to cross the border illegally. Emigration control is "path dependent" in
the sense that early failures, which allowed the establishment of mass emigration against the stated intentions of the government, limited the development of institutions and policies that would effectively control emigration today. Deeply embedded migration streams alter the social
landscape and become part of a process of "cumulative causation" that
propels the persistence of international migration in ways that are difficult for governments to control.[85]

The effects of Mexican emigration policies on shaping migration flows
have been modest. They have had little overall effect on the volume and
types of migrants, with the important exceptions of the 1930s repatriation
and the twenty-two years of the bracero program. Yet even these suc-
cesses were driven fundamentally by U.S. policies and economic conditions. The Mexican state at various levels has enjoyed greater success in
promoting remittances and hometown association projects. Mexico and
other countries of emigration continue to create new policies, which they
then copy from each other. Mexico's success in channeling remittances

into investment and the creation of an ethnic political lobby remains to be determined, but there is reason to be skeptical about the prospects in both areas. The vast majority of remittances remain family-level transfers for household maintenance and housing, and Mexicans in the United States tend to be deeply pessimistic about Mexican political institutions.[86]

The capacity of even an autocratic sending country to shape international migration seems sharply constrained. Mexican migration is socially and economically embedded on both ends of the migration stream in ways that resist government intervention. The political liberalization of Mexican politics did not take root until the 1990s, so political liberalism cannot explain the end of exit controls in Mexico in the 1970s. The contemporary influence of political liberalism has been to restrict the range of coercive exit policy options available today. It may still be internationally legitimate to put up walls to keep foreigners out, but it is certainly not legitimate to put up walls to keep citizens in. In that sense, liberalism constrains the options of source countries even more than destination countries. And the limited capacity of countries of emigration highlights what countries of immigration can do. Relative to their ideal of perfect control, countries of immigration look as if they are "losing control," to use Sassen's language. Relative to countries of emigration, countries of immigration are not doing that badly.

Globalization makes it more difficult for all states to control population movement, but that does not mean the system of sovereign states has collapsed. On the contrary, the sovereign ability of receiving countries such as the United States to make unilateral immigration policies sharply constrains the options for sending countries such as Mexico. The sending state is not the only institution that struggles to manage its mobile membership. It is hard for any organization to exercise pastoral power when its flock's pen is easily breached. The following chapter explains emigration's challenge to the Catholic Church and how the Church in Mexico has developed creative methods of managing a mobile flock. Given the limited capacity of the Mexican state to control outflows, it has adopted many of the Church's strategies for embracing migrants and its basic model of membership.

THREE The Church's Eye on Its Flock

You don't know what's worse—their absence or their return.

Agustín Yañez, *Al filo del agua* (1947)

The Church is Mother, and the Church, while respecting the identity of its peoples and also respecting geopolitical boundaries, is also transcending them.

Emilio Berlie Belaunzarán, president of the Mexican Episcopal Commission on Migration and Tourism

Since the mid-1990s, stories have spread throughout central west Mexico of the "coyote saint" who helps migrants cross the U.S. border illegally. In one version, three migrants stranded in a frontier desert are saved by a man dressed in black who appears out of nowhere to offer them a ride in his pickup. When the migrants later visit their rescuer's home village of Santa Ana, Jalisco, to thank him, they find a photograph of Father Toribio Romo in the chapel where his bones have been kept since he was killed by government troops in 1928 during the Cristero War. The migrants realize that the dead priest was the Good Samaritan who took them across the border.

Today, more than five thousand pilgrims clog the dusty streets of Santa Ana on a typical weekend. Many come to pray for the safety of loved ones heading north or to leave votive images thanking Toribio for helping them

Figure 8. Woodburning left by migrants at the chapel devoted to Father Toribio in Santa Ana, Jalisco, 2003.

cross the border successfully. In one image, two men are heading toward a barbed-wire fence and the arches of McDonald's that beckon beyond. The chapel gift shop sells devotional booklets with prayers for unauthorized migrants, and private stalls offer albums with songs like "Protector del emigrante" (Protector of the Emigrant) and "Milagro en el Río Bravo" (Miracle on the Rio Grande). An energetic local priest is trying to have Toribio, who was canonized in 2000, officially designated by the Conference of Mexican Bishops (CEM) as the patron saint of migrants.[1]

Left silent in this celebration of migrants is that in life, Father Toribio was an outspoken critic of emigration and the pernicious U.S. values that returnees brought back home. A character in Toribio's 1920 play ¡*Vámonos*

Figure 9.   Pilgrims pray at the remains of Father Toribio in Santa Ana, Jalisco, 2003.
Photo by David Fitzgerald.

p'al norte! (Let's Go North!) lambasted Mexican emigrants: "How many
people have we seen leaving home crying, who four or five years later,
have completely abandoned their faith and their families, who don't send
them so much as a letter, not to speak of economic support. . . . They be-
tray the motherland, because they go to strengthen with their work the
tyrant [the United States] who will take advantage of these same energies
to increasingly humiliate and reduce to ashes our unfortunate Mexico."
In Toribio's narrative, returnees have become Protestants, act embar-
rassed to work the fields, and wear such effeminate gringo clothes and so
much jewelry that "one can't tell whether they crow or lay eggs." The
play's protagonist concludes that his community would be better off if the
emigrants would get out as quickly as possible and stay out: "We have a
lot to be happy about when the perverse sons of Mexico leave it, because
they leave behind a more peaceful Mexico."[2] The final historical irony is
that Father Toribio's last surviving family members migrated to northern
California.

Father Toribio's story illustrates a sea change in the Mexican Church's emigration policies since the 1920s and some surprising parallels between Church and government policies. Faced with a recalcitrant population that continued to migrate despite decades of admonitions to stay home, Church and state gave up trying to dissuade emigration and instead emphasize embracing emigrants even after they leave the territorial fold. Since the 1990s, the Mexican state has adopted many of the Church's emigrant policy tools and its flexible model of membership ties—a model that the secular government had forced the Church to create by winning the religious wars of the nineteenth and early twentieth centuries.

ORGANIZING THE FLOCK

The state's adoption of the Church's strategy for dealing with migrants may seem surprising because Church and state appear to be such different kinds of organizations, which in places like Mexico have fought long bloody wars with each other. Why should the Roman Catholic Church, whose very name means "universal" and whose ideology and organization encompass the entire globe, be concerned with the movement of members between nation-states? The answer is that the Church is both an organization of particular members and an organization that presides over particular territorial jurisdictions. The Catholic hierarchy's response to migration around the world reveals two axes of Church organization that have coexisted uneasily at least since the Fourth Lateran Council of 1215. Along one axis the Church is divided into territorial districts for administrative purposes but is otherwise a *trans*national organization for which national differences are irrelevant. Along another axis the Church is divided by the nationality or the language of the faithful rather than . simply their place of residence.[3]

Until Bishop Scalabrini founded the Missionaries of St. Charles to minister to Italian migrants in 1887, a territorial organizational model prevailed in most immigrant-receiving countries. Local priests were exclusively responsible for everyone in their territory, including new arrivals.[4] The modern Vatican has attempted to integrate settled immigrants into destination parishes, while providing a missionary-style ministry run by conationals for temporary migrants. In the United States, "national parishes" adopted European languages and imported European clergy corresponding to each major Catholic immigrant group during the last great wave of European migration at the turn of the twentieth century.[5] Following Scalabrini, who emphasized that the intertwining of Catholicism and Italian identity implied that cultural retention also would keep them safe from conversion and apathy, the 1952 papal encyclical *Exsul Familia* stressed ministering to all migrants in their native language. *Exsul Familia* laid out a series of regulations for integrating the ethnic and territorial forms of organization. Resident Catholics fell under the authority of the local territorial parish, but the authority of the ethnic parish was limited to immigrants and their children. Vatican documents from the 1950s and 1960s are replete with detailed instructions about how to negotiate these different ways of organizing the Church's ministry to migrants. Pope Paul VI's 1969 *De Pastorali Migratorum Cura* assigned primary responsibility for the migrant ministry to the parish of destination, while recognizing a principle of extraterritoriality in which the Church in the origin community had "co-responsibility" for migrants. The authority of sending and receiving parishes over the same person has created a dual parish membership akin to dual nationality. Defining the conditions under which status as a "migrant" ends is another strategy the Church has developed to file its mobile members in the right slots of the Church administration. The status of contemporary Catholic migrants is determined by the possibility of immediate "naturalization" into a new parish and a sort of double jus soli by which the third generation automatically belongs to the territorial parish. As organizations with jurisdictions over both people and places, the Church in a given country and the nation-state face similar problems of exercising pastoral power over a flock that moves across borders.

SECULARIZATION AND ITS LIMITS

Around the world, the Church's ability to exercise its pastoral power has waned with the secularization of government. In Mexico, the Church's model of membership has changed over the past two centuries from one based on coercive authority over the entire populace to one in which its secular power has been stripped away and it must rely on ideological influence to embrace the faithful. During the Spanish-American colonial era, the right of the Spanish Catholic kings to nominate bishops meant "Church and State were one."[6] Although Catholicism continued to be the official religion immediately following Mexican independence in 1821, the Church was eventually disestablished, and much of its temporal power was stripped by liberals, prompting the 1858–61 War of the Reform. The secular government has long resented the Church's ties to a foreign pope and control of vast swaths of Mexican real estate and other resources coveted by the state. The Church's alliance with Mexican conservatives and France to crown the Austrian Archduke Maximilian emperor of Mexico in 1864 lent credence to the charge that the Church was an agent of foreign influence.[7] Anticlericalism was institutionalized in the waning years of the Mexican Revolution. In a country where 99 percent of the population was at least nominally Catholic, the 1917 Constitution expelled foreign priests and nuns, nationalized Church property, prohibited public worship and religious education, and gave the government the authority to regulate the numbers of priests. As in secular France following its revolution, the Mexican state in 1920 aimed to replace Catholicism with revolutionary nationalism as the cement holding together a fractured populace. The attempt by President Plutarco Calles to enforce anticlerical laws led to the 1926–29 Cristero War between Catholic rebels and the federal government. Calles promoted a schismatic Mexican Apostolic Catholic Church independent of the Vatican, though the autonomous church never built a mass membership. The Roman Catholic Church continued to be excluded formally from political life until President Carlos Salinas de Gortari reformed most of the anticlerical constitutional provisions in 1992.[8] Tensions eased further with the center-right National Action Party administration of Vicente Fox, whose open Catholicism stood in sharp contrast to seventy-one years of secularist predecessors from the Institutional Revolutionary Party. Although the Church continues to exercise ideological influence, the state has effectively crushed the Church's secular power and its ability to make the population tithe and follow Church rules.

Despite these setbacks, Catholicism continues to dominate the Mexican religious landscape. In 2000 92 percent of Mexicans identified themselves as Catholic.[9] Los Altos de Jalisco is even more conservative and Catholic than the Mexican norm. In 2000, 98 percent of the population of Arandas self-identified as Catholic; in 2003, 98 percent of Arandense and Agua Negran household heads reported attending mass, with a median attendance of six to seven times per month.[10] The Catholic Church in Los Altos is a true "church" in Max Weber's sociological sense of an organization with a monopoly on religious matters.[11] When the faithful migrate to the United States, they encounter a "religious marketplace" where the Catholic Church is simply another de facto denomination among many. Consequently, membership in the U.S. Church is even more voluntaristic than in postrevolutionary Mexico.[12] Aware that migrants might drop out of the Church altogether, Mexican clerics such as Father Toribio for decades encouraged the faithful to stay home.

A "HOLY CRUSADE"

In 1920, the archbishop of Guadalajara called for a "holy crusade" against emigration in a circular read aloud in Sunday mass throughout the archdiocese and published under the banner headline "Against Emigration" in the regional Catholic weekly.[13] The following year, a weeklong conference in Guadalajara on agrarian problems developed a national Church response to emigration.[14] In the evocative language of the keynote address, emigration "is a demolishing act, a devouring act, an act that every day rips shreds of flesh and soul from the motherland." As a result of emigration, Mexico "is losing a great part of its vigor, a great part of its energy, and if now we are almost a cadaver, then we are probably heading not to the grave, but rather to complete decomposition."[15]

In the eyes of the Church hierarchy, emigration's perils included foreign ideas and U.S. attachments introduced by returnees. These ideas endangered the purity of Mexican culture and even Mexico's very existence as a sovereign state:

Another evil that should not pass unmentioned is the loss of patriotism. When the Mexican worker has spent just a year in the North, he becomes a panegyrist for everything North American. He is an admirer of that country's customs, of its organization of work, its pastimes, its language, and even its vices, and he looks down on everything about his motherland with a certain sadness because he considers it inferior to that country of gold and liberty. Now one understands how in such conditions, he would not care if his motherland were annexed by the United States, and he might even celebrate that it happened.[16]

Memories of the 1848 annexation of what became the southwestern United States were still fresh in the 1920s, and fears that migrants would make invidious comparisons between Mexico and the United States were not unfounded. In his study of Arandas, Taylor found that returnees had a much more positive view of the United States than Arandenses who never left. He even interviewed one returnee who welcomed rumors that the United States was massing troops on the border to invade: "I don't care. I'd rather work for Americans than for the government here. I'd rather be under American laws than under the Mexican government; I had more guarantees over there than in my own country."[17] Even if this peasant expressed a minority view among returnees, such a perspective was enough to frighten clerics, government officials, and other Mexican elites that returnees would be agents of U.S. influence.

In the eyes of the Church, family disintegration was the second major problem caused by emigration. Husbands returned to Mexico to find their household in ruin with "wife or daughter dishonored" and "sons abandoned to their instincts, prepared for crime." A mostly male migration left women back home "unprotected" and exposed to the temptations of infidelity and even prostitution when men did not provide for their family.[18] Family separation threatened nationalist as well as gendered obligations. In the view of one presenter at the Guadalajara conference, the absence of fathers and husbands "crumbled," "destroyed," "split in half," and "annihilated" the worker's family—the basic unit of society's moral and material strength. Workers' families were the "soul of the motherland," "a redoubt of national traditions," and the "solidification of the national spirit."[19] By threatening the worker's family, emigration threatened Mexico itself.

Religious apathy and conversion made up the third set of problems caused by emigration. According to Church records from the 1920s, migrants in the United States lost their faith because few priests could minister to them in Spanish and Protestant missionaries took advantage of Catholic weakness by offering needy migrants relief in exchange for conversion. Even though the Catholic clergy portrayed Protestantism as a fundamentally Anglo-Saxon religion, they argued that Catholic migrants were still vulnerable because migrants identified Protestantism with the power and prestige of the United States. The United States was an inherently dangerous religious environment because of its "cosmopolitanism." In the words of the 1921 address: "What can a worker do in the fields in the United States . . . among what is truly a cosmopolitan people? There he comes unexpectedly in contact with Jews and Protestants. He has to encounter a heap of different tendencies. And we know what is most influential in our lives. It's daily conversations; it's ordinary and trivial contact with the world. And it's clear that this man, upon finding himself in that heterogeneous, dissolvent environment, must feel a great deal of doubt in the middle of that religious apathy."[20]

In effect, Mexican clerics were folk sociologists of assimilation, and perceptive ones at that. They understood that acculturation happens not only because of a conscious decision or forced compliance, but also because of quiet adjustments to daily exposure to difference.[21] A priest in Arandas noted that emigrants lose their religious conviction because they "see a different mode of life, go to dances, movies, etc., and have other diversions. The propaganda of the *evangelistas* is not so important."[22] Even in the deeply racist context of the 1920s, Mexican Catholics interacted with different kinds of people in the United States to the extent that it was difficult to maintain their religious boundaries.[23] Another argument against emigration, which was not made publicly, was that material progress would weaken religious sentiment. A Guadalajara priest complained to Paul Taylor in 1931 about workers returning from the North with newfound wealth: "When the Indian wears shoes, he does not go to mass. And when he wears pants, he does not believe in God."[24] The solution to these problems was to discourage the rapid material progress and exposure to heterogeneous beliefs implied by emigration. Priests saw preventing exposure to the United States as the best way to maintain religious orthodoxy.[25]

The economic effect of emigration was also seen as threatening, not least because it eroded the tithe base. In 1912, Church officials in Arandas complained to the archdiocese that tithing income had declined due to "the considerable emigration of its inhabitants to the North and losses of harvests."[26] Labor shortages jeopardized production of agricultural goods and primary industrial materials. Despite pervasive discrimination against Mexicans in the United States, they came back to Mexico with impossibly high expectations of wages and working conditions that generated an agrarian radicalism bitterly opposed by the Church.[27] The parish priest of San Juan de los Lagos reported in 1920 that returnees were introducing anarchist ideologies learned in the United States.[28] As the agrarian conference speaker described the problem on a more mundane level, "Men who upon returning to their homes do not find work conditions here that satisfy them spend the first days sometimes in full orgy, and almost always in full laziness."[29] To make matters worse, demands spread to the population that never left Mexico. The conference speaker told the story, perhaps apocryphal, of one hundred workers harvesting wheat who refused to obey their foreman's instructions. When the workers heard the whistle of a northbound train, they piled their baskets together in the field and set them alight, shouting, "Long live the United States!"[30]

For the archbishop, the emigration of Mexico's workers was especially egregious because they were being lost to Mexico's northern nemesis. His position followed the mercantilist logic that population is a source of national strength that should be protected from the predations of foreign competitors. The demographic disaster of the recent revolution and ongoing tensions with the United States made retaining population all the more important for Mexico:

> In the first place, with their separation from the country, emigrants contribute to the decline of the motherland, which has been almost ruined by the internal wars that still have not ended. Emigrants are needed to reconstruct the country's ancient splendor; and if there has already been much anger about the loss of so many sons left on the battlefield, there will be even greater difficulties in agriculture, industry, etc. . . . because

of the absence of those whose work could contribute to national reconstruction. Therefore, the abandonment of the country in these precarious conditions it faces is a lack of patriotism; and this lack of patriotism takes on greater significance if one considers that they go to work in, and thus to aggrandize with their work, a nation that has always been considered an enemy of our own and the cause of our greatest national disgraces.[31]

Given the many perceived threats to the Mexican family, Church, and motherland, the archbishop urged priests and leaders of Catholic associations to fight the "fever of expatriation that seems to have seized all Mexicans." Peasants were to be told that stories of an easy life in the North were lies, that in fact conditions were miserable in the North, whereas work was plentiful in the archdiocese. The 1921 agrarian conference continued the crusade with plans for a national office that would coordinate an anti-emigration propaganda campaign, send priests on missions to workers in the fields in the United States, and fund repatriations with special tithes.[32] The economic push factors would be mitigated by training peasants to become small private landholders and establishing Catholic consumers' and producers' cooperatives. In 1929, the Mexican episcopate drew up a fifteen-point plan that focused on working with U.S. bishops and Catholic organizations to remedy the familiar "consequences of decatholicization that are being brought from the United States." Parishes in Mexico would report to a binational liaison office in the United States on whether repatriated Mexicans maintained their faith and good customs, identify the specific destinations of renegades, and investigate the cause of their perversions.[33] Churches took up special collections every year from Mexicans on both sides of the border so that U.S. bishops would not have to pay for all of the ministry's expenses.

Even as the Mexican and U.S. clergy began to cooperate in fits and starts, a strong sense that emigration was a national menace continued to inform the Mexican Church's policy. Mexican clergy thought that emigration threatened to sever the tight connection between Catholicism and mexicanidad. As the archbishop of Guadalajara expressed the problem in private correspondence to a priest in the United States, "With the loss of their religion, [emigrants] often lose their love of the motherland." Mexicans in the United States were encouraged to join Guadalupano clubs paying homage to the Virgin of Guadalupe or parallel organizations of lay Catholics on both sides of the border that would "sustain their faith and love of their nationality."[34] Local U.S. Catholic responses to Mexican immigration varied during this period. Many U.S. parishes had asked for Spanish-speaking priests since the 1920s and 1930s. While sometimes encouraging a sense of mexicanidad to preserve migrants' faith, U.S. priests generally made a stronger effort to assimilate Mexicans by celebrating holy days on the U.S. calendar and encouraging them to speak English. Historians suggest that, in general, priests in the Southwest treated Mexicans as second-class citizens.[35]

FROM TURNCOATS TO PRODIGAL SONS

Cooperation between the U.S. and Mexican Churches improved by the late 1930s. Pope Pius XI in 1937 ordered Mexican and U.S. bishops to work together to minister to Mexican migrants and meet the threat of conversion through transnational organizations such as Catholic Action.[36] Two years later, U.S. and Mexican Church authorities agreed to ensure that Mexican, or at least Spanish-speaking, priests were available to minister to Mexicans in the United States. Parallel to the government's efforts, parishes in source areas were urged to form committees to help repatriates find work. The episcopate told parish priests to develop registries of emigrants in the United States that could be used to send them invitations to the towns' patron saint fiestas. Rather than the usual condemnations of emigrants, the episcopate publicly acknowledged that emigrants "have had to estrange themselves from the motherland." It suggested that emigrants were forced to leave by circumstances at home, rather than because they were dupes or adventurers.[37]

The growing accommodation of emigrants was likely the result of papal pressure insisting on cooperation between U.S. and Mexican bishops and general improvement in U.S.-Mexican relations during the Good Neighbor Policy of President Roosevelt. In a complementary explanation, the sociologist Victor Espinosa argues that a more conciliatory attitude toward emigrants was the result of the 1926–29 Cristero War, when the Church hierarchy and local priests fled to the United States. An unknown number stayed after the war to minister to Mexicans and established a seminary for exiles in Montezuma, New Mexico, in 1937. Local priests recognized that haranguing parishioners for migrating was ineffective when they owed their lives to the migrants who had spirited them to safety. Migrants' resources were also needed to finance the reconstruction of churches damaged during the fighting.[38]

The emigrant program in Arandas was a model for the entire archdiocese of Guadalajara. In 1944, the archbishop instructed priests to form a Pro-Emigrant Section of the Mexican Catholic Union in each parish, following the Arandense model established in 1942. Section members in the county seat of Arandas and subcommittees on eleven ranches were asked to work through their friends and family to find addresses of Arandenses living in the United States or other parts of Mexico. Secretaries scoured notary records looking for migrants who had asked for copies of their church records. Once a directory was compiled, the parish sent emigrants local news, invitations to join pious associations, and postcards to stir their hometown memories. The section sent patron saint fiesta programs to more than 300 families in 1942, 700 in 1943, and 1,160 in 1944.[39] Emigrants responded to these overtures by sharing intimate details about their lives, which became the basis for pastoral intervention. Priests reunited several marriages, separated couples living in free union, and even "pulled out of the bosom of Protestantism, three of ours that had affiliated with that sect, one of whom was already a pastor."[40] Throughout the 1940s, 1950s, and 1960s, absent Arandenses in Mexico and the United States donated money for the construction of the cathedral in Arandas and other parish expenses.[41] These donations reversed the old problem of peasant flight eroding the tithe base. Now emigrant contributions were a source of the parish's economic revitalization, as the following chapter on hometown associations describes in detail.

MEETING NEW CHALLENGES

Following the mass repatriations of the 1930s, the 1942–64 bracero guestworker era renewed emigration's challenge to the Church. The archbishop of Guadalajara told priests in 1951 to warn prospective migrants of the spiritual and material dangers facing them "so they will not abandon their homes, families, work, and motherland for this adventure." He said the public should be warned that illegal immigrants went hungry waiting for false promises of contracts. Even the legally contracted "live in miserable pigsties, face high costs, are taken out by brute force to work on rainy days, and are given opportunities to spend what they earn on vices." The parish priest of Arandas took the initiative to reprint a thousand copies of the archbishop's warning.[42] As in earlier migrations, a lack of Spanish-speaking priests in the camps invited Protestant inroads. In 1957, there were only twenty to thirty U.S.-based priests assigned to care for braceros living in the three thousand labor camps scattered throughout California. Nationally in 1960, sixteen Mexican priests attended to braceros for three- to four-month stretches, hardly adequate for a population of 315,000 braceros and an even higher number of unauthorized workers.[43]

By 1960, the clergy recognized that simply telling workers to stay home was not working. As voluntary members of the Church, migrants could choose to leave it altogether. Given the fact that migration had become deeply established in the sending communities and the Church was limited to wielding ideological tools, priests were forced to innovate to keep migrants within at least a partial embrace. The Church's policy changed from simple dissuasion against emigration to a campaign to prepare braceros heading north for the moral dangers they would face. The new campaign included a "Manual for Braceros," special masses and charity in Mexican contracting centers, and a "Bracero Hour" radio broadcast about conditions in the United States.[44] The emphasis was on managing the effects of emigration rather than hindering departure.

When it became clear that the bracero program would not be renewed following its 1964 demise, the CEM's emigrant commission met to plan the Church's response. The CEM promoted a pastoral tour of Mexico that would bring U.S. priests south for three to six months and include a tour of the historic migrant-sending regions. The episcopal leadership understood that migration patterns were already beginning to change from circular migration back and forth across the border to permanent settlement in the United States, a tendency that was to accelerate in the coming years.

Permanent emigrants represented a different kind of challenge to the Mexican Church than seasonal migrants, who had regular contact with priests in Mexico. Priests based in the United States, supplemented by visiting Mexican clergy, would now have to do the heavy pastoral lifting.[45]

UNIVERSAL RIGHTS

The rise in unauthorized migration spurred by the end of the bracero program meant that human rights concerns became ever more important to the Church. Following meetings between U.S. and Mexican bishops, the Missionaries of St. Charles (the Scalabrinians) opened a seminary in Guadalajara in 1980 to attend to migrants in transit, prepare priests for ministering to the growing Latino population in the United States, and convince the Mexican Church to develop a more consistent policy toward emigrants.[46] Priests on Mexico's northern border were most intensely involved in migration policy during the 1970s and 1980s because they directly dealt with denouncing abuses of unauthorized workers and providing charity to migrants trying to make it across the border. During the heyday of open illegal migration across the U.S.-Mexican border at Tijuana, Scalabrinian priests running a shelter held daily outdoor masses in the shadow of the border fence to bless the scores of migrants waiting for nightfall to cross. As a transnational order operating migrant ministries and research centers around the world, including a center in New York that publishes the premier migration studies journal *International Migration Review*, the Scalabrinians have institutionalized a more universal outlook on international migration than existed in Mexico prior to their arrival.

By the turn of the millennium, the migration policies of the Mexican and U.S. episcopates had almost completely converged in a strong transnationalist stance. A 2002 joint pastoral letter began by declaring, "We speak as two episcopal conferences but as one Church, united in the view that migration between our two nations is necessary and beneficial." The letter is one of the clearest justifications of a right to emigrate and immigrate:

The Church recognizes the right of a sovereign state to control its borders in furtherance of the common good. It also recognizes the right of human persons to migrate so that they can realize their God-given rights. These teachings complement each other. While the sovereign state may impose reasonable limits on immigration, the common good is not served when the basic human rights of the individual are violated. In the current condition of the world, in which global poverty and persecution are rampant, the presumption is that persons must migrate in order to support and protect themselves and that nations who are able to receive them should do so whenever possible. It is through this lens that we assess the current migration reality between the United States and Mexico.[47]

At the same time that it promotes universal rights, the Mexican Church has continued to worry about emigration's effects on Mexican culture and the economy. Acknowledging the Vatican's position on freedom of emigration, the CEM has argued that emigration and immigration are qualified human rights that do not exempt citizens from their communal obligations. Especially in poor regions, the emigration of productive forces and "those gifted with genius and skill" is blamed for depriving the community of the "material and spiritual benefits it needs."[48] The Scalabrinian seminary's weekly, *Migrantes,* has warned of a drain of brawn as well as brains. The editorial board rejected the consensus in the 1980s that emigration was an escape valve for a Mexican economy that could not provide enough jobs for its workers. As late as the 1980s, *Migrantes* portrayed temporary migration, permanent settlement abroad, and repatriation as detrimental to Mexico. A sedentary population has generally been the Mexican Church's ideal, but unattainable, preference.[49] It emphasizes universalism largely because the nationalist policy failed.

MANAGING SETTLEMENT: THE VIEW FROM LOS ALTOS

Massive emigration and permanent settlement in the United States are the facts on the ground, and the Church has attempted to manage that reality as best it can. Concerned with the potential effects of the 1986 Immigration

Reform and Control Act, the diocese of San Juan de los Lagos (which includes Arandas) conducted a study in Los Altos to determine the extent of
emigration and its effects. According to the study, 75 percent of Alteño
families had at least one member working in the United States; 20 percent
of the Alteño population lived in the United States permanently; 20 percent of Alteño families included married couples who had permanently
separated, and 5 percent had members who were divorced, usually because an emigrant man had abandoned the family.[50] In light of these perils, a new bishop in 1988 gathered addresses of emigrants from all fifty-six
parishes and mailed them letters pledging to work for the salvation of
the entire diocese, including "the *hijos ausentes* [absent children], whom the
further away you are, the more you are respected and loved."[51] While the
usual anathemas of Protestantism, materialism, family disintegration, and
ostentatious behavior are mentioned, the most striking feature of the letter from a historical perspective is its blessing of the decision to migrate:
"The determination that you took to find, in far-away lands and with great
sacrifice, the work that permits you to secure your future and the happi-
ness of your families, has been very just and very Christian."[52]

According to a 1993 diocesan survey, fewer than 1 percent of returned
migrants in Los Altos have left Catholicism for another religion: "Emigration has brought changes in religiosity, but those changes have been
greater in religious practices and human conduct than in belief." For example, emigrants attend mass less often, but they remain Catholic.[53] The
disconnect between a significant Protestant conversion of Latinos in the
United States and the near hegemony of Catholicism in the historic migrant source regions may be explained by the fact that some migrants
identify as Protestants while in the United States and as Catholics while
in Mexico.[54] Another possibility is that converts to Protestantism in the
United States are less likely to maintain ties to the home region, particularly when Protestantism is viewed so negatively in the rural areas and
small towns of central west Mexico.

Contemporary diocesan policy makes familiar claims about the negative effects of emigration on family life and the social order. Church officials lament the fashions, tattoos, body piercing, and gangs introduced by
returning migrants or their U.S.-born children. The diocese also argues

that marital separation creates mutual suspicions of infidelity, greater opportunities for bigamy and cohabitation, and an absence of male role models that leaves children "virtual orphans." Emigration is described as changing "values typical of our towns," such as fidelity, solidarity, honor, and sacrifice for the common good. Despite these problems, internal diocesan documents say that, "in general, family customs have not suffered significant changes" due to emigration. Similarly, while warning of "the scarce social control of a plural culture" in the United States, official diocesan policy states that cosmopolitan environments should not be "a source of division or conflict, but of mutual enrichment."[55] Following the Vatican's lead, Mexican bishops and diocesan officials now argue that emigration even presents an opportunity for migrants to evangelize in their destinations. The shrill warnings of the 1920s crusade have been toned down.

The editorial board of *Migrantes* in 1988 urged every diocese to develop a pastoral plan for emigrants that would follow the model of the diocese of Zamora, Michoacán, another city in the heart of the historic sending region. Local clergy were told that given the problems created by emigration, it would be best if the faithful did not leave home. Those who insisted on emigrating, however, should be prepared to confront the cultural, religious, and economic problems they would face.[56] During the economic crisis of the 1980s, some local priests even encouraged young men to emigrate to find work. Bishops of northern Mexican states called on priests in the source areas to discourage emigration, but to recognize that, "if there is no alternative, the whole family should look for a way to emigrate to preserve family unity." The diocesan policy in San Juan urges wives to follow their migrating husbands as soon as possible. This increases the number of emigrants, but at least it keeps couples together and puts wives in a position to channel more of the family income into savings than solitary husbands might be inclined to do.[57] Seminarians in San Juan de los Lagos have circulated the questions on the U.S. naturalization exam so they can teach migrants how to become U.S. citizens. Actually encouraging family reunification migration and U.S. naturalization is a conspicuous reversal of the relentless dissuasion of emigration that marked the 1920s through the early years of the bracero program.

The tools of contemporary pastoral power directed at emigrants include publications, clerical training, and surveys. The diocese of San Juan de los Lagos has distributed thirty-five thousand copies of a migrant's devotional booklet small enough to be carried in a shirt pocket while crossing the border. The precursors of the devotional were the 1960s "Manual for Braceros" and a devotional written by a Scalabrinian priest in Zamora.[58] The San Juan version includes special prayers for migrants who are leaving home, crossing the border without papers, facing deportation, and looking for work. "I feel like a citizen of the world and the Church that has no borders," it reads. The devotional includes prayers for family members back home and even the Mexican government. Another section lists Catholic shelters on the border and summarizes Church teachings on the legitimacy of migration, noting that Jesus, Mary, and Joseph were migrants in Egypt.[59] The Mexican Episcopal Conference published a similar devotional for migrants in 2003. These Catholic guides predate the secular migrant guides distributed by the Mexican government beginning in 2005.

In an effort to institutionalize its pastoral plan for migrants, the diocese of San Juan produced a 119-page migration policy book for local priests in the late 1990s. The book provides a sophisticated sociological understanding of the causes and effects of Mexico-U.S. migration and templates for celebrations of the return of the hijos ausentes. It replicates government and social science research techniques in its profile of migrants from Los Altos based on the seminary's 1993 survey and a database of information collected from priests in sixty Los Altos communities. The database estimates the numbers of emigrants from each parish living in the United States, their principal destinations, seasonal migration patterns, local ministries for migrants, and information on hometown association leaders.[60] Seminarians in the diocese take an obligatory class on the sociology of migration and the theological underpinnings of the migrant ministry. The director of the diocesan migrant program teaches that farmers' cooperatives and economic development generating better-paying jobs are the best long-term alternative to emigration. Price supports and trade protection for local meat and dairy products are suggested "not as a solution, but as an aid, because migration will not be stopped." In the director's final analysis, even if it were possible to stop emigration through economic development, emigration is a "human right."[61]

Following the Flock North

One of the most effective ways of managing the flock is by following it across the border. The Church hierarchy has sent Mexican priests to minister to Mexicans in the United States at least since the 1920s. Pastoral visits to braceros targeted a seasonal population of workers from all over Mexico scattered across the United States. Following the end of the program in 1964, social networks increasingly channeled migrants from particular source communities to specific U.S. destinations.[62] By the 1970s, Mexican parish priests were able to target large concentrations of paisanos by making short trips to U.S. settlements. The CEM developed a standardized policy for diocesan emigrant programs and the exchange of priests, in which bishops in both sending and receiving areas were required to give their authorization for pastoral visits. The slow bureaucratic process was resisted by parish priests seeking the right to make brief visits north without authorization.[63] The hierarchy drew up further regulations for long-term exchanges of priests between the United States and Mexico in 1969, 1985, and 1991. Local priests still consider these exchanges highly bureaucratic, and many Mexican priests visit family, friends, and paisanos in the United States for short periods outside the formal framework. One Michoacano priest I interviewed spent a summer in California without a visa or the authorization of his superiors. He helped celebrate mass at a Los Angeles church on the weekends and earned enough money washing dishes during the week to buy a used car back in Michoacán.[64]

The binational hierarchy encourages priests to take a sacred image of a hometown saint with them on their tours of communities in the North. During these visits, paisanos usually organize a mass or party in someone's backyard or a public park, where the visiting priest may even baptize a baby or celebrate a first communion. These rites are supposed to be coordinated with the U.S. parish priest, though the rule sometimes is ignored, which can create tensions between visiting and resident priests. Collection plates are often prominent in these events as part of a secular

Figure 10.   A Mexican priest tries to "shear sheep" in the United States in a Scalabrinian editorial against the practice, 1984.

trend away from raising money *for* migrants, as in the repatriation campaigns of the 1920s, to raising money *from* them. The first project of many migrant hometown associations (HTAs) is to renovate the church or sponsor charity work back home. A priest in the parish of origin is often involved in these efforts as a coordinator or trusted conduit for the donations. In a typical example, the Comunidad Arandense in Anaheim raised US$2,000 to US$3,000 a year in the mid-1990s to give gifts to the children, poor, and imprisoned of Arandas.[65] Three priests in Arandas worked with the migrants and arranged the use of a private Catholic school for the annual event at which the gifts were presented.

Official promotion of binational visits was tempered in the 1980s by the recognition that fund-raising was sometimes at odds with the priests' pastoral mission. An editorial in *Migrantes* lamented that many priests visited the United States not so much to maintain spiritual contact with their flock as to "shear sheep" by asking the faithful for dollars. The money was used "for their personal lucre, or under the pretext of social or religious projects, for prestige." The editorial accused such priests of exploiting their migrant brothers by playing on their "psychological weakness of affection for their homeland."[66] *Migrantes* called on bishops to control the visits by eliminating fund-raising, enforcing the rule that the diocese approve all trips, and ordering visiting priests to coordinate their activities with the destination parish.

Many priests in the traditional source regions are former migrants themselves, including two officials in the Los Altos migrant ministry who went to work in California during a break from their seminary training. Although they had tourist visas, they said they chose to cross illegally to gain a better understanding of the experience of many Jaliscienses. One spent five years in Los Angeles packing plastic utensils for an airline catering company; another spent four years near Los Angeles picking strawberries. They both assisted priests in Santa Monica on weekends. The former leader of the ministry explained their decision to work in California: "Our diocese sends a lot of migrants, so it's necessary to attend to them. How can we do that if we don't have a personal knowledge of this phenomenon? . . . It was easy to judge [emigrants] from here. We said that someone who goes to the United States goes to ruin—that's what you heard from a lot of people, from parents or sometimes priests . . . so we went to get to know a little about migrants' experiences."

The U.S. Catholic hierarchy prefers long-term or permanent postings of Spanish-speaking priests in the United States. In 2003, U.S. bishops filed fourteen formal petitions and many informal requests in the San Juan diocese alone asking for Mexican priests. A diocesan official said one bishop from California visited the seminary openly asking "Who can I take?" Asked if recruitment by U.S. bishops was causing a clerical brain drain in Los Altos, the official laughed and said that on the contrary, priests there "come out even from under the rocks." Local clerics say Los Altos has produced a quarter of all priests in Mexico.[67]

Whether a Mexican priest permanently transfers to the United States or makes a short visit changes the scale of cross-border ties that are promoted. Priests permanently posted in Spanish-speaking areas of the United States minister to Mexicans from all over Mexico. Depending on the host city, they may also find themselves ministering to Catholics from other parts of Latin America. The U.S. Church is an institutional promoter of Latino pan-ethnicity because the Spanish language, not national origin per se, is the basis of organizing the ministry. Mexican priests or lay leaders in the United States may have a special relationship with their hometown paisanos, but their pastoral portfolio extends far beyond them. There simply are not enough Mexican priests in the United States to minister to separate paisano clusters. When priests based in Mexico visit the United States for short trips, they usually seek out satellite communities of their Mexican parish. Their visits bring together paisanos in the United States to renew hometown solidarity through contact at masses and parties, collectively paying homage to the touring patron saint and sponsoring Church projects back home.

Welcoming the Hijos Ausentes

Priests in Mexico have become part of their members' migration circuits. Partly as a consequence, their strategies for dealing with emigration and emigrants have become much more sophisticated. In some parishes, workshops on the Day of the Emigrant educate returnees about their rights in the United States and provide telephone numbers in the United States and Mexico where they can report abuses.[68] The workshops are also a sort of purification ritual where migrants confess to the sins they committed in the North and are then reintegrated into the home community in a cathartic mass.[69] The Catholic weekly newspaper in the diocese of San Juan carries a constant stream of news about patron saint festivals and returning migrants. Interviews with local Church leaders, fiesta sponsors, and migrants give the impression that such practices developed organically in each locality. However, their nearly universal dispersion and similar format is due to a recurring set of instructions from the archdiocese, beginning in the early 1940s, and instructions from the Vatican in 1952 to hold a special day of the migrant modeled on the Day of the Italian Migrants.[70]

In 1988, *Migrantes* directed priests to avoid using the Day of the Emigrant for the economic benefit of the parish.[71] The current stance is a backlash against the 1940s Arandas model, in which the fund-raising possibilities of such a day were cited as a reason to establish it widely.[72] In practice, migrants continue to pay for a significant share of the cost for the fiesta's musicians, fireworks, decorations, food, and drink. Local churches can even turn a profit. In Agua Negra, the rectory was renovated with the equivalent of US$2,200 cleared by the 1997 fiesta. As the priest noted in the official record of vicariate business, "The earnings from this fiesta were absolutely fabulous, since when the faithful receive their program, they give an offering, and the hijos ausentes send their donation from wherever they are living."[73] In 2003, of the equivalent of US$9,000 raised by donations, 42 percent was raised directly from Agua Negrans living in the United States and 9 percent from Agua Negrans living elsewhere in Mexico. These figures do not include indirect migrant contributions, as a further 23 percent of the donations came from local family sponsorships, which interviews show are heavily dependent on remittances.

Administering Migrants

To *minister* to a mobile population effectively, the Church must first be able to *administer* that population. Raising funds from emigrants first requires keeping track of them, a formidable challenge in a diocese that estimates that three-fourths of its families have at least one member in the United States. Just as states must document their populations to extract resources such as taxes and conscripts in exchange for protecting their welfare and security,[74] the Church hierarchy must first identify its members and record its interactions with them to receive financial resources and deliver spiritual services. Even within the Catholic Church, migration creates profound challenges for filing members in the right place. Bishop Scalabrini refused to allow his Italian parishioners to emigrate without a letter of recommendation addressed to clergy in the destination. Pope Pius XI in 1923 ordered that Italian migrants be provided with "ecclesiastical identification cards" from the local Church authority before departure, so that they could be more readily recognized in their new homeland. The order was renewed in a 1952 papal encyclical.[75] Management of migrants extends to the most literal aspect of filing: ensuring that different parts of the Church have access to a member's records and are aware of the rites conducted in multiple locations. Even long-time residents of the United States often return to

Mexico to celebrate sacraments such as marriage. The sequential ordering of rites—for example, the fact that marriage builds on baptism—means that the ritual life course of a member must be tracked by coordinating the exchange of documents across ecclesiastical jurisdictions. In the 1930s, the archbishops of Guadalajara and Los Angeles instructed Mexican parish priests to be more careful about investigating the backgrounds of brides and grooms to avoid binational polygamy. The policy appears to have been practiced; in the 1950s, for example, prospective grooms in Arandas who had lived in the United States had to produce witnesses testifying that they had not married while they were abroad.[76]

In Agua Negra, a team of young volunteers went door to door in 2002 surveying the population and asking for addresses of family members in the United States so the priest could send them invitations to participate in the patron saint fiesta.[77] Half of the invitations are sent to Agua Negrans living in the United States. Such censuses build on the 1940s parish registries of migrants in places like Arandas that used less scientific methods. Like many churches, the Agua Negra vicariate also keeps records listing the names of fiesta donors, their addresses, and the amounts they gave to the church.

Effective administration of a mobile population requires a population that is willing to be administered. Migrants can opt out of the filing system the Church tries so hard to construct, underlining migration's fundamental challenge to governmentality. As the hierarchy recognizes, collecting information on individuals for fund-raising can impede the Church's embrace of its absent population for other pastoral purposes. The sensitivity of clerical fund-raising became clear during the homily of the parish priest in Arandas during the 2004 Day of the Hijos Ausentes. The previous year, none of the hundreds of migrants or their family members in attendance had given him their address, despite his pleas for their help in creating a migrant directory. In 2004, he again asked for addresses and assured his audience that the information would not be used to ask for donations: "Perhaps sometimes you think, no, this priest is already thinking about getting money out of us, because the *padrecitos* only think about that. But no, no, no . . . it's not about that. . . . Perhaps one day I'll visit you, not to raise money, no, no, but rather to go and share with you a moment of faith."[78]

Knowledge about the population at both the aggregate and individual levels is the basis of the Church's efforts to fight religious conversion and a shift in migrants' cultural orientations away from locally accepted norms. At the aggregate level, the clergy uses that knowledge to direct visiting priests to major satellite communities and to sponsor special processions, masses, and purification rituals for returning migrants during the Day of the Hijos Ausentes. Along the border, such information is used to construct shelters providing the undocumented with basic human and spiritual services. Knowledge about specific individuals is used to prevent bigamy and facilitate pastoral intervention in social problems. Priests also identify individual migrants whom they can invite to the patron saint fiesta, visit in the United States, and target for fund-raising. It is in these rationalized forms of gathering and recording information that the bureaucratic logic of the Church in managing members' international mobility coincides with the Church's ideological interests in controlling the effects of migration.

WHAT EXPLAINS CHURCH POLICY?

Mexican Church policies are principally reactive to migration patterns shaped by U.S. immigration policies, economic push and pull factors, and migrants' social networks. A recalcitrant population continued to emigrate en masse despite the Church's sustained campaigns of dissuasion through the 1950s. The effectiveness of Mexican Church policy has been further constrained by a trend toward permanent settlement in the United States that puts migrants out of its immediate grasp.[79] Yet postbracero migration networks have opened new opportunities for local Mexican priests because these networks concentrate paisanos in a handful of U.S. destinations. Migrants' preference for priests familiar with their language, hometown patron saints, and local religious expressions creates the conditions for priests in parishes of origin to maintain ties with paisanos abroad. Consequently, the Mexican Church now focuses on the management of emigrants rather than dissuading emigration.

The Mexican Church addresses the long-term settlement of Mexicans in the United States by working more closely with the U.S. Catholic hierarchy.

Ties to migrants in the United States are especially tenuous because they are no longer bathed in hegemonic Catholicism, so berating them for betraying the motherland might prompt migrants to simply leave the Church's orbit altogether. Vigorous complaints that migrants to the United States are agents of Protestantism or religious apathy threaten to become self-realizing expectations. Expressions of xenophobia are also unproductive. The nationalism promoted by the Mexican Church is now a soft, cultural nationalism based on positive affirmations of being Mexican and Guadalupano. Like the Mexican government, the Church has also carried out a pluralistic cultural mission among Mexicans in the United States. It promotes emigrants' native language by holding masses in Spanish and recruiting Spanish-speaking priests, at the same time encouraging emigrants to become U.S. citizens and learn English. Americanization and maintaining mexicanidad are viewed as complementary. Still, there is a national face to the Church in Mexico that can be seen in the ongoing preoccupations over migrants' introduction of cultural pathologies from the United States.

Processes of nationalization and multiculturalism within the United States have shaped Mexican Catholic emigrant policy as well. The U.S. Church's receptiveness to a binational migrant ministry is largely the result of the incorporation of Catholicism into the U.S. mainstream. The U.S. Catholic hierarchy no longer feels it must stamp out the "foreign" practices of its immigrant members, as it often did at the turn of the twentieth century, when anti-Catholicism and anti-immigrant sentiment were intertwined and Catholics struggled to assert their cultural credentials as U.S. citizens.[80] Expressing disdain for Mexicans or immigrants is no longer culturally acceptable or strategically prudent given that Latinos constitute a rapidly growing part of the Church's membership. Even in places like Georgia that historically have not been Mexican destinations, the Church is learning to adapt to an influx of newcomers.[81] The soft, cultural nationalism of the Mexican Church translates easily into the multiculturalism of the U.S. Church. The impulse to welcome cultural difference and cooperate across borders has also come from the Vatican, particularly following the Second Vatican Council in 1962. Both national branches have followed the Vatican in enthusiastically taking up the global rights revolution demanding an expanding list of protections and privileges based on universal rights of personhood.

EFFECTS OF CHURCH POLICY

Although my emphasis has been to explain changes in how the Church confronts migration, it is worth sketching how those policies have shaped migration between Mexico and the United States. In the first instance, the dissuasion policy was a failure; emigration actually increased during the 1920s crusade against it. It is hard to assess the counterfactual question of whether migration would have been even greater had the Church not opposed it, but the decimation of Mexico's population suggests that dissuasion was futile, and it is no longer Mexican Church policy. The effects of Church policies emphasizing human rights and more open immigration policies are harder to assess, but the Catholic Church has certainly emerged as one of the major interest groups in the United States and around the world promoting a more accommodating stance toward immigration, even when such positions have been politically unpopular.[82]

Other areas of Church policy in Mexico are more obviously consequential. The importance of these policies in promoting cross-border ties begins with migrants' intense devotion to local patron saints. Religious fiestas structure the calendar of temporary returns to Mexico. Most of the fiestas are concentrated between the Day of the Virgin of Guadalupe on December 12 and the end of January. The Mexican government estimates that more than a million migrants return for the holidays every year, sparking the most active phase of the Paisano Program that welcomes vacationing returnees.[83] The U.S. Border Patrol heightens its enforcement efforts immediately after the winter fiesta cycle, when illegal reentries spike sharply as migrants return to work. For instance, between December 2001 and March 2002, apprehensions rose more than 400 percent, and they rose 250 percent the following fiesta season.[84] Communities with patron saint fiestas outside the modal months of December and January receive the greatest returns during their fiestas, providing strong evidence that the fiesta exerts an effect on the migration calendar that is independent of the agricultural cycle or other seasonal conditions. The Church hierarchy promotes activities during the fiesta that cater to migrants and welcome them home. The state has piggybacked on religious fiestas by either cooperating with local priests or, in some communities, attempting to shift the focus to a secular fiesta. In both cases, the religious fiesta predates the government's secular involvement.

The Church promotes cross-border ties and hometown solidarity more generally through its role in forming HTAs, especially the many ad hoc associations that raise funds for church renovation or construction projects. When Mexican parish priests visit their U.S. satellite communities with an image of the patron saint, they bring together paisanos who might not otherwise see each other. Finally, Catholic centers of refuge along the border help to perpetuate international migration. Along with travel agents, human smugglers, and labor brokers, Catholic organizations can become part of a "migration industry."[85] Of course, unlike smugglers, shelters spend money on migrants rather than earn money from them, but both ease the path for travelers who cannot rely on a social network of experienced migrants from their hometown or family.

CHURCH, STATE, AND FLOCK

Comparing the stances of the Mexican Church and state toward emigration shows how population mobility poses similar challenges to organizations of members with jurisdictions over particular territories. The Church has developed most of the policy innovations for emigrants, which have then been copied by the state. During the 1920s and 1930s, both Church and state objected to emigration on the same nationalist grounds that emigrants were building up the demographic and economic strength of the United States while weakening Mexico and introducing foreign ideas upon their return. Both used propaganda campaigns to dissuade emigration, raised funds to repatriate Mexicans, and eased their reentry with help finding jobs. Since the end of the bracero program, both have increasingly acknowledged that emigration is a deeply rooted part of the cultures and economies of the source regions. Church and state

Figure 11. Program cover for mass to celebrate Day of the Absent Jalisciense, 2002.

promote remittances, though the rationale is different for each: The Church emphasizes migrants' responsibility to provide for families left behind, while the government emphasizes spending money on investments rather than consumption.

Even the iconography of the fiestas reflects cooperation. For example, the program for the mass during the 2002 Day of the Absent Jalisciense, an event primarily organized by the state Office of Attention to Jaliscienses Abroad, bore the logo of the federal government's Paisano migrant protection program as well as an image of the Virgin of Guadalupe. Both Church and state promote migrants' intensely localistic affection for the hometown or ranch of origin. Fiestas honoring the hijos ausentes are advantageous from the state's point of view because they promote permanent emigration with continued homeland ties and paisano tourism, considered the best recipe for attracting remittances and forming a Mexican lobby in the United States. The same strategy is useful from a strictly financial perspective on the part of local priests in high emigration areas that rely on remittances. An end to remittances, whether because of an end to migration or because emigrants severed their hometown ties, would be a financial disaster for many parishes. One of the proposals by the diocese of San Juan to the Mexican government in a meeting between Church officials and President Fox in 2003 was to reduce remittance transfer fees.

Beginning in the 1980s, the Mexican Church and state have paid increasing attention to educating Mexicans about their civil rights in the United States and the universal human rights of unauthorized migrants. The Mexican and U.S. episcopates have adopted the current policy positions of the Mexican government concerning Mexico-U.S. migration, though they also criticize the Mexican government for its abusive treatment of Central Americans in transit through Mexico. The 2002 binational episcopal letter calls for an amnesty for undocumented migrants in the United States, a temporary guest-worker program, greater ease of family reunification migration, greater respect for migrants' human rights, and an end to U.S. border enforcement strategies channeling migrants into dangerous wilderness areas. On the Mexican side, it calls for targeted development projects in migrant-source regions to create economic alternatives to migration and matching fund programs multiplying remittances to generate investment in migrant-source communities.[86] While this reflects the basic position of the Mexican government, the goals of the Mexican Church and state differ in important respects. Mexico is one of many migrant-source countries in which governments and political parties are trying to secure domestic political support from migrants abroad—an aim that is not of direct interest to the Church. The Church is also more concerned than the federal government with emigration's moral effects, though, as I describe in chapter 5, at the local level government and Church leaders publicly talk about the same cultural pollutions.

Church and state use similar techniques to govern a mobile population. They survey migrants to determine their demographic characteristics, legal status, migration routes, U.S. destinations, and occupations. Both organizations document the amounts of collective remittances; how they are spent; and the names, addresses, and telephone numbers of the remitters. Just as the Mexican state has at times issued identification documents that also attest to the bearer's moral character, on a smaller scale priests in Mexico have issued ecclesiastical identification documents and letters of introduction to destination parishes. At the local level, the Church often has better records than the state, given that local government bureaucracy is shot through with clientelism, lack of continuity between administrations, and corruption. The state imitates the Church's administrative methods by building on an existing system of baptismal registries to record births and creating directories of migrants from particular hometowns.[87] The techniques of administering a mobile population are similar because both Church and state exercise their power through knowledge about the whole population as well as its individual members.

The Church's embrace of mobile members is facilitated by a hierarchal structure imposed over most of the globe. The consulates of a nation-state attempt similar coverage of its emigrant population, but the fundamental difference is that while a religious organization does not inherently violate sovereignty, a consulate is a sort of sovereign enclave that survives in the receiving country only through the legal fiction of extraterritoriality and reciprocal agreement with the host government.[88] The sovereign nature of the international system limits the sending state's capacity to embrace emigrants. The Church is in a better position than states to embrace emigrants because it has a universalist face and transnational organization, allowing it to organize and direct emigrants in multiple jurisdictions.

In the broad sweep of history, the nation-state's acquisition of temporal power at the expense of the Catholic Church has forced the Church to emphasize universal values and voluntary participation rather than rely on coercion.[89] The Church of the Inquisition is dead. States have monopolized legitimate taxation, which is to say that it is only acceptable for governments to extract money from residents using the implicit threat of force. The Church cannot make anyone tithe, including emigrants, so it relies on religious appeals and affective ties to raise funds at home and abroad. Ironically, the state's monopolization of political power at the expense of the Church during the nineteenth century, which ended forced tithing and stripped the Church of its political autonomy, created a Catholic institutional arrangement for obtaining resources from members and delivering services to them that is highly effective in a context of mass migration. Consequently, the Mexican state is following the Church's lead in shifting to the deployment of ideological power to hold sway over the flock that strays beyond Mexico's borders.

FOUR Colonies of the Little Motherland

Once a year, migrants gather in hotel ballrooms in Los Angeles and Chicago to raise money for their hometowns in Mexico and to select a queen who will represent the local "colony" of paisanos. Mexican mayors, consular officials, and even governors mingle with migrants in dark suits to discuss whether to spend the money to pave roads, open small factories, or renovate churches. Club Arandas is typical of the estimated three thousand Mexican hometown associations in the United States. Its unassuming leader, Joaquín, migrated to Orange County without papers in 1974 to pick strawberries.[1] Now the owner of eight local restaurants and a house on a private street that bears his name, Joaquín has become a spokesman for the Jalisciense Federation in Los Angeles. During major fund-raisers, he lobbies the governor of Jalisco and channels money back to his native town. Several months after the 2003 pageant, his niece, the new Señorita Arandas, joins four other winners for a bus tour of Jalisco sponsored by the state's Office of Attention to Jaliscienses Abroad. They arrive in Arandas with a police escort like rock stars as the mariachis play and a young boy shouts "Viva México!" A welcoming committee of local dignitaries reminds the public that the purpose of their visit is not only for the queens to learn about their roots, but also to promote economic ties between Arandas and the United States.

The geographic dislocation of conducting the business of local Mexican government in distant U.S. cities and the remarkable political mobility of HTA leaders has intrigued researchers, journalists, and policy makers. Scholars of transnationalism present HTAs as the expression of a new kind of "transnational community" or "transnational social field" that is redefining what it means to belong to a community by including people who are physically absent but who make their presence felt through regular visits and remittances and by sponsoring charity and development projects in their hometown. Such migrants are said to transcend the old boundaries of territorial belonging that depended on a sedentary population and call into question basic concepts of citizenship, community, and nation-state. Even the most recent transnationalism literature, which has retreated from earlier claims of novelty to rediscover transborder practices of older migrations, continues to claim that new conceptions of membership are necessary to understand both new and older practices.[2]

What these discussions tend to ignore is that migrants from small Mexican towns have formed HTAs in Mexico City and Guadalajara as well as in Los Angeles and Chicago. This chapter compares domestic and transborder HTAs from the same place: the county of Arandas.[3] Following a push from the Church in the 1940s, domestic HTAs created a legitimate way for internal migrants to continue to be involved in the life of their hometown. Migrants in the United States then built on the domestic model to create HTAs that institutionalize ties between all three levels of the Mexican government and its citizens abroad. Hometown associations can negotiate the terms of their cooperation with the state because their contributions to hometown projects are voluntary and the state is eager to bring the organizations within its consular embrace. Hometown associations have become one of the main expressions of citizenship à la carte.

DOMESTIC HTAS

Massive internal migration from Arandas has fed the growth of domestic HTAs. The Cristero War (1926–29) prompted what is probably the largest exodus from Arandas in the twentieth century. Hundreds of residents fled for the safety and greater economic opportunities of Mexico City; the country's second largest city, Guadalajara; and the industrial powerhouse of León in the neighboring state of Guanajuato. Large-scale economic migration to major Mexican cities continued through the 1960s. From 1960 to 1970, Los Altos lost a third of its population.[4] Internal migration from Arandas has outpaced U.S. migration at least since 1950. In 2000, 27 percent of the county seat's population had domestic migration experience, compared to 22 percent with U.S. experience. Internal migration persists, particularly to Guadalajara, but migration to Mexico City has practically ended as economic opportunities have grown in more livable alternatives.[5]

Although Arandas is just sixty miles east of Guadalajara, most of Los Altos has only recently become integrated into the rest of the republic. Even in the 1950s, the roads out of Arandas were impassable in the rainy season. In the dry season, a trip to Guadalajara was four hours by bus. It took almost two days to reach Mexico City by a combination of bus and railroad, a journey that now takes six hours by car. A former county president recalled that moving to Mexico City in 1968 at the age of ten was like moving to another country:

> I used to go to the ranch with my great-grandfather. I saddled the horse and walked around wearing sandals. . . . I got up early to milk, herd the cattle, and then go to school. It was really peaceful. . . . Then I went to live in Mexico City, and I saw the airplanes I had never seen before in my life, and TV, because [in Arandas] we didn't have anything but a transistor radio we listened to at 10 o'clock at night. Then we prayed and went to bed. You arrive in Mexico City, and it's an abrupt change. The next day I wanted to sell my sandals and come home. . . . It was a cultural shift from heaven to earth. . . . [I felt] like an Arandense feels when he arrives in Los Angeles or Chicago, although maybe one feels better there because there are a lot of Spanish speakers and there's not a lot of aggression, but when someone arrives in the capital, they immediately experience aggression. In what way? In that the *chilangos* [Mexico City

natives] call you *jalisquillo* [little one from Jalisco] in their singsong voice.
They're very tough people, very difficult. . . . If you arrived from the
provinces, they called you *indio* [Indian] or *el provinciano* [country bump-
kin], because that's how the people in Mexico City are.

In the face of this abrupt cultural change, practically every town in Los
Altos developed an HTA in Mexico City during the 1940s. The local
church initiated the first HTAs from Los Altos. Alarmed by massive out-
migration during the Cristero War, local clerics organized absentees in
colonies to aid each other, maintain their conservative religiosity, and fi-
nancially support churches that had been damaged during the war. In
1942, the parish priest in Arandas established a Pro-Emigrant Section of
the Mexican Catholic Union that urged migrants in each destination to establish a "Colonia Arandense." The first domestic HTAs from Arandas
were formed in the mid-1940s in León, Guadalajara, and Mexico City by
seventeen "sons and daughters of Arandas, feeling the loneliness of their
exile from their *patria chica* [little motherland]."[6] The leaderships of the
colonias informed both the county government and parish of their formation, though only the priest was asked for permission to organize a congress of the colonias during the 1947 patron saint fiesta. By the end of the
decade, Arandense colonias had formed in six more Mexican cities and
united in a single federation. A representative coordinated the federation's
relationship with a corporatist County Cooperation Committee of thirty-
nine that included subcommittees representing commerce, agriculture,
workers, industry, professionals, and women. The Mexico City colonia
dominated the activities of the federation. In 1946, it boasted a membership of four hundred, including influential bureaucrats and a radio network magnate. From 1946 to 1951, the Mexico City colonia published a six-
page monthly newspaper, *El Arandense*, and distributed as many as twelve
hundred copies to Arandenses throughout Mexico and even the United
States. The 1949 patron saint fiesta drew five hundred returnees.

What were the aims of these associations? Their formal goal was modernization. In the hopeful words of *El Arandense*, "By achieving the indus-
trialization of our town, all of its problems can be resolved."[7] The lawyers,
merchants, and bureaucrats who formed the backbone of the colonias dis-

pensed money and advice to their paisanos in Arandas. Projects over a five-year period beginning in the late 1940s included reforestation; beautification of the park; providing hospital beds, telephone service, a water pump, and library books; constructing a children's clinic, a chamber of commerce, and a cathedral; holding art and literary competitions; and loaning money to farmers and ranchers. Paisanos in Guadalajara developed a nine-member women's committee in 1946 working for the "redemption of the Arandense woman, especially the peasant woman, to replace her antiquated working methods with modern ones, which will offer her greater comfort with less effort."[8] The colonia in Irapuato, Guanajuato, sent an agronomist to Arandas to teach peasants how to use improved strains of corn and other farming techniques.

Most important, the colonias established political links between Arandas and the levers of power in Mexico City and Guadalajara. Urban Arandenses acted as intermediaries to develop public infrastructure projects in Arandas by sending a delegation to meet with Arandense bureaucrats in the corresponding ministries.[9] Members of the colonias sought and received public recognition for their projects in the county president's public speeches and even on national radio. In return, while claiming to be apolitical, *El Arandense* openly supported the candidacies of local congressional deputies and praised the work of the county president. The director of *El Arandense*, Francisco Medina Ascencio, was particularly adept at using the colonias to access government leaders and the resources they commanded. As a state official and then governor of Jalisco from 1965 to 1971, he funneled money to Arandas for a secondary school, highway improvements, a dam that allowed the first sustained irrigation in the county, paved streets, wells, and a drainage system. Medina Ascencio and other Arandenses in government helped their paisanos get government jobs and admission to public universities. Unofficially, Medina Ascencio had a strong hand in picking county presidents in his hometown.

Colonia leaders often complained publicly about locals in Arandas who did not share the federation's modernizing spirit or questioned its motivations. After sending money to care for a sick child in Arandas, the colonia published the news with the question, "Now will the Arandenses who still doubt our effort believe us?" When it reported that a rich Arandense in Guadalajara donated 10,000 pesos to write a history of Arandas, *El Aran-dense* asked, "Why do many Arandenses still doubt the good faith of our labor?"[10] These questions suggest that extending "the community" of Arandenses to include absentees deeply involved in local politics was contested by political actors who resented the intrusion of emigrants.

Like HTAs around the world, the Arandense colonias also organized mutual assistance and entertainment in destination communities. Monthly meetings in Mexico City drew more than two hundred Arandenses, who sang the "Himno Arandas" and took their leave with a hearty " 'Til Arandas!"—a sort of "Next year in Jerusalem" expression of belonging to a diaspora. They joined Jaliscienses from all over the state every Friday night at the Casa de Jalisco for musical performances. The colonia in León organized an annual picnic that drew as many as three thousand Arandenses and their friends. Like many groups of domestic or international migrants, the colonia developed the social networks of its members as an economic resource. A directory of Jaliscienses living in Mexico City included several pages of Arandenses and Arandense-owned businesses in Guadalajara and Mexico City advertising discounts for paisanos. In 1948, the colonia in Mexico City organized a mutual aid society to insure its members in case of sickness or death and provide submarket interest rates on loans for small grocery and retail businesses. By 1950, the society had seventy members.

The strength of the Arandense federation's clubs ebbed and flowed, but all of the original clubs had disappeared by the mid-1950s. The generation of elites that left during the Cristero Wars settled in destination cities, and the federation organizers tired of devoting time and resources to publish their newspapers. Despite the decline in HTAs' organization of economic and political projects in Arandas, individual absentees remained critical actors in the county's development. A county president during the late 1950s recalled that the county budget was so meager that to fund practically any project he had to visit Arandenses living in Mexico City and Guadalajara. "The three years I was in the presidency, I was always off begging in other cities," he said. Groups of Arandenses in those cities continued to hold parties, but they no longer raised money for development projects in Arandas. The county president usually spoke directly to four or five Arandense business owners or politicians, who then either donated the money directly or arranged funding through their political contacts. Following a reform of state finances in the 1970s that channeled more funds to the counties outside Guadalajara, local leaders began relying on support from paisanos in state and federal government for major projects that entrepreneurs or HTAs could not afford.

By the 1970s, the dairy confection business and factories distilling agave into tequila began to prosper in Arandas. These industries generated more local resources to pay for projects such as paving streets. Nationally, after a long decline in counties' share of government expenditures, from 12.9 percent in 1900 to 1.1 percent in 1980, the 1983 County Reform Act laid the groundwork for an increase in the county's share of government expenses, which rose to 3.4 percent by 1991.[11] The redistribution of government revenues to give the counties larger budgets meant that county presidents no longer needed to ask paisanos for donations to provide basic services.

The Catholic Colonia

The only active organized group of Arandenses in Guadalajara today is an informal religious club of seventy-five families that has its roots in similar clubs that have formed periodically since at least 1967, when an Arandense priest in Guadalajara created a group to revive the Day of the Hijos Ausentes during the patron saint fiesta in Arandas. Every November 12, the Arandenses in Guadalajara hold their signature annual event. Two hundred or more Arandenses gather at the Rosario church for a mass and a simple luncheon. The county president and parish priest of Arandas generally attend, along with the county band. There is no discussion of projects for Arandas. A smaller group of Arandenses meets at a Guadalajara church every month for a *salve*, a procession through the church to honor the Virgin of Guadalupe through song. The salve group historically has comprised mostly middle-class, long-term residents of Guadalajara. It is one of the few remaining venues to reestablish hometown solidarity, as Arandenses are no longer concentrated in one neighborhood as they were in the 1920s. The long-term future of the salve group looks grim in the face of weakening ties to Arandas among the organizers and apathy among the second generation. A sixty-two-year-old organizer who left Arandas in 1967 says he returns to Arandas less and less even though highway improvements have cut travel time: "Every year in Arandas, two or three relatives die . . . and sometimes I think, Why should I go? Sometimes I take the bypass road around Arandas when I'm coming through. Sometimes I don't even stop off." As with most other members, the organizers' adult children rarely attend the salve, although they do return to Arandas for the fiesta. The Colonia Arandense in León has declined in the same way for the same reasons. Arandenses in León have held a monthly salve since at least the 1950s, but around 2000 they ended their other activities, such as picnics and dances. The first-generation leadership has mostly died or become too feeble to organize.

In broad strokes, domestic HTAs initiated by the Church were critical for the economic development of Arandas in the 1940s and 1950s through their direct donations and role as intermediaries between the county government and state and federal authorities. Although they lived outside their hometown, Arandenses were able to voluntarily harness their political and economic resources to great effect and establish an organizational model that migrants in the United States would adopt. But the strength of domestic HTAs did not last. Across the major destinations of internal migrants, Arandense HTAs have declined in the face of assimilation into the metropolitan milieu, the decentralization of government, and economic growth in Arandas that has generated more local resources and access to the levers of power.

ARANDENSES ABROAD

As early as the 1940s, the parish priest in Arandas and colonia federation leaders encouraged Arandenses in the United States to form HTAs along with their paisanos in Mexico City and Guadalajara, but transborder HTAs did not develop until more than a generation after they were first proposed. The earliest known reference to U.S.-based emigrants participating in the hijos ausentes procession through the streets of Arandas is of four Arandenses visiting from Los Angeles in 1949. They reported to the colonia newspaper that they were trying to form an organization of Arandenses in Los Angeles. During the 1940s and 1950s, the only other news in *El Arandense* about paisanos in the United States was confined to social news of musicians on tour and elites living in Mexico who took their holiday in the North. As late as the 1970s, the county president of Arandas did not send invitations to the patron saint fiesta to migrants living in the United States, as he did to migrants in other parts of Mexico; at the time, Arandenses in the United States worked in low-wage jobs and could not afford to support their hometown. For the same reason, the county administration offered awards for distinguished Arandenses only to paisanos living in other parts of Mexico, and the government did not seek donations from U.S.-resident Arandenses.

Settlement patterns also inhibited the early development of U.S-based HTAs. In the early 1930s, Paul Taylor found that "there was no tendency to form large and distinct Arandas colonies."[12] He reported that Arandenses had migrated to at least twenty-four U.S. states, which by 2003 had fallen to sixteen states, according to the MMP study's survey. Groups of Arandenses living in the United States did not organize until the 1970s, when residential concentrations formed in Los Angeles and Orange County, greater Chicago, and Union City in the San Francisco Bay Area. By the 1980s, there were two soccer teams each in Orange County and Union City, one in Los Angeles, and one in Chicago. As often happens among migrant sports clubs, one of the Arandas soccer teams in Orange County grew into the Social Club of Arandas. In 1978, Arandenses from northern and southern California began meeting every July 4th for a soccer game and party; they alternate every year between Union City and Orange County. In its heyday in the 1990s, club members estimated the game drew between two hundred and one thousand Arandenses.

Transborder HTAs have made various charitable donations to Arandas; for example, the Social Club donated four ambulances to the Arandas Red Cross in the late 1990s. An organization of about ninety families in Orange County formed in 1994 to compete with the Social Club as the legitimate voice of Arandenses in southern California. The new club leaders claimed that the older club was dominated by men more committed to increasing their status than following through with altruistic hometown projects. Led by a cadre of six middle-class men in California working with three priests in Arandas, the Arandense Community raised US$2,000 to US$3,000 a year in the mid-1990s for charity projects in Arandas. Like many HTAs, the club also took up collections to help pay for the repatriation of the bodies of Arandenses who died in California. Struggles over who should receive public recognition for developing projects in Arandas, and rumors that county officials in Arandas kept the best donations for themselves, weakened cooperation between the club and county authorities. Arandense Community leaders discussed building a new clinic in Arandas, but before the project began the club disbanded over allegations that club leaders were siphoning off its money.

The timing of the formation of Arandense HTAs in the United States is consistent with the broader binational pattern. As part of the federal government's renewed effort to embrace Mexicans in the United States by appealing to their local and regional ties, the Secretariat of Foreign Relations (SRE) began the Program for Mexican Communities Abroad in 1990. The program encouraged migrants to form new HTAs, register them with the consulates, and cooperate with the Mexican government on hometown development projects. Federations of Jalisciense clubs formed in Los Angeles in 1991 and in Chicago four years later. In response to proposals by the SRE and the Los Angeles federation, the opposition National Action Party (PAN) governor created the Office of Attention to Jaliscienses Abroad (OFAJE) in 1996 and visited Jaliscienses in the United States a dozen times from 1995 to 2001. His PAN successor has been equally active. The OFAJE offers county presidents and migrants detailed practical guidance on how to form an HTA, down to model statutes complying with U.S. law and a directory of the one hundred or so Jaliscienses clubs in the United States.

According to Mexican consular registries, the number of Mexican HTAs grew from 263 to 815 between 1995 and 2005. The social scientists Lanly and Valenzuela estimate that only about a quarter of Mexican HTAs register with a consulate.[13] Hometown associations often disintegrate and then form again a few years later, sometimes under a different name. In some communities, ad hoc groups form and disband with each fiesta cycle. A loose definition of associations that includes the many ad hoc groups would suggest there are around three thousand Mexican HTAs in the United States. Most are concentrated in California, Illinois, and Texas. In a 2004 survey of Mexicans in the United States soliciting a *matrícula consular* identification document, 14 percent reported belonging to an HTA.[14] In 2005, registered HTAs donated US$20 million to hometown projects, which, when complemented with matching funds from municipal, state, and federal governments through the "3×1" program, generated US$80 million in investments. In the first three years since it expanded nationwide in 2002, the "3×1" program supported nearly four thousand social investment projects.[15]

The Arandas clubs have not participated in the "3×1" program because the county government has alternative sources of funding, but the clubs remain socially active. The July 4th soccer game between Arandenses in northern and southern California is now organized by Club Arandas, whose leader began making his restaurant fortune by selling tacos to players during weekly Arandense soccer games in California in the 1980s. When the governor of Jalisco visited California, the club leader lobbied him for a sewage treatment facility and a branch of the University of Guadalajara for Arandas. The outcome of that lobbying was uncertain as of this writing, but it has become increasingly common for Mexican migrants to intervene on behalf of their communities of origin with state and federal officials visiting the United States, sometimes with success. In general, the level of activity of the Arandas HTAs seems typical of Mexican transborder HTAs. They have sponsored hometown projects and made charitable donations, lobbied state and county officials visiting the United States, and waxed and waned with charges of financial shenanigans and leadership struggles.[16]

Visiting Paisanos

Since Arandenses in California and Illinois first invited the county president of Arandas to visit in 1995, he has generally attended at least one of their annual signature events, usually the July 4th soccer game or a Señorita Jalisco competition to crown a young woman to represent Jaliscienses in the

United States. Arandense opinions are split over whether these are serious fund-raising trips, attempts to seek political support indirectly by showing concern for migrants, or simply junkets. In the 1990s, all three PAN county presidents raised funds from Arandenses in the United States for various public-use vehicles and a clinic.[17] A federal deputy noted in an interview that during the 1990s, county presidents throughout Los Altos successfully visited HTAs and sister cities in the United States and brought back equipment for schools and hospitals and vehicles to collect trash and transport students.

The trips are not motivated only by social projects, however. A former county president of Arandas described the fund-raising limitations of the trips in an interview: "My wife went with me every time I went, and I invited several *regidores* [aldermen] too. I also invited two or three people who were not part of the administration. . . . It costs more money to take a trip to visit [the paisanos] than what they can donate at a given moment. I think that going to greet the paisanos there is the true motive for going."

Politicking is part of cross-border trips, although it is subtle. Few Arandense elites see emigrants as having significant political influence. Unlike earlier, domestic HTAs, transborder HTAs do not appear to be vehicles for intensive political involvement or the transformation of Arandas. Indeed, transborder Arandense HTAs have been avowedly apolitical. Joaquín, the current HTA leader in Orange County, has close relationships with both PAN and PRI leaders, and the quality of ties between the HTAs and county authorities does not seem to depend on the party in power. The soft politicking of a visit to paisanos in the United States to show concern for migrants among voters back home jibes neatly with the function of these trips as taxpayer-funded junkets for local officials and opportunities for migrants to demonstrate their ongoing interest in their hometown.

Welcoming the Prodigal Sons

The patron saint fiesta is the main venue for both Church and state to reach out to migrants. In Arandas, the local parish and county government coordinate hijos ausentes activities. The Church takes charge of the procession and mass, and the government organizes the luncheon and recognition of illustrious emigrants. Arandenses living in the United States have been recognized as a corporate group in the Arandas fiesta since at least the late 1970s. In 2004, about two hundred migrants paraded through the streets of Arandas behind a local marching band and banners of the religious Colonia Arandense in Guadalajara. Their number multiplied several times over by the time they reached the church. The parish priest and the visiting Arandas-born bishop of Tlaxcala (east of Mexico City) delivered homilies welcoming the hijos ausentes and asking them to remember their families, origins, and traditions.

Nearly one thousand migrants and their families attended the county luncheon for the hijos ausentes that year. Officials estimated that 70 percent lived in the United States and 30 percent in Guadalajara, Mexico City, and other domestic sites. The organizers honored several Arandenses living in the United States who represent two kinds of ideal migrants. The first is someone who becomes rich in the United States and returns to Arandas to build a house and start a business. Even the federal SRE has printed posters asking "successful Mexicans who have returned from the United States and are now reintegrated into the economic and political lives of the communities of our country" to call the SRE branch office in Guadalajara to identify themselves. The second type of model migrant achieves economic success and settles in the United States more or less permanently, but often returns to Mexico for vacations. Joaquín, who has given money to Arandense charities outside the HTA framework as well, is a prime example of the second type. The SRE also has a program to identify this type of migrant, who is most consistently targeted by the Arandas county government through the HTAs.

In private interviews, county officials described their welcome-home activities for the hijos ausentes as an investment in paisano tourism. "We want them to come here instead of going to Acapulco or Orlando. . . . When they come here, they bring money and spend," said one Arandense official involved in creating a directory of migrants who could be mailed fiesta invitations. Of the many fiestas in Arandas, the patron saint fiesta is the only one that generates net income for the government through sales of commercial licenses and exposition tickets. The absentee luncheon cost the county US$5,000 out of total county fiesta expenditures of US$130,000. The profit of US$80,000 was donated to various social services in Arandas. At the state level, the OFAJE is developing a Paquete Paisano (Compatriot Package Tour) as a collaboration of state tourism officials and private operators offering tourism packages directed at Jaliscienses in the United States. Paisano tourism has advantages over collective projects for a prosperous town like Arandas. Encouraging migrants to return to the fiesta for their own enjoyment and the cultural edification of their children brings diffuse but much more important economic returns than a typical HTA-sponsored project. The median amount of money brought home by migrants who were household heads was US$3,000 in Arandas and US$1,000 in Agua Negra.[18] One family of returnees could easily spend as much as the amount raised at a typical HTA dance or soccer game. An indirect economic benefit is that politicians have less reason to worry about migrants transforming their collective economic capital into political capital and demanding government services or, even worse, political change.

Habitantes Económicos

Although HTAs from the county seat of Arandas have been largely apolitical, HTAs from the delegation of San Ignacio Cerro Gordo in the county of Arandas have been part of a secessionist movement to legally recognize their migrants in the United States as local residents of San Ignacio. Beginning in the mid-1980s, a movement in San Ignacio formed to secede from Arandas and create a new county with access to more resources from the state government.[19] The secessionist committee and its sympathizers at the University of Guadalajara argued that Sanignacienses in the United States should be included in the census to achieve the required population of ten thousand in the new county seat and twenty thousand in the entire county. A 2001 census conducted by the University of Guadalajara showed an average of one member per household living in the United States and added 1,948 "absent sons and daughters" and their 1,952 second-generation descendents to the 9,538 residents of San Ignacio. The secessionists prepared a bill to be presented in the state congress that would officially include *habitantes económicos* (economic inhabitants), who are physically absent most of the year but who remain economically engaged in the community. As the president of the committee explained, "The economic inhabitant is continually sending money. Here he has his houses, his ranches, and his family. Most of them come back three, four, or five months. They live here part of the time."

Returned migrants and Sanignacienses in the United States have played a fundamental role in the secessionist movement. In 2001, the leader of the secessionist committee, who worked as a carpenter in Los Angeles in 1977 before returning to establish his own carpentry business in San Ignacio, traveled to Detroit to form a five-member subcommittee. A second committee member made a fund-raising trip to Detroit in 2004, and a third is the veteran of eight migrations to Detroit and California. The subcommittee in Detroit, the destination of more than half of the Sanignacienses in the United States, conducted a census there with the help of the Mexican consulate, distributed secessionist propaganda, and raised US$10,000 to help pay for legal costs. A smaller group in Los Angeles has also raised funds for the movement. The committee established an Internet site that keeps Sanignacienses everywhere abreast of the movement's progress, with photographs of demonstrations in Jalisco and copies of relevant legal documents.

The debate over the legitimacy of counting Sanignacienses in the United States was never resolved because natural growth eventually enabled San Ignacio to meet the population requirements with residents alone. The secession decree approved by the state legislature in 2003 emphasized the economic contributions of migrants as a pillar of the local economy and noted that remittances were equal to the likely budget of the new county. According to a 2001 University of Guadalajara survey, Sanignacienses in the United States annually remit US$1.7 million, and 15 percent of local businesses were started with *migradólares*. The decree explicitly adopted the language of the secessionist committee in stating that "migrants constitute *de facto* economic inhabitants of the region," but the decree's argument was limited to the notion that migrants help create the economic viability necessary to form a new county rather than arguing that migrants in the United States should be included in the census as extraterritorial citizens.[20] Still, the San Ignacio case represents a further institutionalization of the inclusion of migrants abroad and shows how HTAs can make political demands back home based on their economic power.

THE RISE, FALL, AND RISE OF THE HTA

Why did domestic HTAs grow beginning in the 1940s and then decline, while transborder HTAs have grown since the 1990s? A constellation of factors explains the timing of the waxing and waning of these organizations. The first is external stimuli from above. The Catholic Church promoted the domestic HTAs in the early 1940s to access the financial resources of migrants who had fled a hinterland plagued by violence and poverty for the greater security and opportunities of major cities. Transborder HTAs with both secular and religious orientations began to form on a widespread basis in the 1990s. Their formation accelerated quickly when the Mexican government imitated the Church-inspired associations by institutionalizing its relationships with existing transborder HTAs and promoting the creation of hundreds more. The external stimuli of the Church and state are a necessary but insufficient explanation, because they do not account for the timing of the growth of transborder HTAs in the 1990s, nor the reason that thousands of migrants responded voluntarily to state and Church initiatives.

Migration patterns are a second critical factor explaining HTA development. Both the transnationalism and classic assimilation literatures are misleading, because it is the permanence of *settlement*, rather than increased circularity, that has driven emigrants to claim membership in the community of origin despite their physical absence. Since the end of the bracero program in 1964, and accelerating with the 1986 Immigration Reform and Control Act that granted amnesty to more than two million Mexicans, migrants have become more settled and concentrated in their U.S. destinations.[21] Enough time has passed to allow a handful of Arandenses to claw their way from menial jobs into the middle class and even entrepreneurial wealth. According to a University of Guadalajara study, migrants to the United States generate US$2,500 a year for a typical family in

San Ignacio (county of Arandas), which is ten times more than the average remittances received from internal migrants.[22] Migrants to the United States have much deeper pockets than their domestic counterparts.

A complete explanation of the decline of the domestic HTA and the rise of their transborder counterparts must also include the decentralization of the Mexican government. On the one hand, counties' increasing share of government spending and the spread of branch offices of federal agencies explain why local governments no longer have the same incentive to work with domestic HTAs. Local governments now have budgets based on the collection of property taxes, for example, which gives them money for projects that were impossible in the 1940s and 1950s, when the federal government controlled virtually all government spending.[23] Domestic HTAs are no longer necessary liaisons between the governments of peripheral towns and the state and federal capitals.[24] On the other hand, the literature on transborder HTAs emphasizes that the decentralization of the Mexican government is one of the driving forces behind the accelerated formation of HTAs in the early 1990s. The National Solidarity Program for regional development and the alleviation of poverty, which included sharing planning and costs among the three levels of government and local citizens, was one of the hallmarks of the administration of President Carlos Salinas de Gortari (1988–94). Community participation extended to migrants in the United States, who were encouraged to contribute through the International Solidarity version of the matching fund program.[25] Decentralization has encouraged transborder HTAs and discouraged domestic HTAs. Having lost their secular function, domestic HTAs have retreated to the strictly religious sphere, at the same time that transborder HTAs are expanding from the religious to the secular sphere. But the question remains: Why did domestic HTAs not re-form to participate in Solidarity and similar secular programs when the opportunity arose?

The final piece of the puzzle explaining why domestic HTAs rose and fell even as transborder HTAs continue is nationalization, in the sense of the homogenization of culture and communication within the country's borders.[26] International migrants create HTAs as a means of coping with a sense of difference and alienation in the receiving country.[27] Given the limited nationalization of the Mexican populace during the domestic rural-urban migrations of the 1920s to 1960s, the impetus for domestic migrants to become involved in their sending communities was strikingly similar to the conditions driving contemporary international emigrants to maintain connections to distant hometowns. Over the past eighty years, as source communities such as Arandas have become more nationally integrated through public education and transportation and communication networks, a sense of displacement has dissipated among domestic migrants. Homogenization and integration have weakened localistic ties within Mexico. Indeed, the domestic HTA has dug its own grave by contributing to the decline of local isolation that was the association's raison d'être. The HTA organizers of the 1940s and 1950s, along with individual absentees, improved the transportation, communication, and educational infrastructure of Arandas in a way that eroded the distinctions between the provincial town and the metropolis. "The highway brought in outsiders," explained a seventy-year-old businessman who had organized the Mexico City HTA during the 1960s. Decades of massive, sustained contact between Arandas and other parts of Mexico diminished local distinctiveness. A sixty-two-year-old organizer of the religious club of Arandenses in Guadalajara explained that newcomers to Guadalajara don't join the HTA because Guadalajara no longer seems as radically different from Arandas: "Arandas changed its life—why? Because of the means of communication, the means of transport, because when you're in Guadalajara, you can be in Arandas in an hour and forty-five minutes. . . . There are no longer those red-tiled houses with a little room with wooden doors and a giant key. Now everything you live there, you live here. So I don't think there's much difference."

An Arandense who first arrived in Mexico City in 1951 contrasted the prestige and sense of adventure associated with going to Mexico City then and in 2004: "When people saw someone who had been to Mexico City come back, they said, 'Ooh, look, he's been to Mexico City!' It was a source of admiration back then. Now, going to Mexico City is like going to the corner. Same for going to the U.S., too. In four or five hours, you're there."

One local newspaper has called the modernization of Arandas its *guadalajarización*. The participants in domestic HTAs are mostly older people who remember what a shock it was to move from Arandas to a metropolis. For their children in Arandas who patronize the six Internet cafés and speed to Guadalajara on a divided four-lane highway, the isolated highlands town is gone forever. On the other hand, the nation-making activities of the U.S. and Mexican states will continue to enforce the social cleavages that produce transborder HTAs. Those HTAs, at least among the first generation, are likely to continue to operate while their domestic counterparts decline. The specific *hometown* basis of these Mexican organizations in the United States will likely continue even in the face of growing integration within Mexico, given that hometown networks structure flows of migrants between specific Mexican and U.S. localities by channeling information about how to cross the border and where to find housing and jobs.[28]

WHAT'S UNIQUE ABOUT THE TRANSBORDER HTA?

A remarkable similarity in the domestic and transborder HTAs over the past sixty years calls into question the claim in the transnationalism literature that migrants' transborder ties require a radical new conception of community and membership. At a minimum, the historical timing of the claim is questionable. The domestic HTAs that preceded their transborder counterparts first changed local conceptions of community. Both kinds of associations were driven by similar subjective and structural differences between source and destination, concentrated settlement patterns, political centralization creating spaces for migrants as intermediaries between levels of government, and external stimuli from Church and state. Scholars of transnationalism emphasize that *community* can no longer be defined as a geographic entity alone, because absent migrants create a "deterritorialized community."[29] The HTA crystallizes the territorial unbundling of community membership. However, the discourse explaining the extension of Arandas and its territory to include its hijos ausentes is the same for Arandenses in Mexico City as it is for Arandenses in Chicago. "Although you live far away, you are always close," said the parish priest in 2004 as he welcomed returnees from the United States. Or as the colonia newspaper in Mexico City expressed their long-distance membership to readers in 1950, "In reality we are not outside Arandas; the presence of all of you establishes an extension of the red earth [of Arandas] and our beloved town."[30]

Migrant-sponsored modernization projects in their hometown and fund-raising visits by political and religious leaders to satellites have been basic features of both domestic and transborder HTAs. Local leaders will obtain resources wherever they can get them, whether that requires traveling to Los Angeles or to Mexico City. In both cases, government business may be intertwined with politicking and the desire to take one's holiday at public expense. In Arandas, the domestic HTAs of the 1940s and 1950s were far more important in the development of Arandas than the transborder HTAs have been. An impoverished community depended on paisanos in Mexico City and Guadalajara to secure a highway, telephone service, a dam, paved streets, and other basic infrastructure. The economic development of Arandas would have been impossible without that infrastructure in place to produce goods and ship them to regional, national, and, in the case of tequila, global markets.

The tendency in Arandas for solicitors of funds to approach individual patrons in the United States, such as Joaquín, is a return to the fund-raising style of the county presidents seeking individual Arandenses living in large Mexican cities in the 1950s, when negotiations were direct and problems of collective action avoided. An unstated advantage of private donations, from the perspective of hometown politicians, is that they are not as easily leveraged into political capital for a group of absentees such as the 1940s Colonia Arandense federation. Of course, not all Mexican communities have produced migrants with the wherewithal to make large individual donations. The relative wealth of Arandas derived from the tequila industry and its status as a small city are likely to make Arandense officials more likely to approach their trips to the United States as excursions than are officials from impoverished rural communities desperate for funds. Transborder HTAs are also more influential in communities with strong traditions of collective village labor and mandatory participation in local governance.[31] The importance of HTAs to a source community is inversely related to its degree of economic development.

Both domestic and transborder HTAs have made hometown donations directly, but more important for the HTAs has been their role as intermediaries with state and federal officials. Joaquín's lobbying with the
governor of Jalisco on his visits to California represents an interesting
twist on the notion of HTAs as political intermediaries between the Mexican center and its periphery because the lobbying takes place abroad.
Transborder HTAs have been able to gain political leverage in Mexico not
only through their collective remittances, but also because they are seen
as one of the few legitimate voices to represent the 10 million Mexicans in
the United States in their relations with the Mexican government. The renewal of competitive party politics in Mexico in the 1980s and the expan-
sion of the Mexican political field to include Mexicans in the United States
have driven state and federal interest in establishing ties to the HTAs.
One form of migrant lobbying that distinguishes transborder from domestic HTAs occurs when Mexicans living in the United States act as intermediaries to establish sister city programs between the governments of
their Mexican places of origin and U.S. destinations. Like county governments throughout Mexico, Arandas has attempted such a strategy, but it
has not been successful. A similar call for cross-border lobbying came
during the 2004 hijos ausentes luncheon, when a Mexican diplomat called
on Arandenses in the United States to contact their U.S. congressional
representatives to promote President Bush's proposal for regularizing
long-time undocumented Mexicans in the United States. Mexican HTAs
have been slow to become involved in U.S. politics, but they represent a
potential institutional sphere for mediating between the governments of
Mexico and the United States through ethnic lobbying. Although there is
good reason to be skeptical of the chances of an effective lobby forming,
the point of theoretical significance is that international migrants' place in
two different political systems provides them with a space to act as intermediaries through a transborder HTA, similar to how domestic migrants'
place in a single federal system provides a space for the intermediation of
a domestic HTA.

Certainly, domestic and transborder associations are not the same. The
international border separating HTAs in the United States from Mexican
hometowns complicates the flow of material goods. Although Mexicans

in the United States can act as intermediaries between their hometown governments and Mexican state and federal officials visiting the United States, and between hometown governments and sister city governments in the United States, they are nevertheless in two separate political systems. Migrants who rise to positions of political prominence in the United States can help fellow Mexicans obtain government resources *in the United States*, but they do not channel massive development back home as the Arandenses in Mexico City did in the 1940s.

In the case of Arandas, the domestic HTAs have been far more important in creating hometown development and political change than the transborder HTAs that began forming in the 1970s and widened their portfolio of activities in the 1990s. Even the most stellar examples of transborder HTAs in the contemporary Mexican migration literature, such as the migrants from Ticuani, Puebla, living in New York who developed and then controlled the potable water supply in Ticuani,[32] do not approach the level of hometown influence of the Colonia Arandense federation in the 1940s. In this regard, the experience of domestic HTAs from Arandas is similar to that of Oaxacan HTAs in Mexico City that dominated their towns of origin economically and politically in the 1960s.[33] The experience of Arandas is not idiosyncratic either in Mexico or internationally. Many studies have found similar degrees of HTA influence in developing countries, which in some cases continues to this day.[34]

The history of the domestic HTAs helps explain the source of organizational forms that institutionalize ties between the Mexican government and its emigrants. Internal migrant associations initially sponsored by the Church have been models for government at all levels trying to tap migrants' resources and political support. Whether migrants are in Los Angeles or Mexico City, from the perspective of county governments, they are outside the local cage. Local governments are therefore developing new ways to open their arms to migrants, but migrants safely ensconced in another jurisdiction can decide whether to accept the embrace, which public projects to support, and how many coins they are willing to give from their purses.

FIVE

The Stranger or the Prodigal Son?

Just as they've sent us dollars, they've also sent us their
customs and addictions.

Thirty-one-year-old housing developer in Arandas

When migrants return from the North laden with gifts for the annual patron saint fiesta, the municipal government receives them under a banner
reading "Welcome, Hijos Ausentes." Families reunite and dollars crackle
through the local economy. Yet many residents, and even many migrants,
resent the cultural changes that migrants bring back with them. A 1991 cartoon in a weekly newspaper expressed a common ambivalence toward
norteños, the migrants with extensive experience in the United States. "January is here, it's fiesta . . . and our norteños," reads the headline over a
bird's-eye view of Arandas and a skull and crossbones on a road sign warning "ARANDAS: 15,000 NORTEÑOS." The caption reads, "And the worst part:
in the U.S. they don't go out because they're afraid, and here, even their
moms can't stand them. The solution? A new city for them, special schools,
fines in dollars, concentration camps . . . ?"

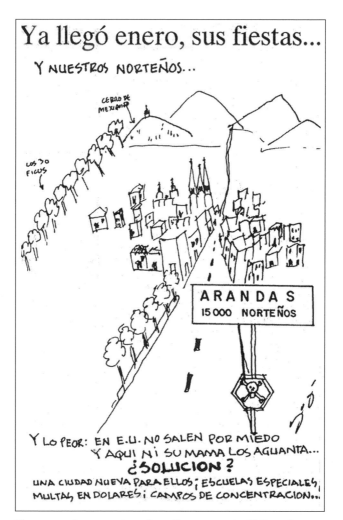

Figure 12. A 1991 cartoon from the newspaper *Notiarandas,*
poking fun at migrants returning for the January fiesta.

The supposed transgressions of migrants are amplified because they
take place during the fiesta celebrating the Virgin of Guadalupe, patron
of Arandas and Mexico. The fiesta is also the town's main civic event,
when the government self-consciously promotes local traditions of
tequila, mariachis, and *charro* horsemen. Jaliscienses pride themselves

on being the most Mexican of the Mexicans, and within Jalisco, Alteños pride themselves on being the most Jalisciense and Mexican of them all.[1] Patron saint fiestas are a celebration of the sacred as well as a celebration of the collective self.[2] At a fiesta for the hijos ausentes in a nearby town in Los Altos, a parade float juxtaposes the illegal drugs and homelessness of Chicago with the "idyllic, tranquil, family- and religion-centred life of the home town."[3] Foreign "impurities" introduced by migrants are on public display during the fiesta and generate open controversy.

Asking how actors in the sending community try to maintain the cultural authenticity of migrants and the hometown flips the conventional question about the assimilation of immigrants that dominates studies of international migration. The mirror image of *assimilation,* the process of groups or individuals becoming similar, is *dissimilation,* the process of becoming different.[4] Rather than ask how U.S. institutions attempt to integrate the immigrant population, I ask how Mexican institutions try to prevent the *dis*integration of the community of origin when emigrants leave and return. Those efforts involve a delicate balance between trying to take advantage of the economic and cultural advantages of emigration while trying to prevent the seepage of undesirable foreign ideas and practices into the home community. Long periods of socialization in another state's cage create many problems—and fewer opportunities—for the state, the Church, and other actors in the community of origin. A tension develops between attempts to extend the community by including extraterritorial members, as scholars of transnationalism have emphasized, and attempts to protect the community by monitoring returnees and moderating the effects of migration, a project consistent with the classical view of state-led nationalizing.[5] This tension is obscured by the notion of a "transnational community," which misleadingly suggests a holistic cultural unit. The terms of emigrants' place in the community are up for debate. The objects of contention are not simply abstract identities, though defining a moral sense of self and community are important features of the cultural landscape. The politics of dissimilation extend to fundamental features of state building such as policing and education and to decisions about who does what jobs.

THE CULTURAL PRICE OF AN ECONOMIC REWARD

In the view of Alteños, the economic rewards of migration come at a steep cultural price.[6] Attitudes about economic impacts in Arandas and Agua Negra were generally positive among household heads in the 2003 survey I conducted (see the appendix). Among the migrants, 88 percent thought emigration had a positive economic impact on the community, and 77 percent of nonmigrants thought the same. More surprising is that migrants and nonmigrants in the sample were equally likely to report that migration has had a negative impact on the community's customs and morals; 77 percent of both nonmigrants and migrants held that view. Most Arandenses share an image of who is a good member of the community and who is a transgressor. Just as nonmigrants fear the corrupting influence of American culture on their hometown, migrants fear its corrupting influence on their own children, whether they are in the United States or Mexico.[7] Church and state have developed practices such as the hijos ausentes fiesta to celebrate the "good" migrant, while distancing themselves from migrants who violate cultural norms.

Negative views of the cultural impacts of migration in Los Altos are consistent with national surveys; in 2006, twice as many Mexicans said the cultural influence of the United States has been unfavorable for Mexico (44 percent) as said it has been favorable (21 percent).[8] On the other hand, the level of nationalism directed against the United States is mitigated when Mexicans look northward for a model of modernity. The suspicions of Mexican elites are "often allied to a sneaking admiration" that has become more pronounced with the advent of the 1994 North American Free Trade Agreement and a generation of technocrats schooled in top U.S. universities.[9] Widespread ambivalence toward the effects of migration to the United States reflects a broader ambivalence toward the northern neighbor in general.

With the possible exception of the clergy and a handful of literati, most Arandenses say that the economic benefits of migration to the community outweigh the cultural costs. A former migrant who spent twenty-two years working in blue-collar jobs in factories in Los Angeles before returning to Arandas to become president of the municipal PAN committee and chief of police expressed a common view: "The cultural problem of different customs that are taken from the United States through migration and brought here—customs which maybe don't go with the culture of Arandas, and so people say, 'These noisy characters come here and bring their loud music and walk around all tattooed and this and that'—I think that doesn't have the importance that foreign exchange income has for the country, its economic development, the transformation of the towns to a much better level of living, and better dwellings for its residents."

Alteño families often depend on remittances for economic survival, or at least have grown accustomed to the material comforts that remittances offer. Seventy-eight percent of households in Agua Negra and 44 percent in Arandas include at least one migrant. The norteño is not an exotic character, but one's husband, son, nephew, or cousin. Most people know that migrants suffer on their journey despite all their bravado and stories of adventure. An Alteño adage expresses residents' two minds toward migrants who bring home dollars and arrogant attitudes, yet who must often borrow money to return to the North after the fiesta: "When they come, they strike fear, and when they leave, they strike pity."

MONITORING NORTEÑOS

For Arandenses to describe and explain how migrants are changed by their experiences in the United States, migrants first must be identified and monitored. In Arandas, the clearest form of social labeling of emigrants is applied to the subset who have settled abroad for long periods, the norteños. The sociologist Harvey Sacks describes the process of assigning certain people to membership categories as the beginning of social control. Membership categories are "inference-rich," meaning that categorizing someone as a norteño enables categorizers to assume a great deal of information about that individual based on what norteños as a category are expected to be and do. Even if those inferences are inaccurate, they resist refutation once the "membership categorization device" is socially rooted. The psychologist David Rumelhart uses the similar concept of "schemas" to suggest that membership categorization devices are like folk theories in the sense that people use them to explain why members of a category behave in certain ways.[10]

How do residents of Arandas, a town of forty thousand, decide who is a norteño? When asked in interviews, Arandenses usually listed the same set of cues: Young, male, urban migrants wear baggy or short pants, tattoos, earrings, and gold necklaces. Their head is shaved or they wear their hair long. Both men and woman dye their hair, the only cue Arandenses mentioned for (young) migrant women. Most Arandenses called this a *cholo* style. Labeling migrants is an inexact science: Imitators who have never left Los Altos have access to migrant styles through locally produced copies or the gifts of returnees, and migrants who avoid the cholo aesthetic do not display obvious cues. It is harder to tell a returned migrant from a nonmigrant when both sport the popular ranchero look of boots, jeans, sombrero, and buttoned shirt, though the apparent expense of these fashions and accompanying gold chains are more subtle indicators of migrant status. The behavior of migrants dressed in a ranchero or generic urban style is not as readily categorized as norteño. Consequently, the behavior of the cholos receives greater scrutiny and disproportionately influences the public sense of how migrants behave. All of my local informants expressed negative views of cholos.

The personal presentation of earlier generations of migrants was the object of similar negative reactions from a government preoccupied with sculpting the modern Mexican man while maintaining social solidarity. The Secretariat of Labor's 1946 surveys of returning braceros found that more than a third of the returnees had changed their "normal" way of dress to clothes that were "expensive, flashy, exaggerated" and "uncomfortable and inappropriate for the milieu of their origin." The study's authors argued that "this mutation in their clothing can be explained as the satisfaction of desires unsatisfied and repressed for a long time, and the desire to appear original and to distinguish themselves in their home environment and signal themselves as recent visitors from the United States."[11]

Vehicles also telegraph signals that identify migrants. Symbols of Americana such as decal flags, U.S. license plates, English-language music pulsating from sound systems, chrome detailing, and dramatic driving styles all display migrant status. Newspapers identify and monitor such norteño behavior at the most mundane level. For example, a regional daily reported the death of a returned migrant in Los Altos in the following news brief, which is typical of media reports that mention migrant status:

> Teocaltiche, Jal. A young man from Teocaltiche who was driving like he was possessed ended up dead when his vehicle overturned in a ditch while he was celebrating Mother's Day. The man was Martín Cuevas, 30 years of age, who was driving a gray Blazer pickup 4x4 with California plates 82 2MZH037 in a state of intoxication. After spending the day drinking and "spinning" the truck, it finally turned over in an area known as El Barrio, leaving him trapped in the pickup. He was still alive when police rescued him but died while being transported to the hospital. This young man had recently arrived from the neighboring country of the North, but he lost his life to alcohol. His body was taken to the morgue for the autopsy mandated by law.[12]

An almost infinite number of categories can be applied to an individual, but only some categories are considered relevant in a given context.[13] Categorizations are especially condensed by the limited space of a newspaper brief. Here, the reporter did not include other potential categories based on occupation, ethnicity, or height because they were not considered relevant to explaining the narrative. The inclusion of the categories of young, male, and returned migrant implies a theory about why Martín Cuevas died that any reader in Los Altos would recognize and probably share: Young male returnees drink and drive recklessly in Los Altos because they can't do so in Los Angeles.[14]

The disorder created by returned migrants can become a policing issue. Just across the Guanajuato state line in Manuel Doblado a government billboard reads, "Welcome to your land, paisano. We invite you to respect the rules of your town." In neighboring parts of Michoacán in 1907 police opened a checkpoint at the local train station to register returnees by collecting information on their Mexican place of residence, the weapons they carried, and details of their migration to the United States.[15] Today even the police use informal membership categorization to monitor migrants, rather than checking official identification papers.

In Arandas, police trouble with returnees does not generally include serious, sustained violence. A former municipal president who served in the 1950s said that rambunctious returnees are "a bother, but there are other, more important crimes for the government to worry about." Another former municipal president from the 1990s said he ordered police to confiscate the car stereos of those who played their music too loud. The incoming police chief, a former migrant himself, launched a publicity campaign promising to crack down on people who drive aggressively and play loud music. He aimed the measures at the entire population but considered norteños the primary offenders.[16] The hundreds of shots fired in the air by residents of Arandas celebrating the New Year indicate that guns are widely available, but Arandenses usually settle fights with fists or a knife. The police chief said there are no organized gangs in Arandas that originally formed in the United States; some returnees have formed new gangs upon their return, however. Many walls are tagged with U.S.-style gothic graffiti, though the messages suggest local groups proclaiming neighborhood pride, with slogans like "¡Rifa San Pedro!" (Up with San Pedro!) rather than the violent behavior associated with transplanted gangs from Los Angeles or Chicago. Police consider gangs more of a problem in San Ignacio, where teachers say that returnee gang members from Detroit sometimes bully other school kids.

CONTROLLING THE BODY

Control over members' bodies is one of the goals shared by Church and state in their exercise of pastoral power. Migrants are blamed for the introduction of illegal drugs and increased consumption of alcohol. In 1946, the Secretariat of Labor found that braceros drank more alcohol upon their return than before they had left.[17] According to a 1997 study by the government of Jalisco, in rural communities with high levels of emigration migrants were eleven times more likely than nonmigrants to have used at least one of a set of drugs including solvents, marijuana, cocaine, and heroin. And a 2003 report on the condition of migrants commissioned by the government of Jalisco warned of "the presence of mental health problems and addictions originating in the loss or alteration of their original customs and the necessity to adopt new ways of life." Jalisco has a

"Go Healthy, Return Healthy" program in twenty-seven counties of high emigration to discourage drug use and other unhealthy behaviors.[18] In Arandas, the portfolio of one of the council members includes combating drug addiction. "There is a very close relationship between the addiction of the Arandense and traveling to the United States," he said. While the overwhelming weight of the public discourse in Arandas about drugs blames outsiders in general and migrants in particular, there are exceptions. At the outset of an antidrug crusade in the 1980s sponsored by the Church with support from local government, a prominent editorial from an ex-migrant in *El Arandense* urged Arandenses to stop pointing the finger at outsiders and start recognizing their own culpability for the drug problem in Arandas.[19]

Blaming sexually transmitted diseases on outsiders is another way for Arandenses to set themselves apart from the rest of Mexico and the United States as more Catholic and morally pure. There were twenty-two known cases of AIDS in the county of Arandas in 2003. Arandenses blame migrants for bringing back AIDS from the United States, though according to the government of Jalisco, of the nearly seven thousand cases in the state reported from 1983 to 2001, only 6 percent were people who had lived in the United States for more than six months.[20] The county doctor blames venereal diseases such as syphilis on men who have returned from northern fleshpots, rather than the clandestine sex industry in certain roadside bars outside Arandas.[21] Several of the local elites I interviewed, including priests and a prominent PAN politician, claimed that migrants were responsible for the introduction of homosexuality to Arandas. They contrast the supposed freedom (*libertad*) that migrants feel with what is really libertinism (*libertinaje*). Police do not regulate migrants' sexual practices, though to the extent that those practices are associated with disease, they come under the gaze of the state's statisticians and medical apparatus.

The prevailing folk theory of why young male returnees are so disorderly in Mexico is complex. On the one hand, migrants are more constrained by the police in U.S. public spaces, so many compensate by "letting loose" in the public spaces of Mexico, behaving like U.S. college students on spring break in Cancún. Residents often say that migrants behave worse in Mexico than they do in the United States. The director of the secondary school in Agua Negra explained that migrants suffer the humiliations, privations, and discriminations of life in the North. "Everything they repress there, they come here to vent," he said. Male migrants refer to the sense of freedom they feel in Mexico. Much of that sense of freedom is derived from less state surveillance and regulation over their daily movements, recreation, and work. In Mexico, they can drive without seatbelts, drink alcohol in the street, litter, raise chickens in their backyard, and enjoy the tax-free rewards of informal commerce—all without fear of *un tiket* from an agent of the nanny state. Parents can discipline their children as they see fit, unlike in the United States, where they say children misbehave because they are taught in school that if their parents spank them, they can call the police and have their parents thrown into jail.[22] The sense of relief of being in a place with less government control over daily life is particularly dramatic for unauthorized workers, many of whom complain of feeling "locked up" and fearful of *la migra* (the U.S. immigration authorities) while they are in the United States.

On the other hand, many Mexicans believe that the lack of moral discipline in private U.S. religious and family life promotes undisciplined behavior in both countries. They see migrants as cut loose from the conservative Catholicism of Los Altos and adrift in a heterogeneous religious environment where they are preyed upon by the proselytizing of Mormons, Jehovah's Witnesses, and Evangelicals, or simply lured into religious apathy by a more secular U.S. society. The loosening of family bonds generally and the absence of watchful wives in particular are also thought to promote vice and immorality among men. Even if migrants take their families with them to the North, a culture of individualism, the anonymity of the city, and high levels of residential and job mobility weaken the social controls on behavior that operate in the towns and villages of Jalisco. The greater use of illegal drugs and liberalized sexuality resulting from weakened social controls in the United States are then imported back to Mexico.

Most Arandenses think that cultural dissimilation, becoming less like "us" and more like "them," is usually a bad thing. Government employees, priests, and the press monitor migrants to mitigate those cultural impacts and reinforce their pastoral power. The drugs, criminality, and disease that North Americans often blame immigrants for importing to the United States are seen in Mexico as *exports* from the United States to Mexico via emigrant carriers. On both sides of the border, the same practices are viewed as foreign pathologies. For those in the business of maintaining national and local purity within the territorially defined community, migration is a threatening conduit of cultural change.

DENATIONALIZING

One of the legal indicators of dissimilation is the loss of Mexican citizenship when migrants naturalize in the United States. Residents of Arandas and Agua Negra draw a distinction between migrants in general and migrants who become U.S. citizens. Many Alteños object to the transformation of Mexicans into U.S. citizens and the idea of dual nationality. The extent of this contention belies the notion that migrants and those who stay behind form part of one "transnational community."[23] The old-fashioned nationality in a single nation-state apparently matters to many residents of source communities, who are not all enthusiastic about the possibilities of a "trans-" or "postnational" society.

More than 80 percent of my respondents in Arandas and Agua Negra had a neutral or positive impression of people from their locality who migrate to the United States; 64 percent of migrants and 35 percent of nonmigrants expressed a positive view, and 9 percent of migrants and 20 percent of nonmigrants expressed a negative view.[24] Respondents' views of migrants who become naturalized U.S. citizens were much more negative than their views of migrants to the United States generally: More than 33 percent of the sample expressed a negative view toward naturalized migrants, twice as many as expressed a negative view toward migrants in general. Nonmigrants were twice as likely as migrants to express a negative view of naturalized migrants.

The more negative views regarding migrants who nationalize in the United States are accompanied by negative attitudes toward dual nationality. Since 1998, Mexican law has allowed Mexicans by birth to hold both Mexican and foreign nationalities. Ninety-two percent of migrants and only 68 percent of nonmigrants support the right to dual nationality. A logistic regression found that nonmigrants, people without a migrant in their household, women, and Agua Negrans were significantly more likely than migrants, people with a migrant in their household, men, and people living in the city of Arandas to oppose the right to dual nationality.[25] Dual loyalties appear more threatening to people with less direct experience with migration or the greater social diversity found in towns.

Interviews with Alteños show that they are more ambivalent about migrants who become U.S. citizens because adopting another citizenship is a sign of national dissimilation. Fears of migrants becoming American at Mexico's expense have been common at least since Paul Taylor's 1931 visit.[26] In 2003, a fifty-year-old former municipal official said that when he was young, Arandenses scorned their paisanos who had become U.S. citizens, leading naturalized migrants to hide their new status while they were in Mexico: "They came back to their community and didn't tell anyone that they were now U.S. citizens. They didn't say anything because there were criticisms and misunderstandings, and people even said things that were false, no? That you had to trample the Mexican flag [to naturalize in the United States]. . . . It was a tremendous achievement to have a U.S. residency permit, but a U.S. citizen hid his citizenship. . . . I remember people here saying, 'This guy came back from the United States and he renounced his motherland.' "

The myth of being forced to trample or spit on the Mexican flag as part of the U.S. naturalization ceremony remains ubiquitous in Mexican migrant source communities and among many immigrant Latinos in the United States. Negative attitudes toward migrants who become U.S. citizens have probably contributed to historically low naturalization rates for Mexicans in the United States, but such attitudes may be waning. The percentage of Mexican immigrants in the United States who have naturalized climbed from 15 in 1994–95 to 25 in 2000–2001.[27] Growing public acceptance of naturalized emigrants in Mexico would likely contribute to a further rise in U.S. naturalization, especially as Mexico has legally recognized dual nationality since 1998.

MALINCHISMO

Arandense intellectuals complain in public about the cultural side of denationalizing. According to editorials in the local newspapers, U.S.-style Christmas and Halloween celebrations are two of the biggest expressions of migrants' cultural degeneracy.[28] For example, in a front-page Christmas Day editorial in 1993 headlined "Santa Claus Should Disappear," *El Arandense* decried the displacement of nativity scenes by Christmas trees and the invasion of secular, materialistic values from the United States that pollute the local religious tradition. A municipal president in the 1990s ordered the publication of material condemning Halloween as a foreign import and promoting the celebration of the authentically Mexican Day of the Dead. A 1990 editorial in *Notiarandas* took up the same crusade against Halloween, which it saw as part of the cultural "invasion" of migrants "who come to Mexico to do what they can't do in the United States, and in so doing trample on our beautiful traditions." Migrants are proximate, accessible targets for Mexican cultural nationalists who feel plagued by broader diffusions of American culture through media and commerce. The same article complained, "What sort of culture, based on vandalism and vagrancy, will our Mexican-Americanized paisanos feel they are complying with in their mission as half-Mexicans? I say half-Mexicans, because you will understand that they don't know either the North American culture or the culture of our towns. As Doña Marina would say, '[They're] neither from here nor there.' "[29]

Doña Marina is the name that the Spanish conquistadors gave to La Malinche, an indigenous woman who betrayed her people to become the mistress of leader Hernán Cortés. *Malinchismo,* a syndrome of preferring the foreign to the authentically native, has its modern incarnation in *pochismo,* the phenomenon of people of Mexican descent born in the United States acting like gringos. Malinchismo and pochismo loom large in Mexican nationalism and are rhetorically powerful slurs used by Arandense elites during interviews.[30] Even college-educated nonmigrants tend to see norteños' U.S.-born children in subtractive cultural terms as having "no culture" because they fall between two discrete cultural systems. The Mexican essayist Octavio Paz made this subtractive argument most forcefully in his influential, damning account of the *pachuco*, a sort of proto-cholo living in Los Angeles during the 1940s. For Paz, the pachuco is neither Mexican nor North American: "His whole being is sheer negative impulse."[31]

Some migrants see themselves as "taking the best from here and there" in what researchers would call an additive cultural hybridization of two systems. A former migrant who lived in California and Illinois for ten years before returning to publish *El Arandense* subscribes to the additive view of culture, but he said he was socially rejected when he returned. He blamed the negative reception on the "inferiority complex" of Arandenses who stayed behind: "If you said that you were coming from the United States, many people scorned you. . . . A lot of people here, for this same inferiority complex, wanted to tell you that the culture there was not appropriate for the culture here, that it was a lower culture, that it would harm them." His description of a psychological mechanism in which an inferiority complex turns into an assertion of superiority has a sociological counterpart in the concept of "normative inversion," in which despised groups reverse an established social ranking to assert their moral superiority over the dominant group. In this new ordering, *norteamericanos* may have more money and be more organized, but they are sexually loose, individualistic, cold in their interpersonal relationships, irreligious, and materialistic.[32]

Linguistic shifts are another site of cultural contention. During summer vacation and the patron saint fiesta, groups of returnees can be heard speaking English in the streets of Los Altos. The lay head of the migrant ministry in Agua Negra says that when returnees speak English with each other, she and her friends tell them, "Shh, shh, you're in Mexico!" Residents complain that "mental *gabachos*" born in Mexico or the "pocho" children of Mexican origin born in the United States anglicize their Spanish pronunciation and invent hybrid neologisms such as *parquear* (to park) and *marqueta* (market).[33] Learning English is seen as an accomplishment, and nonmigrant elites often send their children to learn English in local private classes, but "losing" Spanish is viewed as a moral failure and a rejection of being Mexican. Arandenses who have visited the United States as tourists often tell stories of interacting with people of

Mexican origin there "who don't want to speak Spanish even though you can tell by looking at them" that they do speak Spanish. The folk theory is that their reticence is "because they are ashamed of their roots." Mexican visitors often fail to understand that many of the second or later generations simply don't speak proficient Spanish, and perhaps never had a facility to lose in the first place. For all the fears in the United States that immigrants and their children are not learning English fast enough, the second generation prefers to speak English, and away from the border region the third generation rarely speaks Spanish with any proficiency.[34]

Concerns about the purity of language are not new. A Mexican born in California and living in Guadalajara in the 1930s told Paul Taylor about the reaction he faced when he arrived in Mexico: "It's good to be able to talk English. They call me *gringo* and say, 'Why don't you go back to your country?' They say I'm *agringado* [gringoized]. I say to them, '*Gracias*.' They don't hate the American. They hate *us*."[35] In this essentialist understanding of the world, being a gringo is not an offense per se, but imitating gringos is an unacceptable transgression of a national cultural boundary. Returned migrants usually say the greatest discrimination they face in the United States is from other Mexicans or people of Mexican origin who have forsaken their national roots to act like gringos. They single out Mexican-origin officers of the U.S. Border Patrol for particular criticism. It is not clear if migrants really are more likely to suffer discrimination at the hands of coethnics than from Anglos, or if migrants simply perceive coethnics as more discriminatory for having violated expectations of solidarity, but Arandenses commonly made the claim in interviews and even in public. For example, during a speech at the 2004 municipal luncheon to celebrate the Day of the Hijos Ausentes a returned migrant contrasted Mexican Americans who disdain Mexicans with the illustrious absentees officially recognized for helping their fellow Arandenses in the United States. "We always remember who we were, many times insulted by each other, by our own co-nationals, who while in foreign lands don't understand us, because our own brothers see us as foreigners. Sadly, this has happened many times, and therefore we want to recognize people who have achieved success abroad and who have given a helping hand to our people."[36]

Other symbolic displays that ostensibly suggest denationalization are considered irrelevant even by elites who otherwise see themselves as the guardians of local and Mexican culture. Returned migrants often sport the American flag on their clothing or vehicle as a way to make claims to a higher status based on their experiences and the money they earned in the North. Nonmigrants wear similar clothing to trade on the youth culture cachet of the United States. Surprisingly, even local elites do not see displaying the American flag as a culturally obnoxious act, like wearing a Halloween mask, at least if those displaying the U.S. flag are working class. A PAN federal deputy explained a commonly held view of returned migrants who display American national symbols: "It's not seen as bad. What happens is, normally people who go to the United States have a low cultural level. The great majority are workers. And one understands that they don't do it because they feel more norteamericano than Mexican. One understands that it's a way for them to say, 'Look, I've been successful.' If someone with a university degree or someone with another cultural level did this, I would see it is a bad thing, like, 'Hey, your motherland is Mexico, not the United States.'"

In interviews, elites frequently referred to the problems putatively caused by Mexicans in the United States as an embarrassment to Mexico. The middle and upper classes emphasize that migrants are drawn disproportionately from the ranks of people "sin cultura" (without culture)—a category that captures both the economic class and cultural status dimensions of "low-class." The distancing of Mexican elites from migrants has been a regular theme since the early twentieth century, when Mexican consular officials called on officials in Mexico to stop the emigration of poor workers because it was giving Mexico a bad image abroad.[37] Resentment of migrants' class mobility is also a factor. The wage differential between Mexico and the United States means that people with little education who migrate to the United States and then return are often richer than professionals who never left Mexico. As one entrepreneur described his youth in Arandas in the 1970s, "I was studying and saw migrants returning. I asked myself, 'How come someone who doesn't even read or write is doing better than me?'" Professionals are frustrated by the economic success of nouveau riche migrants who return to Arandas.[38]

Resentment of class mobility is only a partial explanation for the negative attitudes about the cultural transformations wrought by migration, however. Such negative attitudes are the norm among nonmigrants and migrants across the population. Migrants often fear the cultural shifts in their own Americanizing children. Household heads in Agua Negra were just as likely as household heads in Arandas to say they had a negative view of migration's cultural effects, even though there are no real "elites" in Agua Negra, where social stratification is limited to the division between poor farmers with their own land and even poorer day laborers. The class dimension of talk about emigration's negative effects is subsumed by culturally driven fears of destructive influences.

PATRIOTISM AND THE EMPTY CLASSROOM

Many of the problems attributed to migration, and state responses attempting to manage those problems, become visible in public education. Teachers throughout the historic sending areas complain that widespread migration encourages adolescents to drop out of school and migrate themselves. In an interview with a Catholic weekly newspaper, the director of the technical secondary school in Arandas said the principal problem with the student population was the dropout rate: "Many students go to the United States. A very large number of boys come and enroll, but come December, their friends from the North come back with cash, and off they go [in January]."[39] In the primary school in Agua Negra, the director said the students were too young to talk about their plans to migrate, but the school's population fell 20 percent between 1980 and 2003 as whole families migrated to the United States, León, and Arandas. Consequently, the Secretariat of Public Education stripped the school of one of its seven teachers. Migration also contributes to school absenteeism for the estimated 7 percent of students who join the corn harvest in November and December because their fathers left crops in their care. All ten of the educators interviewed agreed that migration was implicated in disciplinary problems at school. Sara, a former migrant with three children whose husband is still working in California, teaches primary school in Agua

Negra: "It's more difficult to control adolescents when only the mother is there, and there are a lot of problem kids in the school. I think many of the problems have to do with this, but well, you can't do anything against necessity, right? . . . [The migration of the father] is a necessary evil."

Educators have long been concerned about emigration's "demexicanizing" effects as well, particularly during the period of intensive state-led nationalizing in the 1930s.[40] The attempt to sculpt a modern Mexican citizenry coincided with mass repatriations from the United States and land reform that distributed large private holdings to a corporatist tenure arrangement called the *ejido*. In a 1934 government school primer, a fictional rural schoolmaster adjudicates between a member of an ejido and an engineer discussing whether returnees from the United States should be given rights to farm ejido lands. One argues that migrants had little choice but to leave, given the wretched economic conditions prior to the agrarian reform, and that migrants should be welcomed back. The other worries that the returnees are lazy, ridden with vices, and gringoized. After "rejecting their motherland," they don't deserve rights in the ejido, "which is the most Mexican thing we have," he says. After hearing their arguments, the schoolmaster tells them, "We are all Mexicans, and if among us there are some *hijos pródigos* [prodigal sons], we should receive them and offer them [the benefits of] what Mexico is doing for her sons." Still, the prodigal sons are on probation. In the schoolmaster's words: "Only if they keep thinking that the Yanqui is better and that the dollar is worth more than all of us, then . . . it will be necessary to remove them from the ejido, because the ejido is a place only for Mexicans who are Mexicans with their entire soul." In the primer's conclusion, the repatriates split into two groups: those who rediscovered their love for Mexico and settled in the ejido and those "renegades" who were forced to leave because they did not love Mexico.[41] The state's message for schoolchildren was clear: Migration is a national threat, but returnees should first be given a chance to become good Mexicans again.

The perpetuation of migrants' cultural nationality through state education in Mexico and the United States is an explicit policy of the government of Mexico and the state of Jalisco. In their 2000 Declaration of Puebla, the directors of state offices of attention to migrants abroad said their sports and cultural programs were designed to keep paisanos "away from the vices and practices alien to our values, principles, and customs." Mexican consulates have distributed thousands of Spanish-language textbooks to schools in the United States, raising the hackles of U.S. nationalists for referring to the stars and stripes as "the enemy flag" and portraying the 1846–48 Mexican-American War as a disaster.[42] According to a 2003 report, the state of Jalisco seeks to "preserve and strengthen our traditions, values, and national identity" for the benefit of 4.5 million Jaliscienses abroad.[43] Thirteen Jalisciense teachers that year participated in an exchange program to teach in public schools in areas of Jalisciense concentration in California, Michigan, and Illinois.

On the local level, the director of the primary school in Agua Negra explained that the civic education classes are designed to inculcate patriotism. On September 16, when Mexico's independence from Spain is celebrated, schoolchildren parade through Agua Negra. "We want them to learn to be well cemented in their values here so that they don't adopt the customs of the North. In the United States, morals are more liberal than they are here," he said. When asked what values are important to inculcate in Agua Negra, he mentioned honor, solidarity, antimaterialism, family unity, and patriotic values "so they don't disown their motherland when they're in the United States." Similarly, the director of the *telesecundaria*, a secondary school that instructs rural students via television, complained of the loss of patriotic values among the current generation, but he singled out U.S. mass media more than migration:

> There's a culture that's not ours. It's from the United States, because we're neighbors, and well, everything is almost a *transculturalización* that's happening little by little. But we do try to maintain the culture, no longer the purest part, but the most that we can of the values from here—like the music and food. . . . In our parades on the 16th of September [celebrating independence] and the 20th of November [celebrating the revolution], we try to play revolutionary music that is from here. And it seems the students don't like it. They say, "No, we should play English [U.S.] music."

Perhaps more than any other group of residents, and certainly among government employees, educators believe that migration is prejudicial to the culture of source communities. Migration lowers school attendance, missing parents contribute to student absenteeism and disciplinary problems, and migrants are conduits for the U.S. music and language that allegedly threaten the status of formal Spanish and regional and Mexican music. Further, migration is thought to contribute to a decline in the Mexican patriotism that teachers promote. The extent to which migration, media, and commerce independently diffuse North American cultural practices is just as difficult to determine now as it was when Taylor wondered how to weigh the effect of migration against U.S. radio broadcasts that reached Arandas in 1931. But in the minds of educators, migration is a major channel for the introduction of undesirable American culture.

"MENTALITIES" OF WORK

Return migration presents challenges and opportunities for local economic development. Optimists, including many government officials, have long hoped that returnees will be agents of economic modernization who will bring back new technologies and entrepreneurial ideas with their capital. There is also hope that workers will undergo a cultural transformation in the United States that will make them more disciplined. Pessimists maintain that migrants do indeed undergo a cultural transformation, but with the opposite effect: Once returnees think about work from a U.S. frame of reference, they become lazy and no longer want to work in Mexico. Local employers have developed folk theories to make sense of how migration affects the culture of work, and they use these theories in their hiring decisions.

Agents of Modernization?

Many scholars and policy makers have hoped that return migrants will modernize their home communities based on their exposure to the United States. Such modernist projects are explicit in the works of early twentieth-century researchers who studied whether returnees were more likely than nonmigrants to wear shoes and eat with utensils rather than tortillas.[44] The Mexican anthropologist Manuel Gamio and other policy makers believed that migration would transform the supposedly backward character of the Mexican peasant. A 1946 study by the federal Secretariat of Labor found that returning braceros changed their clothes and bathed more frequently than they had before migrating, proving that peasants were dirty only because they were poor and that they would become cleaner if given better economic opportunities. A psychiatric study of eighty-nine braceros who returned with mental illnesses rejected the prevailing idea that their problems were caused by a "psychosis of expatriation" and a "clash of cultures" in the United States, noting that such experiences could only exacerbate an existing condition.[45] Counting the number of baths and mental breakdowns was part of the state's exercise of pastoral power to improve the discipline and morals of poor Mexicans while preserving their mexicanidad.

What do returnees themselves think about whether their U.S. experiences have improved their work back home? In my 2003 survey, only 35 percent of working Agua Negran returnees said that they had learned something useful and applicable to their work in Jalisco, compared to 60 percent of Arandense returnees. The difference between the two communities lies in the limited agricultural economy of Agua Negra, where it is much more difficult to put into practice the skills learned in the U.S. economy. The experience of Agua Negra in 2003 is reminiscent of the pattern Taylor found in the exclusively agricultural economy of Arandas in the early 1930s, in which a few returnees made productive use of trucks and sewing machines acquired in the United States, but most found the skills they had learned in U.S. industry and on the railroads to be irrelevant in Jalisco.

Timoteo, a migrant who returned to the county seat from working on a southern California melon farm to become a wealthy rancher, credited migrants with modernizing agriculture based on their exposure to the United States. He said that as late as the 1970s, pack animals were widely used in Mexico, but migrants in the United States learned the use of machines and even brought back secondhand tractors. The use of fertilizer and chemicals was also adopted from the United States. "People learned a culture that was more advanced than ours," he said. On the other hand, a former veteran of five bracero contracts and five more years in Illinois said that the knowledge he gained in the United States repairing farm machinery was of little use in Agua Negra, where agriculture was not mechanized. Several former braceros said their work in U.S. fields and orchards was the same kind of manual labor they did in Mexico. If the work in the United States is too different from the types of jobs and technology available in Mexico, the new skills are irrelevant to the needs of the local economy; if the work is too similar, such as harvesting crops manually, no new skills are learned. The ideal match for the transfer of technology and skills occurs when jobs in the United States require only moderately more advanced skills and technology than jobs in the same sector in the specific Mexican source community.

The Disciplined Worker

Migrants may be a modernizing force as entrepreneurs and innovators, but from the perspective of local residents, have they become better workers? Seventy-five percent of household heads in my 2003 survey said that migrants returning to their hometowns from the United States did not work as hard as they did before they left; only 14 percent said returnees worked harder. There was not a statistically significant difference between migrant and nonmigrant views. Clearly, returnees do have higher expectations of pay and work conditions than those who stay behind. Arandense migrants have what the labor economist Michael Piore calls a "dual frame of reference," in which they assess their options in one labor market based on their experience in another. Even if most Arandenses are on the bottom of the U.S. labor market, the dollars to be earned there make the work preferable to similar unskilled work in Arandas.

Employers view most repatriates' reticence to work, and their refusal of agricultural work in particular, as a moral failure rather than a rational analysis of the returns to be gained by choosing one national labor market over the other.[46] Taylor found that employers preferred workers who had never been to the United States. One employer complained that repatriates were "lazy" because they were accustomed to daily wages of 2 to 4 dollars and did not want to work for 1 to 2 pesos. Another told Taylor:

"Farm labor has been very docile and none made trouble [or] could change others. Now [they] come back with Bolshevik ideas, [are] not so respectful, [make] demand[s] . . . and are troublemakers."[47]

Although contemporary employers often mentioned the problem of "lazy" returnees who had unreasonably high expectations of wages, they also tended to prefer the *disciplina* of older returned workers, which made them better employees than their nonmigrant counterparts, particularly in factory settings. Almost all of the employers and working returnees I interviewed mentioned that the U.S work experience teaches greater discipline. The discipline of the labor process is most effective when it does not require constant surveillance because migrants internalize their U.S. habits.[48] A former PRI municipal president who owns several agribusinesses praised the quality of his returnee employees: "They're people who come back accustomed to a schedule in which one has to earn his salary; one has to sweat. You don't have to spend half your time watching them or pressuring them. That is to say, they come back with a mentality that they [will work] eight hours, but they will be eight hours of real work—not simply time passed, but time *worked*."

As early as 1908, studies found that some Mexican employers believe returnees will work harder in Mexico to afford their new lifestyle.[49] In Arandas, the owner of a tequila distillery with 460 employees said returnees at his factory "have acquired culture" in the United States, by which he said he meant that they are "more responsible" and have "a better understanding of how to work in a company" by being punctual and running machinery. Their U.S. frame of reference extends beyond higher wages to expectations of owning houses and cars, and they have to be more disciplined at work to keep a steady job to save the money to acquire those goods. "They want to live more comfortably and so they act more responsibly," he said.

Most employers of campesinos did not see much difference in migrants' work ethic, though one former bracero in Agua Negra said that when his day laborers don't come to work, he tells them, "Go to the United States, you bastards, so you'll know what it's like. There, if you're ten minutes late, you come on time the next day, and if not, you're fired!" In general, employers believe the discipline of the U.S. labor market is most useful for improving the quality of factory employees, an effect that matters in the mixed economy of Arandas but is irrelevant in the agricultural economy of Agua Negra.

"Arandas Is Their North"

For Arandense employers, U.S. migration may prepare some Arandenses to become more disciplined workers. In the short run, however, the availability of an alternative labor market in the United States creates problems for local employers in some sectors of the economy. Locals are decreasingly willing to work in the agave fields doing the hard, boring work of weeding and tending the spiny plants, despite a US$20 daily wage that is twice as high as other agricultural work in the region. Arandenses are acutely aware that they could do similar unskilled work in the United

Figure 13.   An Arandense foreman hires internal migrants from Chiapas at a day laborer hiring corner in Arandas, 2004. Photo by David Fitzgerald.

Figure 14.   A Chiapan internal migrant weeds the agave
fields near Arandas, 2004. Photo by David Fitzgerald.

States for much better pay. Labor shortages in the agave fields, distilleries, and construction have been filled by several hundred men and a
handful of women from Chiapas, Mexico's poorest state. A cattle rancher
in a neighboring county initiated the migration stream around 2000 by
making the one-thousand-mile trip to recruit fifteen workers. Since then,
migrants have arrived on their own and found lodging and work via their
hometown social networks or simply by waiting outside the Arandas
cathedral at sunrise, where an informal market for hiring day laborers
functions like the parking lots outside home improvement stores in Los
Angeles, where many Jaliscienses seek jobs. Employers of unskilled labor
in Arandas generally prefer Chiapan to Arandense workers, as even
Arandenses who never migrated are considered contaminated by re-

turnees' unreasonable expectations. The Chiapans, with their frame of reference in the extremely low-wage environment of Chiapas, are considered better workers because, as Arandense employers say, "Arandas is their North." Indeed, the 4-to-1 wage differential for agricultural work between Arandas and Chiapas is slightly larger than the 3.7-to-1 gap between what Arandenses earn in the United States and Arandas.

The personnel director of the local agave growers association explained how Chiapans are solving sectoral labor shortages left by migrants in the United States: "What is the problem? We're being left without people. People from Los Altos go to the United States, they go to Canada, and they go other places to work, and we are left without a strong supply of labor, right? So, these people [from Chiapas] come, and say we are their United States. Why? Because here they earn a good salary. They're accustomed to live in very poor conditions, very extreme poverty, so it's not hard for them to adapt here."

Despite the advantages of access to cheap labor, prominent Arandenses publicly express their resentment against the influx of Chiapans. The incoming mayor and developers have publicly spoken of the need to give Arandenses preference in hiring, though that has not stopped some of those who complain about Chiapans "taking jobs from Arandenses" from hiring Chiapans themselves. In an interview, a university-educated leader of the local PAN explained the costs and benefits of the Chiapan migration to Arandas: "Benefits, in that their labor is cheap, and detriment—well, because of their customs and traditions that they've brought here—that they walk around wearing a machete, their dress is irregular to us, they have mixed genetically with the girls from here. And they're Chiapans, they're darker, shorter, and they keep degenerating the race [*degenerando la raza*] that we have here. We have a race that is more Spanish or French or Jewish. And when it is mixed, people come out more creole [*criollo*], no? . . . With facial features that are wider, cruder, darker."

Alteños openly celebrate their reputation for the white skin, light hair, and blue or green eyes that distinguish them from most Mexicans. Despite the biological racism that characterizes many Arandenses' views of Chiapans, Chiapan migration is likely to continue. A long history of exposure to the United States by direct migratory experience and returnees' hyperbolic reports of easy money have prompted many Arandenses to refuse the worst jobs and to expect middle-class comforts. The worst jobs have been defined as a Chiapan niche. Mass emigration prompts businesses to resort to internal migrants to fill jobs, which then prompts more international migration because there are even fewer acceptable jobs to accommodate the growing native workforce. This is the sending-country version of the social labeling of particular kinds of work as "immigrant jobs" in the destination country.[50] Employers are not adapting to labor shortages caused by an absolute dearth of workers; in fact, underemployment is rampant. Rather, employers are creatively managing a shift in workers' expectations of wages and conditions and the prestige of specific jobs caused by their dual U.S. and Mexican frames of reference.

Cultural representations of migrants are sometimes contradictory in rural communities, whose residents already feel unsettled by the pace of change as they become more integrated into the rest of the nation and the world. Celebrations of the "absent son" who leaves to provide for his family contrast with more ambivalent representations of the "prodigal son" who returns to his family after learning that the American dream is an illusion. The norteño can even become like Georg Simmel's "stranger," who reminds the community of what its culture is by showing what it is not.[51] Representations of the norteño-as-stranger allow Arandenses to invert the status hierarchy by asserting the moral superiority of local traditions and ways of life against the agringado customs of the migrant. These culture wars *a la mexicana* influence outcomes as diverse as how migrants maintain ties with their hometowns and employers' hiring decisions.

For migrants, events such as the Señorita Arandas pageant and the winners' tour of Jalisco discussed in the previous chapter are ways to claim that migrants still are moral members of the community. Neatly coiffed young women dressed in styles reminiscent of the nineteenth century are attempting to establish an alternative schema for norteños, in contrast to the predominant cholo schema of a young man with shaved head and tattoos driving recklessly through the plaza, playing rap music and shouting out the window. The religious procession of hijos ausentes and the luncheon with mariachi music extolling the absentee and his nostalgia for Arandas are institutional venues where mainstream migrants, the Church, and the state join to display their idea of a proper moral order. The Mexican government at various levels attempts to socialize the population in Mexico and even Mexicans in the United States through educational and cultural programs that promote a sense of mexicanidad and local ties. Hometown association projects such as donating an ambulance create prestige by showing not only that migrants have wealth, but that they are using their wealth for the benefit of the community. All of these activities are important ways to maintain hometown ties.

Migrants' expectations of higher wages and better working conditions and employers' theories about who is a desirable worker are transforming the local labor market. Although many returnees are no longer willing to work in Mexico and some employers reject returnees even if they are willing to work, factory owners prefer returnees who have been disciplined to internalize punctuality, a consistent work pace, and sobriety. Most strikingly, employers' preference for unskilled agricultural workers who have not been "contaminated" by the U.S. frame of reference either directly or by diffusion has prompted an unprecedented in-migration from Chiapas.

In short, the cultural transformations wrought by migration crystallize a fundamental ambivalence about the influence of the United States and how to enjoy the fruits of modernity and economic growth without sacrificing patriotism, faith, and social solidarity. Cultural nationalists in countries of emigration are concerned with the dissimilation of emigrants and the disintegration of their communities brought on by emigration. This negotiation takes place in a broad cultural field that transcends the territorial border between the United States and Mexico, but it is hardly the open field of free-flowing people and ideas proclaimed by the globalists. Some actors in Mexico are actively intervening in that cultural landscape with attempts to repair the bars of the nation-state's cage.

Conclusion

Stakeholders in the heated debates about immigration to the United States rarely pay much attention to Mexico's policy toward emigration and emigrants. Conservatives who want to restrict immigration are the most likely exceptions to this rule. The former Republican presidential candidate and pundit Patrick Buchanan summarizes the restrictionist take on Mexico's policies, which he calls "the Aztlan Strategy": "This then is the Aztlan Strategy: endless migration from Mexico north, the Hispanicization of the American Southwest, and dual citizenship for all Mexican-Americans. The goals: Erase the border. Grow the influence, through Mexican-Americans, over how America disposes of her wealth and power. Gradually circumscribe the sovereignty of the United States. . . . Stated bluntly, the Aztlan Strategy entails the end of the United States as a sovereign, self-sufficient, independent republic, the passing away of the American nation. They are coming to conquer us."[1]

The hyperbole and patently false claims in such accounts might be risible were they not politically influential and if they did not reproduce some of the analytic assumptions of serious scholarship about how migration changes the nation-state. The argument that Mexico's policies threaten U.S. sovereignty is exactly wrong. Most of Mexico's emigration policies failed in large part because of the *strength* of U.S. sovereignty and the (often unintended) consequences of its immigration laws and practices. An international system based on each country's sovereignty has further constrained Mexico's policies toward emigrants already abroad. Mexico can engage its emigrants directly only to the extent that the U.S. government allows it. And notwithstanding the alarms of the restrictionists, the U.S. government has increasingly recognized that Mexico's efforts to embrace its emigrants in U.S. territory fall within the legitimate practices of the international system. Although in 1958 the U.S. Supreme Court in *Perez v. Brownell* found that a U.S. citizen's voting in Mexico's 1946 presidential elections was constitutional grounds for involuntary expatriation, in 1967 the Court's decision in *Afroyim v. Rusk* opened the door to allowing U.S. citizens to keep their citizenship despite voting in foreign elections. Since the 1990s, the State Department has not sought to involuntarily expatriate Americans even if they naturalize in a foreign country or work for a foreign government.[2]

This book concludes with an analysis of how the Mexican government has met emigration's challenges and, to a lesser extent, its opportunities for building state and nation. I concentrate on ten critical domains of statecraft, including controlling the labor supply, policing, taxation, education, and foreign relations. Given the fundamental importance of emigration to many of these domains in Mexico as well as other countries of emigration, the fusion of a territory, a government, and a people has cracked apart to create a particular kind of nation-state. Yet the Westphalian system of sovereign states is not in decline. In fact, it is so robust even when confronted by mass international migration that it has shaped a new social contract between emigrants and their home country that I call citizenship à la carte.

EMIGRATION AND THE MEXICAN NATION-STATE

Mexico has used a variety of policy tools over the past century to meet emigration's challenges and opportunities in ten critical areas of nation and state building.[3] In general, the challenges of emigration have been most significant for cultural nationalizing, with a greater mix of costs and benefits in areas such as taxation and managing foreign relations.

Labor Control

The Mexican government tried to control the volume, trip duration, skills, and geographic origin of emigrants from 1900 to the early 1970s. The instruments of emigration control included propaganda campaigns, the 1942–64 bracero program, refusal to issue travel documents to certain occupational and geographic categories of workers, requirements that emigrants first work in domestic agriculture, and even coercion at the border. In the face of its failure to control emigration by preventing some Mexicans from leaving, the Mexican government since the late 1980s has turned to an emphasis on the management of emigrants who are abroad or visiting Mexico. For example, the Fox administration tried to negotiate an amnesty for unauthorized Mexicans in the United States and a bilateral temporary worker program.

What explains this shift? As shown in chapter 2, the failure of emigration control and the current abandonment of serious emigration restrictions are explained by a combination of external constraints, imposed by a highly asymmetrical interdependence with the United States, and internal constraints, imposed by actors within the fragmented Mexican state who undermined federal emigration policy through contradictory local practices. The state's lack of cohesion is more visible in the history of labor control policy than in any of the other domains considered here. Indeed, the Mexican policies that most affected migration flows were not emigration policies at all. To the extent that Mexican policies have shaped labor migration to the United States, they have been policies primarily concerned with agriculture, demography, and the ravages of civil war.

Policing

Just as criminals' option of hiding out south of the border complicates policing in the United States, Mexicans' ability to move back and forth across the border challenges policing in Mexico. Absent migrants are difficult to surveil and arrest because they are in another country's jurisdiction. As early as 1907, police in the state of Michoacán complained that the promise of impunity by fleeing to the United States was encouraging crime. In recurring cases in the Arandas County archives, officials grumbled that it was impossible to serve summonses for judicial proceedings because the suspects or witnesses were in the United States.[4] Between 1980 and 1994, the United States extradited an average of only two fugitives a year to Mexico, rising to a still paltry fifteen annual extraditions between 1995 and 2003.[5] However, the absence of migrants wanted by the police is not considered a particularly serious problem in Mexico because policing is so inefficient generally. Between 1996 and 2000, only 14 percent of arrest warrants were enforced in Mexico. The best estimates suggest that between 1996 and 2003, 96 percent of crimes committed went unpunished.[6] On a daily basis, the problem of tracking criminals who escape to the United States pales in comparison with the problem of tracking criminals locally.

The presence of returned migrants creates more immediate policing challenges to the extent that migrants are associated with disorderly behavior and the formation of gangs. Criminal returnees have learned new organizational models abroad, and they make use of the obstacles to cooperation between sovereign policing agencies as they move between jurisdictions. The sociologist Robert Smith has highlighted a serious gang problem in a migrant-source community in the state of Puebla. A great deal of policy and media attention has focused on violent gangs reconstructed by deportees from the United States living in Central America. Several of these gangs prey on Central Americans in transit to the United States through the southern Mexican state of Chiapas. The strength of those gangs can be attributed to their operation in an area with very limited state policing capacity.[7]

The fact that so much Mexican migration to the United States is illegal according to U.S. law also presents a policing challenge for Mexico, even though Mexico's Constitution generally supports the right of exit. The U.S. Border Patrol made 1.16 million apprehensions of Mexicans along the U.S.-Mexico border in fiscal year 2004.[8] Increased U.S. border enforcement since the mid-1990s has spawned an increase in migrants' use of smugglers, higher fees, and smugglers' willingness to take greater risks to penetrate militarized U.S. border defenses. The unintended consequence has been a boon for the coyote industry, which, though illegal in Mexico as well as in the United States, rarely is prosecuted in Mexico; in fact, coyotes pay Mexican police to look the other way. Clandestine migration also leaves migrants vulnerable to banditry along the border, which has contributed to levels of lawlessness that the Mexican government has had difficulty controlling.[9]

Financial Extraction

Normal modes of political power don't work very well to extract resources from an absent population.[10] Frustrated by their inability to collect debts from absent migrants, Mexican federal and state governments have increasingly seen migrants as a font of resources that can be acquired creatively without coercion. The government's three main strategies are indirect extraction, use of persuasion rather than coercion, and wielding the ideological power of long-distance nationalism and appeals to hometown ties.

Remittance policy is the principal tool of indirect extraction. Since the late 1990s, the Mexican federal government has publicized the use of automatic teller machines in Mexico linked to U.S. bank accounts as the cheapest way to send remittances home. Consulates compile weekly lists showing the most affordable wire transfer companies and complain vociferously about the high fees charged by some companies. Remittances spent in Mexico generate fiscal revenues through the value-added tax at the federal level and through property taxes at the county level. Agricultural economists estimate a multiplier effect of remittances that indirectly increases Mexican GDP by US$2.69 for every US$1 of remittances to urban households and US$3.17 for every US$1 of remittances to rural households.[11] Since the late 1990s, the Mexican government has encouraged migrants to channel their remittances into business investments and "productive projects." Government support of migrant-financed business incurs a cost in the short term, but in the long run it presumably generates economic activity that can then be taxed.

As shown in chapter 4, the Mexican state has imitated the Church's emigrant policies based on voluntary cooperation. The state's use of coercion and its monopoly on taxation in the nineteenth century forced the Church to establish a voluntaristic relationship with its membership, which has proven advantageous for the Church's maintenance of cross-border links with migrant members. The Mexican government at the federal, state, and county levels has successfully promoted the hometown associations that were pioneered by the Church and migrants themselves. Migrants fund hometown projects not because they are required to by law, but because they can use such projects to increase their prestige, claim to be good members of the community despite their absence, and enjoy the psychological rewards of charity. Arandenses in the United States have not tried to mobilize their resources through HTAs on a large scale, however, underlining the state's limited room for maneuver if emigrants do not want to cooperate.

The promotion of HTAs and individual migrant donations is based on ideological appeals to the community of origin. County and state governments promote "paisano tourism" and develop fiesta activities emphasizing local traditions that cater to the nostalgia of absentees. The government of Arandas has even sent its migrants cassettes and compact disks featuring odes to Arandas. On the national level, the rhetorical embrace of Mexicans abroad has become de rigueur in policy pronouncements on migration. President Zedillo famously included Mexicans abroad in his definition of the Mexican nation, and President Fox repeatedly called migrants "heroes." Officials promote the ideology of the homeland and the hometown because migrants are outside the state's territory and its immediate administrative reach.

Social Welfare

One of the functions of modern states is to redistribute some of a country's wealth to alleviate poverty and inequality. Remittances arguably retard the development of redistributive mechanisms such as social welfare programs. As early as the 1950s, annual bracero remittances were Mexico's third largest source of foreign exchange; by 2005, remittances of US$20 billion were the second largest source of foreign exchange after petroleum exports. Eighteen percent of the adult Mexican population receives remittances.[12] Those dollars support the maintenance of millions of poor and lower-middle-class Mexicans without any state intervention. In addition to funding an alternative to social welfare, emigration is an escape valve. Citizens who might otherwise increase demands on Mexico's social services remove themselves from the country and then generate resources via remittances that alleviate the poverty of those who stay behind. From the sending state's point of view, emigrants who remit are perfect citizens: They indirectly give to the state while taking little in return.

Documentation

Simply counting and contacting the emigrant population are a bureaucratic nightmare for all levels of government. One way the state is attempting to embrace its emigrants is by imitating the Mexican Church's system for tracking migrants who agree to register themselves. In the early 1990s, the county administration of Arandas began sending U.S-based migrants invitations to the annual fiesta using a directory of addresses that has since disappeared. A new impetus to create emigrant directories came from above in the late 1990s, when the governor of Jalisco asked all county governments to compile directories that could be used to encourage migrants to remit with a designated wire transfer service as part of the FIDERAZA investment program, discussed in chapter 2. County administrations have compiled new directories by installing a booth at the patron saint fiesta, leaving stacks of forms at travel agencies, and sending county employees from table to table at the emigrant luncheon.

There are several major obstacles to creating these directories. Migrants cannot be forced to participate because they are usually absent, and coercion when they are present would alienate them. Many migrants do not trust the government, especially undocumented migrants who fear that the directory could somehow be used against them. The government draws on HTA membership lists, but the HTA structure of Arandenses in the United States is unstable over time and uneven across destinations; Arandenses move frequently, so most of the addresses and phone numbers are useless within a couple of years. Different organizations in Arandas create directories independently of each other. At any given moment, the county government, the Catholic Church, and a weekly newspaper are each compiling addresses that they do not share with each other. Finally, there is very little continuity of policies, files, or personnel between three-year county administrations. Even the secretaries in the presidency are political appointees who are sacked by the incoming administration, and departing officials take many documents with them. In a common refrain, a former elected official explained, "Here we are pillagers of information. The outgoing president doesn't give a fig if he leaves his administration destroyed or well organized." The result is that each new administration usually begins a new directory. The local government cannot develop the administrative capacity to extract resources from migrants more successfully, not only because of its inability to coerce them, their refusal to participate, and diffuse migration patterns, but also because the local government has such a weak bureaucracy. The files simply disappear.

At the national level, residents are required by law to cooperate with the census,[13] but citizens abroad do not participate, nor could they easily be coerced into participating if the government so desired. The primary tool used to identify individual migrants as well as their aggregate characteristics has become the matrícula consular, an identification document issued by the forty-six Mexican consulates in the United States. The majority of matrícula holders are unauthorized migrants who need the document because they did not obtain a Mexican passport before migrating.[14] There has been an intense debate in the United States about whether the matrícula should be accepted as a legitimate identification document, allowing the bearer to open a U.S. bank account, board a commercial flight, and prove identity to U.S. police. The Mexican government has actively promoted the matrícula for all of these purposes,[15] but it serves another, less recognized, function: Matrícula registrations are a way to collect detailed data on Mexican nationals in the United States that are not available from other sources. The foreign service collects information on migrants' places of origin and destination, which it then shares with Mexican state offices of migrant services and county governments so they can more efficiently target migrant populations from their areas. The matrícula serves some of the functions of a census, but it is based on voluntary participation because the citizens are outside the Mexican government's sovereign grasp.

The Mexican state has comparatively little to offer its emigrants, which is why, of the several million people thought to be eligible to regain their Mexican nationality when a dual nationality law went into effect in 1998, only sixty-seven thousand applied during the initial five-year window the law was in effect. In comparison, 4 million Mexicans in the United States have voluntarily obtained the matrícula because they cannot obtain identification documents from the U.S. government, with the partial and perhaps fleeting exception of driver's licenses in some states.[16] It is the demand of the *U.S.* government and civil society that individuals be able to document their identity for routine transactions that has driven Mexican emigrants into the embrace of the Mexican state.

Education

Migration presents a multifaceted challenge to public education. Of all the agents of the state interviewed in Arandas, educators were most likely to say that migration is prejudicial to source communities. Teachers blame migration for providing an alternative to schooling and elevating dropout rates. Permanent emigration represents a loss of the human capital invested in migrants by the Mexican state. The United States "didn't just take our land [in 1848]; they're even taking our people," explained a high school principal in Arandas. According to a 1998 estimate, the Mexican government spent between US$40 billion and US$50 billion to educate Mexicans who left to live in the United States.[17] When fathers are in the United States, student absenteeism and disciplinary problems increase back in Mexico. The educational system relies on the exercise of power over a whole population rather than students alone. For example, schools rely on the cooperation of parents to discipline students and ensure their attendance and diligence in completing school assignments, so the absence of these social supports undermines the school.

Although migrants have left the state's territorial cage, federal- and provincial-level programs reach beyond Mexican territory to target young Mexicans living in the United States through teacher exchange programs and Spanish-language texts delivered through the consulates. The goal, in the words of one of the architects of Mexico's consular programs, is "to foster Mexicanness among its absent children."[18] Within Mexico, migrants are seen as conduits for the U.S. music and English, or "Espanglish," that some educators view as threatening Mexican music and "high" Spanish. Teachers in Arandas say that migration contributes to a decline in the Mexican patriotism that they work so hard to inculcate. Formal educational policy emphasizes the pragmatic management of youth migration through agreements with the United States that recognize the validity of school records and thus smooth transfers between schools. Yet there are no special programs for students returning to Mexico that address their sometimes limited command of Spanish. In practice, Mexican policies for returnees are implicitly assimilationist, as they bring migrant students back into the national fold with no provision for the different experiences they have had in the United States.

Cultural Nationalizing

Teachers are not the only leaders who fear the effects of emigration and return migration on nation building. As detailed in chapters 3 and 5, the Mexican Catholic Church, public intellectuals, and the public in general have long been concerned that migrants lose their Mexican characteristics when they move to the United States and introduce U.S. cultural pathologies into the source communities when they return. Migrants are portrayed as drug users, gang members, and carriers of disease contracted in the North. Their tattoos, piercings, and hair and clothing styles are considered deviant. Although speaking English generally is seen as an enviable accomplishment, losing Spanish is portrayed as a moral failure and a rejection of being Mexican; in other words, linguistic assimilation from a U.S. perspective is national dissimilation and betrayal from a Mexican perspective. Migrants are denigrated by cultural nationalists, who already feel beset by a pervasive U.S. influence. In a process of normative inversion, cultural nationalists flip the geopolitical hierarchy to assert Mexico's moral superiority over the United States. Local elite resentment of migrants' class mobility partly explains negative attitudes about the cultural transformations wrought by migration, but survey evidence from Arandas shows that the majority of migrant and nonmigrant household heads view migration as exacting a cultural price for an economic reward. Migrants and nonmigrants express more negative views about Mexicans who become naturalized U.S. citizens than they express about migrants to the United States generally. And they share a negative image of young cholo returnees who disgrace the community.

Conscription

I expected to find that at least in the 1920s, Mexican officials would express concern about the loss of potential soldiers to a country that took half of Mexico's territory in 1848 and intervened militarily as recently as 1919. During World War I, the Mexican government negotiated an end to the U.S. conscription of Mexican-born citizens living in the United States, but the rights of Mexico over its citizens abroad was the issue, not the loss of potential conscripts for the Mexican army. Prior to Mexico's alliance with the United States in World War II, the military was composed of volunteers supplemented as needed by a system of press-ganging. The arbitrariness of conscription meant that the loss of potential conscripts to migration was not viewed as a problem either. There was not even the pretense that military service was an experience shared by all men.[19]

Since the onset of a rationalized conscription policy in 1942, when Mexico joined the Allies in World War II, migration has posed an administrative challenge. The first attempts to enforce universal male conscription were met with draft riots and even bands of armed resistance. Open hostility was most common during World War II because of a widespread but false rumor that conscripts would be shipped overseas to fight, which prompted some men from the ranches around Agua Negra to migrate to northern Mexico and the United States. Arandense officials complained throughout the 1940s and 1950s that men selected for active service could not be found because they had moved away. In Arandas and around the country, authorities sometimes arrested men who failed to report for service, but periodic nationwide amnesties allowed men who had not registered at age eighteen to register late without penalty. Braceros were required to fulfill their military obligations before leaving during the early years of the program, but in 1955 they were allowed to petition military authorities to leave Mexico without completing their military service, on the understanding that they would register upon their return.[20] In 2002, the government stopped requiring the fulfillment of military service obligations as a condition for obtaining a passport.[21]

The government's relative lack of concern about emigration's effect on conscription is explained by a weak military, which conscripted only 0.3 percent of the population in 1930, falling to around 0.2 percent in 1960, where it has remained since. Mexico ranks 88th out of 133 countries surveyed by the International Institute for Strategic Studies in the percentage of its population serving in the armed forces. The small size and limited political influence of Mexico's military has been deliberate. With only tiny Guatemala and Belize to its south and a hegemon to the north against which military resistance is futile, Mexico has opted to maintain a small military for internal policing rather than fighting external wars.[22] In short, although emigration has presented an administrative challenge for rationalized conscription, the challenge is largely irrelevant because the manpower needs of the military are so modest and rampant corruption allowing draftees to avoid participation undermines the pretense that military service is an evenly distributed, nationalizing experience.

Political Stability

One of the main goals of state building is to achieve political stability and restrict the activities of dissidents. Aristide Zolberg has observed that the countries with the most severe restrictions on their citizens' exit have been illiberal. Despotism without exit controls would drive away the population. By the same token, the population's ability to leave the country may deter the extreme concentration of state power, particularly in countries with long open borders such as Mexico.[23] The Mexican case suggests that the effect of emigration on political stability varies according to two stages of state building. From the nineteenth century through the 1910–20 revolution, when the Mexican state was extremely weak and shot through with internal conflict, the availability of the U.S. exit option promoted instability. Political exiles such as President Benito Juárez in the 1860s and the anarchist Flores Magón brothers and Mexican revolutionary leader Francisco Madero in the early twentieth century operated from bases in the United States. In 1928, Mexican presidential candidate José Vasconcelos campaigned in Chicago and the Southwest against Pascual Ortiz Rubio, the official candidate. Ortiz Rubio received support from clubs in California organized by the Revolutionary National Party, precursor to the Institutional Revolutionary Party (PRI). Following the consolidation of the Mexican state in the 1930s, however, cross-border organizing of political exiles ceased to play a significant role in Mexican politics until the failed 1988 presidential campaign of center-leftist Cuauhtémoc Cárdenas.[24] When an opposition again became active in the United States, it engaged homeland politics through peaceful democratic channels rather than through the cross-border raids of yesteryear.

In July 1996, the PRI-dominated Congress amended the Constitution to allow Mexicans outside their district of residence to vote for president.[25] The amendment hypothetically allowed Mexican citizens to vote from abroad, but it did not include the necessary enabling legislation directing the Federal Electoral Institute to organize elections outside Mexico. The opposition-controlled federal Chamber of Deputies passed the implementing law in July 1999, but the PRI-controlled Senate killed the measure.[26] The PRI intended to incorporate emigrants symbolically to protect itself politically and to create a Mexican ethnic lobby in Washington, DC, but the party inadvertently opened the door to a Mexican emigrant lobby in Mexico City. Various emigrant groups affiliated with the Party of the Democratic Revolution expanded to include activists from across the political spectrum. They formed the Coalition for the Political Rights of Mexicans Abroad, which successfully pushed through a bill in 2005 that enabled Mexicans to vote from abroad by absentee ballot in the 2006 presidential elections. The emigrant lobby had achieved a dramatic success, pointing to the possibility of binational grassroots mobilization on both sides of the border. Ironically, the migrant vote was not a factor in the closest election in modern Mexican history, decided by only half a percent of the ballots cast. Three million out of 10 million Mexicans in the United States were eligible to vote in the 2006 Mexican elections, but only 57,000, or half a percent, tried to register to vote, and fewer than 33,000 cast valid ballots. Fifty-eight percent voted for the candidate of the incumbent National Action Party.[27] The reasons for low turnout include the absence of a Mexican voter registration program in the United States, a series of bureaucratic hurdles to obtain absentee ballots, and a new ban on Mexican presidential candidates campaigning in the United States. The ostensible reason for the ban was that the Mexican government could not enforce its electoral regulations in another country's sovereign territory, so it simply prohibited campaigning altogether. The more likely reason was that the PRI and PAN in Congress saw migrant voters as wild cards and deliberately sought to suppress turnout by limiting their exposure to the campaigns.

In a 2006 survey representative of Mexican-born adults in the United States, the Pew Hispanic Center found that while 78 percent of the sample was aware that Mexicans could vote from abroad, 55 percent did not know there would be elections that year. Only 13 percent of the sample had a positive opinion of the way Mexican political institutions function; 32 percent had a negative opinion.[28] In short, migrants' widespread dissatisfaction with Mexican politics has not generated widespread political action. Given the apparent consolidation of Mexican democracy in the 2000 election, migrant participation in the future may affect partisan outcomes but is unlikely to have a transformative effect on the political characteristics of the state or its stability.

The strongest political impact of emigration since the postrevolutionary consolidation of the state has been its function as a systemic safety valve that decreased pressure on the Mexican state to transform itself politically. For example, the Mexican anthropologist Andrés Fábregas has argued that there would have been further Cristero violence in the 1930s and 1940s if fewer Cristeros had migrated to the United States.[29] At times of economic crisis in Mexico, such as the 1980s, emigration has risen dramatically. The exit option for revolutionary émigrés that decreased political stability in the first stage of mass emigration by the 1930s became an escape valve that has supported political stability through the early twenty-first century.

Foreign Relations

To the very limited extent that emigrants become involved in U.S. politics and share the policy preferences of the Mexican government, their political resources present an opportunity for strengthening Mexico's position in the bilateral relationship. In what must be one of the earliest attempts to form a Mexican lobby, Juárez Clubs in the 1860s supported Republican candidates in U.S. elections because Republicans were thought to be more favorable to exiled president Benito Juárez. President Luis Echeverría (1970–76) saw Mexican Americans as a potential ethnic lobby and met with Chicano leaders, though these contacts were not institutionalized. The creation of a Mexican lobby in the United States has become one of Mexico's serious foreign policy goals only since the 1990s, beginning with the campaign to negotiate and pass NAFTA in the U.S. Congress. The Mexican government advertised heavily in U.S. Spanish-language media urging Mexican Americans to contact their U.S. congressional representatives to approve fast-track negotiating authority. It spent at least US$30 million promoting NAFTA in Washington—an effort that catapulted Mexico from a conspicuous absence among foreign powers lobbying on Capitol Hill to one of the most prominent. The Mexican NAFTA lobby worked with Latino organizations such as the National Council of La Raza and the National Hispanic Chamber of Commerce to hire former administration officials and pay for U.S. policy makers' junkets to Mexico. In 1993, all but one of the Mexican American members of Congress voted to approve NAFTA. Yet most studies by Mexican and U.S. authors of Mexico's NAFTA lobbying agree that the ethnic factor was not a decisive factor in NAFTA's passage. Only five of thirty major lobbyists contracted by the Mexican government were Latino, and only two of the major lobbyists focused on promoting NAFTA among Latino voters. Many Mexican American congressional representatives agreed to vote for NAFTA only at the last minute, after funding for a North American Development Bank to cultivate community projects was added to the agreement. As the political scientist Rodolfo de la Garza summarized, "There is no evidence . . . that Mexican American members of Congress voted for NAFTA because of Mexican lobbying or because they supported Mexican interests."[30]

In 1994, Mexican consulates and Mexican American political organizations unsuccessfully worked together to try to defeat Proposition 187, the California ballot measure endorsed by Governor Pete Wilson that would have restricted a wide range of services for unauthorized immigrants had it not been thrown out by the courts after it passed. Mexico's dual nationality law that took effect in 1998 was intended in part to encourage Mexican nationals to become U.S. citizens so they would vote against measures like 187 and the politicians who supported them.[31] Most of the Mexican-origin population in the United States and the Mexican government might view politicians such as Wilson as a common enemy, but that does not make Mexican Americans a lobby for the Mexican government's efforts to ease U.S. restrictions on immigration or immigrants. According to the 1989–90 Latino National Political Survey, more than three-quarters of Mexican American citizens feel that there are "too many immigrants in the United States," virtually the same proportion as among Anglos.[32] The overwhelming Latino vote against Proposition 187 apparently reflected these voters' perception of a thinly disguised attack on Latinos in general rather than their support for increased immigration.[33] To quote de la Garza, "If Mexican Americans do not rally to support Mexico around policies such as NAFTA and immigration even after [Mexican consular] officials invested substantial resources to woo them, it is unlikely they will do so on issues that do not directly affect them or are on behalf of the Mexican government per se."[34]

Dissimilation is the main challenge to developing an ethnic lobby among Mexicans in the United States. The same apathy toward Mexican politics (outside a committed core of activists) that prevents contemporary emigrants from threatening Mexican political stability also makes them an ineffective ethnic lobby. Interest in Mexican politics among U.S. residents of Mexican origin generally declines over time and generation. In the 1988 National Latino Immigrant Survey of adult Mexican immigrants either eligible for naturalization or already naturalized, 58 percent said their "primary national identification" was with Mexico, but that identification decreased with length of residence in the United States. The 1989–90 Latino National Political Survey found that, among respondents of Mexican origin, 2 percent of U.S. citizens and 20 percent of noncitizens said they were more concerned with Mexican politics than with U.S. politics, while 90 percent of citizens and 38 percent of noncitizens said they were more concerned with U.S. politics than with Mexican politics.[35] Not surprisingly, Mexico-born immigrants appear much more likely than U.S.-born Mexican Americans to be interested in Mexican politics. Carlos González Gutiérrez, one of the founders of the Program for Mexican Communities Abroad, has argued that the Mexican government should act quickly to build ties with the Mexican-origin population in the United States before the relative share of immigrants declines.[36] Mexico-born immigrants were 38 percent of the total Mexican-origin population in 2000, which is unusually high by a postrepatriation (post-1930s) yardstick.

Another challenge to creating an ethnic lobby is that Mexican Americans and Mexicans in the United States tend to have negative views of the Mexican government even if they are favorably disposed to Mexico as a country.[37] Immigrants who come to the United States seeking a better life are not likely to follow the distant call of a Mexican government that many blame for their predicament. Finally, while ethnicity is an established basis for political organizing in the U.S. political system, overt attempts by Mexican authorities to promote an ethnic lobby risk a backlash from nativists who raise the specter of divided loyalty. Consequently, talk of ethnic lobbies by high-ranking Mexican government officials visiting the United States has been limited to their interactions with Latino audiences. Mainstream Latino organizations are also reluctant to embrace the notion of an ethnic lobby tied to the Mexican government. Latino organizations are clearly oriented toward U.S. domestic politics and do not want to suffer a nativist response by linking themselves to a foreign government. The Mexican project of seeking political favors from its emigrants abroad is challenged by the same factors that make maintaining the cultural nationality of citizens abroad so difficult. Efforts to embrace emigrants outside the Mexican cage collide with the powerful forces of assimilation in the United States.

THE NATION OF EMIGRANTS PARADIGM

The relationship between nation and state lies at the heart of the modern organization of politics. The institutional and territorial borders of the state are supposed to overlap with the imagined borders of the nation.[38] How do sending states' efforts to embrace emigrants complicate that relationship? Scholars of transnationalism give one answer in their claim that "transmigrants," a new kind of international migrant, "build social fields that cross geographic, cultural, and political borders." In doing so, transmigrants are said to create new forms of transnational membership and a "deterritorialized nation-state."[39] Yet by conflating borders of state, nation, culture, and geography, the concept of transnationalism forecloses the possibility of analyzing state-nation relationships. This conflation is particularly problematic in the claim by the anthropologist Linda Basch and her colleagues that nation-states have become deterritorialized through the inclusion of emigrants. In a more nuanced explanation of the Mexican case, the sociologist Rachel Sherman identifies the primary shift in Mexican emigrant policy since the 1920s as one from "state introversion" to "state extension"; in the latter case, state policy is directed toward maintaining relationships with citizens permanently abroad. Yet even here, Sherman makes the unsustainable claim that the state "transnationalizes and deterritorializes itself."[40]

Modern states are a set of administrative institutions exercising control over a defined territory. If the nation-state has not been deterritorialized, how should the relationship between nation and state be conceptualized in Mexico and similar countries where governments try to incorporate "their" emigrants? Studies of nationalism point in a useful direction. *Nation* has two meanings that may overlap in practice to describe the same set of persons, but that remain analytically distinct. In the first sense, the nation is a community claimed on the basis of a shared language, history, region, phenotype, or culture. In the second, it is a political unit of the citizens of the state. The sociologist Rogers Brubaker distinguishes between "state-framed" and "counter-state" understandings of nationhood. In the former, national and state boundaries are congruent; the state institutionally and territorially frames the nation. France is considered the paradigmatic example of state-framed nationhood; in oversimplified terms, everyone who lives in France is French, and all the French live in France, or are at least French citizens. Germany is considered the paradigmatic example of counterstate nationhood, where the nation is conceived in opposition to the territorial and institutional frame of an existing state. Not everyone in Germany is German, and many ethnic Germans are noncitizens who live outside the country.[41]

If the distinction between state-framed and counterstate understandings of nationhood captures many configurations, it still does not fit a set of important cases of mass emigration in which governments frame the nation as extending beyond the state's territorial borders *without trying to change state borders*. Given the Mexican government's embrace of emigrants, Mexican nationhood cannot be considered state-framed in the sense that the entire nation is contained within the state's territory. Neither are any politically significant actors in Mexico framing nationhood in counterstate terms. Some Mexican and Chicano writers have facetiously promoted the notion of a *reconquista* of the U.S. Southwest. This is exclusively a symbolic statement of ethnic pride rather than a political program of actual conquest. Authors such as Patrick Buchanan have willfully misrepresented the symbolism of reconquista as if it threatened U.S. sovereignty, but no one is seriously calling for adjusting the U.S.-Mexico border to better fit the imagined boundaries of the Mexican nation. Although the history of Mexican nationalism has been shaped by the 1848 Treaty of Guadalupe Hidalgo, which left one hundred thousand Mexican nationals in the northern half of Mexico ceded to the United States,[42] there is no irredentist movement, if only because of the overwhelming power asymmetry with the United States.

How, then, should cases like Mexico be conceptualized? I argue that typologies of state-framed understandings of nationhood should distinguish between two aspects of *state:* The first refers to government agencies; the second is the territory controlled by those agencies. Governments claim that the nation extends beyond the state's territory to encompass a population in another country, believing that such a frame reinforces the government's capacity to realize its economic and political projects *within* the existing borders of the Westphalian system. Countries of former mass emigration such as Spain and Italy and contemporary countries of emigration as diverse as China, India, Turkey, the Philippines, Armenia, Morocco, and the Dominican Republic have invoked a form of nationhood that reinforces government capacities by extending ties to nationals living outside the country's territory.[43]

While the *form* of nationhood is similar in all of these countries of emigration, the *content* driving that reformulation varies with the domain of nation and state building in which emigration is most deeply implicated. Policies of emigrant inclusion are driven by multiple logics. The sociologist Barbara Schmitter Heisler argues that sending states tend to encourage long-term but temporary emigration. Emigrants who stay abroad for long periods are more likely to achieve the material success needed to send more remittances, though at the risk of decreasing remittances as they settle. When emigrants eventually return, the sending country retains the human capital that it invested in them by paying for their education before they left, and it reaps the rewards of their investments and expertise.[44] This characterization applies best to emigration policies driven by economic calculations, whether North African policies encouraging guest-worker labor migration or countries such as India and China encouraging the temporary migration of highly skilled or entrepreneurial migrants.

External politics is a primary motivation for sending states to embrace their emigrants when they move to politically powerful countries that allow political integration. Throughout Latin America, governments hope to turn their emigrants into an ethnic lobby in the United States, and sending countries such as Turkey, with established populations in Europe, have tried to do the same.[45] In contrast to the economically driven policies, the logic of developing a lobby requires more or less permanent settlement in the destination country. Effective lobbying requires citizenship in the host country and a long-term investment of time and money in its political processes. Of all the principal forces driving emigrant inclusion, external politics carries the strongest argument for encouraging dual nationality.

Internal politics can also drive policies of emigrant incorporation in Mexico and beyond. New York has become an extension of the Dominican campaign trail, featuring visits by candidates such as Manhattanraised President Leonel Fernández (1996–2000, 2004–8), permanent offices of the major Dominican political parties, and fund-raisers that finance 10 to 15 percent of Dominican presidential campaigns.[46] Promoting the vote abroad and establishing extraterritorial parliamentary districts are the main cards that partisans at home play to attract the support of expatriates, though this can be a dangerous game. Italian prime minister Silvio Berlusconi dug his own grave when he pushed through a measure allowing Italians abroad to vote in 2006 for twelve deputies and six senators to represent them in Parliament. Against his calculation that conservatives would be most likely to participate in homeland politics, expatriate voters decided the narrow election by casting their ballots for the victorious center-left opposition.[47]

The embrace of emigrants may be driven more by demography than by a ploy for remittances, lobbies, or emigrant votes. Contemporary states facing a demographic deficit tend to be rich, industrialized countries. Australia, which has always tried to increase its population through immigration, in 2002 extended the right to dual citizenship to the 4.3 percent of its population abroad.[48] In Israel, the exit of potential soldiers is considered a threat in its demographic race with the Palestinians. Consequently, though Israel upholds the right to emigrate in principle, it actively restricts the emigration of young people who have not fulfilled their military obligations. The main tactic for deterring emigration has been discursive. Former prime minister Yitzhak Rabin famously described emigrants as "deserters" and "the fallen among the weaklings" in a 1976 televised interview. Former prime minister Menachem Begin lamented to the Knesset that same year, "Since the state was founded we have lost [through emigration] four Divisions, or 12 Brigades." These tactics did not endear their home government to Israelis abroad, and Israeli politicians now avoid such language and promote better consular services to keep Israeli expatriates in the national orbit.[49]

Finally, emigrant inclusion may be driven by a search for prestige from international and domestic audiences. In the 1920s, Benito Mussolini redefined Italian emigrants in places like Buenos Aires as Italian "colonizers," creating the pretense that Italy was keeping up with its European competitors in the scramble for empire. Following Spain's international isolation in the immediate postwar period, Francisco Franco's administration negotiated twelve bilateral dual-nationality treaties with Latin American countries in the 1950s and 1960s as part of an effort to reposition Spain as the center of a "Hispanic community." More recently, Russia has reached out to ethnic Russians who had migrated within the Soviet Union and become foreigners in the "near abroad" when the Soviet Union broke up in 1991. The Russian government offers them dual citizenship and claims to speak on their behalf. Despite a stunning demographic deficit of 8.7 million more Russian deaths than births since 1992, the main goal of these policies has not been to encourage return, but to make claims on citizens abroad to enhance Russia's prestige in its sphere of influence.[50]

Whatever their motivations, countries extend their embrace to absentees in a way that reinforces the government's domestic and international capacity. Extraterritorial citizenship is not *trans*nationalism, which suggests the superseding of the national along the universalistic lines of the Catholic Church, but rather a manifestation of long-distance *nationalism* that seeks to link a particular people to the government of a particular place.[51] This framework linking mobile citizen, state, and nation has historical precedent in earlier cases of mass emigration, yet its analytical conceptualization is only now being understood.

CITIZENSHIP À LA CARTE

The territoriality of political power is being reconfigured through the embrace of citizens abroad, a condition I have called *emigrant citizenship* (or *extraterritorial* citizenship, when extended more broadly to include the ancestral citizenship of emigrants' descendents). Resident citizens can make only narrow choices about which resources they are willing to exchange for benefits from a monopolistic state; emigrants have more choices. Emigrants can take their business elsewhere and vote with their feet, giving them leverage to demand new terms of exchange with the state. The leviathan becomes a supplicant. Consequently, emigrants and the governments of their countries of origin are negotiating citizenship à la carte based on voluntarism, citizen rights over obligations, and multiple affiliations.

The capacity of a state to make its citizens fulfill duties such as conscription is severely restricted once those citizens leave the country. The Westphalian system of territorial sovereignty both enables the state's range of action in its own territory and sharply limits its ability to project political power beyond its borders. Some emigrants may voluntarily return to their country of origin to perform the duties of citizenship or send their "voluntary taxes" from abroad, as in the exceptional case of overseas Eritreans in the 1990s, but these are tenuous arrangements. The system of sovereign states remains so robust that governments of sending countries must rely on the coercive intervention of the government of the country of immigration, penalize emigrants' family or take their property left behind, rely on emigrants' voluntary cooperation, or wait until emigrants return home, when they are once again available to the state's direct embrace.[52]

None of this is to claim that coercion is the daily mode of state action anywhere. Even the most totalitarian states find that the constant use of force is expensive and ineffective. State building works much more efficiently with the exercise of ideological power, in which citizens are instilled with the habitus of yielding themselves and their resources without resistance.[53] The ultimate triumph of the state's ideological power occurs when citizens not only accept taxation, conscription, and constant regulation, but see these activities as moral obligations. To borrow from Michael Mann, states wield the ideological power derived from deploying symbols as well as the political power of centralized regulation over a specific territory.[54] Resident citizenship differs fundamentally from emigrant citizenship because the state can much more easily coerce resident citizens to comply when ideological power is insufficient. Within Mexico's territory, the state wields power over its population in both a political and an ideological mode, but when part of the flock strays from the territory, ideological power is a more effective mode of embracing them. The Mexican state has modeled its policies for managing emigrants on the ways that the Catholic Church in Mexico has wielded ideological power at home and abroad.

Emigrant citizenship is based on the notion, dating back to Roman times, that citizenship is a right that is "owned."[55] Citizens are owed protection by their community, and that right to be protected can be transported. The legal scholar Kim Barry rightly points out that according to the logic of international law, intervention by states of origin to protect citizens abroad "is not a right of the citizen abroad, but rather is a prerogative of that citizen's state," because "the state has been injured via the alleged harm to its citizen and is asserting its own right by protecting its citizens."[56] Yet public discourse and even some constitutional laws imply an emigrant's right to protection by the home state. For example, in a passage that enshrines its labor-export policy in constitutional law, the 1987 Philippines Constitution specifies, "The State shall afford full protection to labor, local and overseas." The 1978 Spanish Constitution stipulates, "The state shall pay special attention to safeguarding the economic and social rights of Spanish workers abroad."[57] Moreover, both the right to exit one's country of citizenship and the right to return to it are enshrined in international law.[58] While countries of emigration are obliged to let returnees back in, citizens have a recognized human right to leave their country of origin and in many cases renounce their nationality. Westphalian sovereignty creates a structural imbalance favoring the rights owned by emigrants over their obligations.

In the context of international migration, there is a double disjuncture between the Aristotelian principle that the ruled should be the rulers. Most attention has focused on the problem of noncitizen residents without a voice in ruling the state that rules them.[59] From the perspective of extraterritorial citizenship, there is a second philosophical problem. To the extent that emigrants are among the rulers of their homeland, they make rules to which they are not directly subject; resident citizens must face the consequences of emigrant actions in a more direct way. Emigrants can enjoy the substance of their homeland citizenship à la carte from a menu of rights and obligations, whereas residents must take the rights and obligations together at a relatively fixed price. Communitarians following the political philosophy of Rousseau have long complained that citizenship is generally tilted too far away from collective obligations.[60] This tilt becomes even more pronounced in the state's social contract with emigrants.

The disjuncture between rights and obligations is most extreme when citizens migrate to a country where they receive substantial benefits of denizenship even if they are not full members. Many migrants to the global North enjoy more substantive benefits and protections from destination-country governments than they did in their country of origin. Emigrants in such settings are better able to parlay their absence into greater emigrant rights from their country of origin.[61] The possibilities of citizenship à la carte are expanded when immigrant integration policies promote ideologies of cultural pluralism that translate easily into the legitimacy of holding dual ties. Class also patterns the extent to which citizenship is flexible. Professionals and entrepreneurs are best positioned to use their high levels of human and social capital to take out multiple citizenships as an "insurance policy" in case conditions deteriorate in a given country.[62] On the other hand, migrants from a country that provides meager resources to its citizens, who then move to a country that provides meager resources and protections to noncitizens, may end up with practically no protection at all. For example, Filipina maids in the Persian Gulf abused by their employers may hold a passport but often are effectively stateless in terms of the substantive practice of citizenship.[63] Unauthorized immigrants are less able to negotiate a new bargain with their home state than immigrants who can entertain the possibility of dual nationality and full integration in the host country. This sets limits on the voluntary quality of emigrant citizenship for the 54 percent of the Mexican immigrant population without papers in the United States. Authorized immigrants who cannot naturalize in the United States, such as the 374,000 Central Americans under a tenuous "Temporary Protected Status" issued by the U.S. government after natural disasters at home in 1998 and 2001, are in a similar bind.[64]

Historically, dual nationality has been anathema to governments. The nation-state is based on a political philosophy according to which each nation has one state and each individual belongs to only one nation. During the heyday of the model of "perpetual allegiance" in the mid-nineteenth century, national loyalties were expected to be enduring and exclusive. Plural national citizenships have become increasingly common in the postwar era, however, as the decline in wars between countries makes dual loyalties seem less threatening and the mobility of citizens creates substantive ties to more than one country. Countries of emigration such as Turkey, India, the Dominican Republic, Brazil, and El Salvador now *promote* dual nationality among emigrants and even their descendents abroad. In Mexico, the abrupt shift from a 1993 law affirming that nationality should be singular to the 1997 law recognizing dual nationality was one of the primary strategies by the state to embrace emigrant Mexicans. Political figures in Mexico from the president down have encouraged Mexicans in the United States to assimilate into the United States while maintaining their mexicanidad. This shift supports the argument that assimilation and ongoing transborder ties are not mutually exclusive.[65] The effectiveness of Mexicans as an ethnic lobby in the United States requires the ability to function well within the political systems of both countries. Within both sending and receiving states, dual nationality remains contested by conservatives who try to maintain the principle of national exclusivity. Nonetheless, the promotion of a dual nationality that weakens the exclusive bond between national member and state is an institutionally sanctioned and dramatic departure from the ideal typical form of the nation-state.

AN ENDURING FORM OF CITIZENSHIP?

How long can citizenship à la carte be maintained? History gives some surprising answers. Close to a quarter-million second- and third-generation Brazilians of Japanese descent have successfully drawn on their ancestry to gain preferential access to a Japanese labor market that formally has been all but closed to immigration. From 1988 to 1997, 2.2 million ethnic Germans from formerly communist countries such as Kazakhstan were given preferential access to Germany and substantial resettlement benefits. Many of these "resettlers" had only remote ancestral ties to Germany. Several thousand Israelis, either refugees of the Holocaust or descendents of refugees, have acquired German nationality too. Once Poland became a member of the European Union, some Israelis began applying for the Polish nationality of their parents as well. These "rediscovered" Poles and Germans followed an example set by Argentines of Italian and Spanish ancestry at the turn of the twenty-first century, who drew on generous jus sanguinis provisions to escape the economic misfortunes of Argentina for the benefits of living in the European Union. As the sociologist David Cook-Martín has argued, the lagged importance of emigrant citizenship would have been impossible to predict at the moment of migration, particularly in the case of the migration circuit between southern Europe and Argentina, where the relative economic fortunes of the countries of origin and destination flipped between 1960 and the mid-1970s.[66]

The long-term salience of emigrant citizenship is sensitive to economic and political conditions in both source and destination countries. Relationships between emigration and nation building beg to be understood not only for their effects in contemporary countries of origin and destination, but also because the descendants of today's emigrants may return to their ancestral homeland tomorrow. The reconfiguration of a nation-state through emigration is not always a linear process, and it may eventually be reconstituted as a community in a territory sharing a government. Understanding those processes requires a sociology of exit, of absence, and of return—in short, a political sociology of emigration.

In general, though, the voluntaristic quality of emigrant citizenship is a structural limit to its endurance over time and generation abroad. Resident citizenship is reproduced ascriptively as an accident of birth, whereas ties to emigrants and their descendents tend to fade away. When it comes to Latin American immigration to the United States, there is no reason to expect a massive return of migrants or their descendents. Mexicans in the United States have shown minimal interest in acquiring dual nationality, and on the whole, identification with Mexico decreases with length of residence in the United States and between the first and subsequent generations.[67] The substantive practices of emigrant citizenship for the people of Mexico and other Latin American countries may well be limited to the first generation.

Still, the first generation alone is vast: roughly 10 million people, representing a tenth of Mexico's population. That population will continue to be replenished given the two countries' increasing economic integration, the ongoing wage differential, the strength of migrants' social networks, and a shared two-thousand-mile border that is extraordinarily difficult to seal. As a returned migrant creating a directory of Arandenses in the United States for the county government put it:

> If you put up a wall 10 meters high, 10 Mexicans will climb over it.
> If you put up a wall 20 meters high, 20 Mexicans will climb over it.
> If you put up a wall 50 meters high, 50 Mexicans will climb over it.

Try as the nation of immigrants might to fortify the bars of its cage, southern neighbors will still slip through. And the nation of emigrants' leaders will call over the border, pleading with the hijos ausentes to remember Mexico.

APPENDIX   Survey Methodology

In 2003, my two research assistants and I conducted a household-level survey using the standard questionnaire and methodology of the Mexican Migration Project (MMP) in 97 households in Agua Negra representing every inhabited household where a household head or acting head could be contacted after multiple attempts, a random sample of 200 households in Arandas, and a snowball sample with multiple points of entry among 10 Arandense households in Chicago and 10 Arandense households in Orange County, California. The rejection rate was 1 percent in Agua Negra, 6 percent in Arandas, and 5 percent for the snowball sample. We collected migration and labor histories for a total of 317 households, yielding data on 1,503 persons. For the analyses in which the samples were pooled, we weighted the cases by the inverse of the sampling fraction at each of the sites, following the procedure established by

Massey and Espinosa (1997: 941–43). We administered a second questionnaire, the 2003 Los Altos Household Head Survey, about individual attitudes to the head of household, or the acting head of household at the moment the survey was conducted, in the same 317 households surveyed for the MMP.

The 2003 Los Altos Household Head Survey gathered data on attitudes and practices related to migration, politics, and participation in civil society. With the exception of ten households in Orange County and one household in Arandas that I surveyed, all surveys were administered by two MMP-trained Mexican assistants working under my supervision. For details of the MMP methodology and a copy of the questionnaire, see http://mmp.opr.princeton.edu. On the rationale for the MMP and the "ethnosurvey" generally, see the work of Massey and Capoferro (2004).

The characteristics of the individual-level samples drawn from Agua Negra, Arandas, and among Arandenses in California and Illinois are shown in table 1. The major difference between the Jalisco samples is that in Agua Negra, about half the respondents were the wives of the household head, while in Arandas, about three-quarters were wives. In Agua Negra, male heads of household were more likely to be home from the fields in the afternoon, when most of the surveys were conducted. Arandense men were often working away from the home in nonagricultural occupations during the afternoon, so their wives answered in their capacity as acting head of household. The major differences in the Jalisco samples that reflect variation in the real characteristics of the two communities is a lower level of median education and a much higher incidence of migration in Agua Negra.

Massey and Capoferro (2004) found that the eighty-one communities surveyed by the MMP from 1982 to 1997 yielded a sample of migrants that closely matched a nationally representative sample of migrants in the Mexican government's 1997 National Survey of Demographic Dynamics (ENADID), with the exception of region of origin, which in the MMP overrepresents the historic migrant source region of the Central West, and the underrepresentation of rural communities and large metropolitan areas. However, given major changes in the characteristics of Mexico-U.S. migration following the passage of the U.S. Immigration Reform and

Table 1   Characteristics of Agua Negra, Arandas, and Arandenses in California
and Illinois household head samples, 2003

	Agua Negra	Arandas	Arandenses in California and Illinois
MIGRATION STATUS			
Respondent is a migrant	44%	16%	100%
Household has a migrant	78%	44%	100%
RELATIONSHIP TO HOUSEHOLD HEAD			
Household head	65%	38%	75%
Spouse acting as head	33%	61%	20%
Son/daughter acting as head	1%	2%	5%
Other acting as head	1%	0%	0%
SEX			
Male	54%	28%	70%
Female	46%	73%	30%
Median age	49	40	48
EDUCATION			
Fewer than six years of schooling	62%	50%	20%
Six to eight years of schooling	31%	22%	30%
Nine to eleven years of schooling	1%	11%	20%
Twelve or more years of schooling	6%	18%	30%
Median years of schooling	3	6	8.5
RELIGIOSITY			
Attends mass	98%	98%	96%
Median masses in previous month	4	4	1
Mean masses in previous month	7	6.1	3.2
Sampling weight	1.24	59.16	100
N	97	200	20

Table 2   Characteristics of migrants from Arandas, Agua Negra, and the MMP36

Migrant Characteristic	Arandas	Agua Negra	MMP36 Average
Male	83%	73%	72%
Median age	36	37	35
Currently married/free union	78%	78%	80%
Median years of schooling	6	6	6
Median months of U.S. experience	42	90	48
Undocumented on last trip	72%	86%	59%
Unweighted N	167	225	4,475

SOURCE: MMP 1998–2002 PERS File; MMP 2003 Los Altos Survey. Available at Mexican Migration Project, http://mmp.opr.princeton.edu.

Control Act in 1986 and stricter U.S. border enforcement since the mid-1990s (see Massey, Durand, and Malone 2002), I restrict the comparison of Arandas and Agua Negra to the thirty-six communities surveyed by the MMP from 1998 to 2002, which I call the MMP36. The MMP36 yields a representative sample of those thirty-six communities rather than a strictly representative sample of all Mexican migrants, but the diversity of communities chosen and relatively large number of migrant cases on which it gathered data (N=4,475) make it a useful point of comparison. The characteristics of all migrants from Arandas, Agua Negra, and the MMP36 are shown in table 2.

Notes

INTRODUCTION

1. *La Opinión*, "Incidente en la frontera," Jan. 27, 1954.

2. Craig 1971; Cohen 2001.

3. Transactional Records Access Clearinghouse, http://trac.syr.edu/immigration/reports/143, http://trac.syr.edu/immigration/reports/141.

4. United Nations 2007.

5. For a sampling of the postmodern perspectives on globalization and transnationalism, see Appadurai 1991; Kearney 1991; Basch, Schiller, and Blanc 1994; and Urry 2000. Held and McGrew (2000), Levitt and de la Dehesa (2003), and Portes (2003) offer more cautious approaches.

6. Sutherland 2001. See also Huntington 2004 and Buchanan 2006.

7. Massey et al. 1998: 73.

8. The figures in this paragraph are drawn from Zogby and Rubio 2006, IFE 2006, and CONAPO 2006.

9. Taylor 1933: 1. See Taylor 1928–34 for his U.S.-based research. County archives record Taylor's visit to Arandas in a 1931 letter from an Arandense in

Guadalajara to the county president warning that Taylor had been reproducing photographs of roads, hills, and other strategic sites. "This *gringo* is a little suspicious," the letter concludes. AMA P/ 1931.

10. Durand, Massey, and Zenteno (2001) review the geographic origins of Mexican emigrants over the past century. Cornelius (1976) and Massey et al. (1987) conducted the earliest quantitative surveys of multiple migrant source communities in the region, which have continued in the Mexican Migration Project (Massey, Durand, and Malone 2002) and the Mexican Migration Field Research Program (Cornelius, Fitzgerald, and Borger, forthcoming). See Durand 1994 (15–17) for a comprehensive list of earlier Mexican source-community studies and Durand and Massey 1992 for an analytic review. The Colegio de Michoacán continues to publish anthologies of qualitative migration research from the region, including Calvo and López Castro 1988 and López Castro 2003.

11. Haydu 1998. See also Burawoy 2003 for an extended discussion of the methodological value of revisits and Fitzgerald 2006a on revisits in the context of migration studies.

12. See Brubaker 1992, Soysal 1994, and Joppke 1999 for a sampling of the diverse theoretical perspectives within this macro perspective. See Joseph and Nugent 1994 on "everyday forms of state formation" in the Mexican case.

13. See the appendix for a description of the survey methodology.

14. See Massey, Durand, and Malone 2002 for a discussion of the MMP's methodology.

15. The 2000 census found seventy-six thousand residents in the county. Researchers have studied migration from three of its five rural delegations (*delegaciones*). See Cornelius 1976 and Arias and Durand 1997 on Santa María del Valle (pop. 3,582), Orozco 1992 on Los Dolores (pop. 694), and Valenzuela 2002 on San Ignacio Cerro Gordo (pop. 9,496).

16. See Meyer 1976 and González Navarro 2001 for the history of the Cristero War in this region and Taylor 1933 for its effects in Arandas.

17. Taylor 1933: 43.

18. Table 2 in the appendix gives a detailed comparison of the migrant populations of Arandas, Agua Negra, and the MMP36.

19. Martínez Saldaña 1985; Luna Zamora 1990; personal communication with José Hernández López at the Colegio de Michoacán, July 3, 2004.

20. See Grindle 1988.

21. In 1988, Arandas ranked in the 24th percentile ("medium") in a marginalization index in the state of Jalisco. Just twelve years later, it had improved to the 57th percentile. On the national level, the county ranked in the 78th percentile in its overall level of development (CONAPO 2000; INEGI 2000; Enciclopedia de los Municipos de México, www.elocal.gob.mx/work/templates/enciclo/jalisco/mpios/14008a.htm.)

22. Calculated from the 10 percent sample of the 2000 INEGI census.

23. Lindstrom 1996.

24. For a description of such a town in Los Altos with extremely high emigration rates, see Cornelius, Fitzgerald, and Borger forthcoming.

ONE. THE POLITICS OF ABSENCE

1. Morgenthau 1967: 305; Weber 1978: 54; Kratochwil 1986; Brubaker 1992: 2.

2. Brubaker 1992; Joppke 1998; Wimmer 2002.

3. Joppke 2005.

4. See Zolberg 1997 and 2006 on Chinese restriction and creating a nation through immigration in the United States; Joppke 2005 on ethnic-preference immigration policies; and Lesser 1999, Andrews 1980, and Buchenau 2001 on the "whitening" project in Brazil, Argentina, and Mexico, respectively.

5. See Geddes 2003 on the European Union and Dib 1988 on the Persian Gulf.

6. See Fitzgerald 1996 on the United States; Koslowski 2000 on the European Union; and Cornelius et al. 2004 and United Nations 2000 on a wide range of cases in the rich countries of the Global North.

7. Smith and Edmonston 1997, but see Borjas 1999: 121–26.

8. Guiraudon and Joppke 2001: 16–19.

9. Exceptions to the neglect of the politics of emigration include Sayad's (2004) groundbreaking work on Algeria, Schmitter Heisler 1985, Brand 2006, and anthologies by Østergaard-Nielsen (2003) and Green and Weil (2007).

10. United Nations 2003: 47.

11. Godines 2004.

12. The distinction between emigration policy and emigrant policy is adapted from Hammar's (1985) distinction between immigration policies, focusing on levels and kinds of immigration, and immigrant policies, focusing on integration.

13. On the Foucauldian trope of states "embracing" the population through documentation, see Torpey 2000. Brand (2006: 103) describes the Tunisian government's *encadrement* of its emigrants, a similar term implying both a kind of support and political surveillance. On governmentality, see Foucault 2003 [1978]: 244; on state surveillance, see Foucault 1979 and Giddens 1985: 41–49. Brenner (1994) and Fox (1998) critique Foucault's narrow approach to the study of social control that closes off critical lines of investigation for empirically oriented political sociology.

14. See, for example, Sadiq's (2005) work on the Malaysian state's inability to distinguish citizens from noncitizens because of weak documentary controls.

15. Brown 1980; Weiner 1992.

16.   Scott 1998: 1. Although states may themselves be responsible for creating a group's mobility to pursue various ends, that mobility almost always presents administrative challenges.

17.   See Meyer et al. 1997 on the international diffusion of state practices.

18.   On emigrants as a loss of potential soldiers, see Cohen 1988 on Israel; Moya 1998: 20–21 on Spain; Cannistraro and Rosoli 1979 on Italy; and Dowty 1987: 206–7 on Yugoslavia.

19.   Zolberg 2007.

20.   Johnson 2005: 2. On the brain drain, see Kapur and McHale 2005 for an empirical analysis and Johnson 2005: 2 for a typical editorial against the drain.

21.   See Petras 1981 on the world systems approach to international migration theory, which draws heavily on Wallerstein's (1974) work on the relationship between core and peripheral states in the world economy. The quote is taken from Louie 2001: 12.

22.   See Weber 1946: 280 on "ideal interests" that can be as powerful as material interests.

23.   Mann 1993: 59–61.

24.   Sayad 2004: 83, emphasis in original. In contexts of ethnic cleansing, emigration is not a problem from the perspective of the government of the country of origin. The absent population was expelled from the territory precisely because it did not belong to the victor's vision of the nation. Such brutal nationalizing projects have generated massive expulsions of refugees, from the population exchanges between Turkey and Greece in the 1920s to the civil wars in Rwanda and the former Yugoslavia in the 1990s (Zolberg, Suhrke, and Aguayo 1989; Wimmer et al. 2004). For states seeking to build a sense of nation from disparate elements, the problem of denationalization through emigration remains.

25.   See Deutsch 1966: 94 on nationalization.

26.   See Moya 1998 on Spain; Cinel 1991 on Italy; Guarnizo 1997 on the Dominican Republic; Sayad 2004 on Algeria; and chapter 5, this volume, on Mexico.

27.   Mann 1993.

28.   Johnston 1972.

29.   See Basch, Schiller, and Blanc 1994, Østergaard-Nielsen 2003, and Green and Weil 2007 on a wide range of countries of emigration.

30.   Thunø and Pieke 2005: 507. See also Olesen 2002.

31.   For a review of these debates, see Massey et al. 1998: 222–43 and International Bank for Reconstruction and Development 2006.

32.   Shain 1999; de la Garza et al. 2000; Sheffer 2003.

33.   Østergaard-Nielsen 2003.

34.   Held and McGrew 2000: 105.

35.   Castles and Davidson 2000: 6.

36. Held and McGrew 2000: ch. 1; Geddes 2003. Within the EU, restrictions on the movement of nationals of the "A8" countries that joined the EU in May 2004 vary among the fifteen other member states. These barriers must be dropped altogether by 2011 (*Migration News* 2007).

37. Soysal 1994; Jacobson 1996.

38. Massey et al. 1998: 290; Cornelius et al. 2004.

39. Sassen (1998: 5) interprets loss of state control over cross-border movements as a loss of sovereignty. I restrict my use of sovereignty to the Westphalian sense of each state's autonomy from the others and will discuss the state's variable ability to control cross-border movements of people as one aspect of "state capacity," or the ability of a government to enforce its policies.

40. On deterritorialization, see Basch, Schiller, and Blanc 1994; Appadurai 1991; Kearney 1995; Jacobson 1996: 126; Laguerre 1998; Sherman 1999; and Tsuda 2003. For a critique of the transnationalism literature, see Waldinger and Fitzgerald 2004 and a response by Glick Schiller and Levitt (2006).

41. Krasner 1995; Zolberg 1999.

42. Hansen and Weil 2001.

43. See Smith 1990: 11 on ethnic versus territorial nationhood in Latin America generally and Fitzgerald 2005 on Mexico specifically.

44. See Basch, Schiller, and Blanc 1994: 1 on Haiti and Shain 1999: 55 on Poland.

45. Brenner 1999.

46. Ruggie 1993: 165.

47. Spiro 2002; Pastore 2001; Aleinikoff and Klusmeyer 2001.

48. Renshon 2000: 4.

49. Martin 2002; Aleinikoff and Klusmeyer 2001.

50. Fitzgerald 2005.

51. Corchado 1995.

52. González Gutiérrez 1999.

53. Jones-Correa 2000.

54. On the concept of "pastoral power," see Foucault 2003 [1979]: 183 and 2003 [1982]: 131-33.

55. Mann 1993: 7-9.

56. Fitzgerald 2006b.

TWO. INSIDE THE SENDING STATE

1. Zolberg 2007. See Hannum 1987 for a detailed discussion of the right to leave in law and actual practice around the world.

2. Santibáñez 1991 [1930]: 86; Fabila 1991 [1932]: 50.

3. Loyo 1935; Buchenau 2001.

4. Knight 1987: 1–2.

5. González Navarro 1994: 253.

6. AHJ G-8–1904. All translations are the author's.

7. AHJ G-8–1909, 1910, 1911.

8. AHJ G-8–1910; *El Informador*, Sept. 1, 1918.

9. Constitución Federal de los Estados Unidos Mexicanos, 1857, www .juridicas.unam.mx/infjur/leg/conhist/pdf/1857.pdf.

10. Constitución Política de los Estados Unidos Mexicanos, 1917, http://pdba .georgetown.edu/Constitutions/Mexico/mexico1917.html.

11. The 1885 U.S. ban on contracted labor was ostensibly to prevent indentured servitude, but in practice was part of a general restrictionist effort (Zolberg 2006).

12. Reisler 1976.

13. Cardoso (1980) estimated an exodus of 1 million. U.S. authorities recorded 220,000 legal entries from 1910 to 1920 (Bean and Stevens 2003: 55).

14. Alanís Enciso 1999; Aguila 2000.

15. AHJ G-8–1923; Reisler 1976; Alanís Enciso 1999 and 2003.

16. Secretaría de Gobernación 1996: 24.

17. AHJ, *Informe a la Legislatura de Gral. Manuel M. Diéguez, Gobernador*, 1919; Clark 1908: 513–14; Corwin 1978.

18. Martínez 1972 [1957]: 48. See González 1999: 27–36 for a review of the historiographic debates over the extent to which Mexican elites saw emigration as an escape valve or a bleeding of the nation.

19. On migration rates, see Gamio 1930. On the Cristero War, see Meyer 1976.

20. AMA P/ Apr., May 1927; Meyer 1976.

21. Taylor 1933; Krauze 1997; González Navarro 1994.

22. AHJ G-8–1919, 1925; AMA P/ 1929.

23. Taylor 1933; González Navarro 2001.

24. Cardoso 1980; Secretaría de Gobernación 1996.

25. Meyer 1976.

26. AMA P/ 1932, Sept. 1933, Apr. 1934, July 1934.

27. See Craig 1983.

28. In 1940, 73 percent of the men and 85 percent of the women in the ranches around Agua Negra were illiterate. The illiteracy rate in the county seat was 15 percent for both men and women (AMA P/ 1945).

29. Quotes are taken from PSTP, Series 2, Ctn. 1, Field Notes 1: 18, Book 1, Oct. 18–Nov. 8, 1931, and Taylor 1933: 54, clarification in the original text.

30. For political histories of Arandas, see Martínez Saldaña 1976 and del Castillo Vera 1979.

31. Durand and Massey 1992.

32. AHJ AG-1–1911; Aguila 2000.

33. Alanís Enciso 2003.

34. AMA P/ 1932.

35. AMA P/ 1932. Although Mexico encouraged the repatriation of laborers, hundreds of political exiles were denied permission to return (García y Griego and Alanís Enciso 2003). As in the Soviet Union and other cases, the government distinguished between labor emigrants and political dissidents, trying to keep the former in and the latter out (Dowty 1987).

36. Cárdenas 1934.

37. Carreras de Velasco 1974.

38. AMA P/ Oct. 1940, Sept. 1941.

39. García y Griego 1983; Cohen 2001.

40. See Morales 1989; Knight 1987.

41. AMA P/ May 1948.

42. AMA P/ Jan. 1954.

43. Craig 1971; Cohen 2001.

44. Lázaro Salinas 1955; Craig 1971; de la Garza and Szekely 1997.

45. AMA P/ Aug. 1943, Mar. 1944.

46. AHJ, *Informe a la Legislatura de Gral. Marcelino García Barragán, Gobernador,* 1945.

47. Hancock 1959; González Navarro 1994.

48. AMA P/ July 1951, Apr. 1953, July 1963; Hancock 1959.

49. AMA P/ May 1948–1952.

50. Craig 1971: 134. See also Spener 2005.

51. Secretaría del Trabajo 1946.

52. AMA P/ Mar. 1951, Sept. 1951, Feb. 1952, May 1953, Mar. 1953, May 1961.

53. Clark 1908: 513; AHJ T-1–920–925; AMA P/ Aug. 1935.

54. AMA P/ Mar. 1953.

55. Reisler 1976.

56. AMA P/ May 1959.

57. Hancock 1959; González Navarro 1994; AMA P/ Mar. 1953.

58. Corwin 1978; Rico 1992; Secretaría de Gobernación 1996; de la Garza and Szekely 1997.

59. Massey, Durand, and Malone 2002.

60. Martínez Saldaña 1993.

61. The earliest demand for the absentee ballot in Mexican elections came from the opposition leader José Vasconcelos, who campaigned among Mexicans in the United States for the Mexican presidency in 1928. The proposal lay dormant until the 1990s (Fitzgerald 2004b).

62. *Plan Nacional de Desarrollo 1995–2000.*

63. A *paisano* is a compatriot at the national level, as well as someone from the same town.

64. Fitzgerald 2005.

65. Smith 2006.

66. On emigration policy since 1989, see Fitzgerald 2004b and Godoy's (1998) analysis of Mexican congressional debates. Intensive Mexican government ties with Mexicans in the United States have precedent in the 1920s, when Mexican consulates organized unions, social assistance, and Mexican patriotic organizations among the Mexican and Mexican American populations (see Gutiérrez González 1999). These organizing efforts faded when Mexican government policy turned to repatriation in the 1930s, and they never reached the level of institutionalization or prominence in Mexican politics of contemporary agencies such as the IME.

67. www_chambanet_gob_mx.htm. *Chamba* is slang for "work."

68. Lowell and Findlay 2001; Licea de Arenas et al. 2003; Docquier and Marfouk 2005. The three largest source countries of university-educated migrants in the OECD are the United Kingdom, the Philippines, and India.

69. Associated Press 2001a, 2001b; *Migration News* 2001b.

70. Instituto Nacional de Migración, www.inami.gob.mx.

71. Secretaría de Gobernación 1996.

72. *Migration News* 2001a.

73. Rosenblum 2004.

74. Moctezuma Langoria 2003.

75. Archivo de la Dirección de Asuntos Internacionales, Gobierno de Jalisco, 1995–2004 (ADAI).

76. ADAI, 1995–2004; author interviews with Jalisco state officials, 2004.

77. See Torpey 2000 on this process in the European context.

78. AHJ G-8–1904, 1919; AHJ G-1–1920; AMA P/ Apr. 1953.

79. Knight 2001.

80. See Durand and Massey 1992 and Cornelius 1998 for a discussion of other ways that the agrarian reform spurred more emigration.

81. Grindle 1988.

82. Bean and Stevens 2003.

83. See Keohane and Nye 1987 on asymmetric interdependency as a more subtle acknowledgment of unequal international relationships than simple "dependency."

84. Zolberg 2006: 21.

85. See Massey et al. 1998.

86. DeSipio and de la Garza 1998; Suro and Escobar 2006.

THREE. THE CHURCH'S EYE ON ITS FLOCK

Epigraphs: Agustín Yañez, *Al filo del agua* (1947; Mexico City: Editorial Porrúa, 1971), 151. "¿Quién es más pobre que un migrante que no tiene ni siquiera una casa, que no está cerca de su familia?," *Migrantes* (51), Jan.–Feb. 1988.

1.   Toribio is the functional equivalent of the Virgin of San Juan de los Lagos. Hundreds of thousands of pilgrims from Mexico and the United States visit the cathedral dedicated to her each year to give thanks and ask for all manner of favors, including matters related to migration (Durand and Massey 1995). Santa Ana is only a half-hour drive from San Juan de los Lagos, facilitating a religious tourism package in which busloads of pilgrims visit both sites on the same day. An informal saint, Juan Soldado, is also venerated by many migrants, who pray at his shrine in the border city of Tijuana before crossing (Vanderwood 2004).

2.   AAG, ¡Vámonos p'al norte! (1920: n.p.), 2–9.

3.   The linguistic model is more common in empires where different language groups share the same territory.

4.   Caliaro and Francesconi 1977.

5.   See Vallier 1971; Dolan 1975; Perotti 1997; and Dolan and Hinojosa 1994.

6.   Quirk 1973: 7.

7.   Turner 1968.

8.   Turner 1967; Quirk 1973; Camp 1997.

9.   INEGI 2000.

10.   Survey data on religious practices in Arandas are based on my 2003 Los Altos Household Head Survey (see appendix). Census figures are from INEGI 2000.

11.   Weber 1978: 54–56.

12.   Herberg 1960; Warner 1993. To continue Weber's (1978: 54–56) distinction, the Catholic Church in the United States is much more like a "sect" than a "church" in the strictly sociological sense.

13.   La Época, Sept. 12, 1920.

14.   Some five hundred clergy, including ten bishops, attended the session on emigration. The main presentation was officially sanctioned by José Garibi y Rivera, who would become the archbishop of Guadalajara in 1936 and then leader of the Mexican episcopate between 1960 and 1963 (Curso Social Agrícola Zapopano, 1921).

15.   Curso Social Agrícola Zapopano, 1921: 229–32.

16.   La Época, Sept. 12, 1920.

17.   Taylor 1933: 54.

18.   Curso Social Agrícola Zapopano, 1921: 231.

19.   Curso Social Agrícola Zapopano, 1921: 230.

20.   Curso Social Agrícola Zapopano, 1921: 231.

21.   See Alba and Nee 2003.

22.   Taylor 1933: 58.

23.   See also Gamio 1930 and Monroy 1999.

24.   PSTP, Series 2, Ctn. 1, Field Notes 1: 22, 1931–1932.

25.   While U.S.-bound migration presented a special challenge for the Mexican clergy because of the Protestantism and extreme heterogeneity of the United

States, the Church considered domestic urbanization to be a threat as well, though a weaker one. In contrast to the piety of small towns in Mexico, "in big cities, and I don't refer to the big cities of the United States here, but to our big cities, we enter a current of complete indifference" that creates religious doubt (*Curso Social Agrícola Zapopano*, 1921: 233).

26. AAG, Gobierno/Parroquia/Arandas, July 13, 1912.

27. See Craig 1983.

28. APSJL, *Libro de Gobierno*, July 6, 1920.

29. *Curso Social Agrícola Zapopano*, 1921: 233–34.

30. *Curso Social Agrícola Zapopano*, 1921: 241.

31. *La Época*, Sept. 12, 1920.

32. AAG, Gobierno/Parroquia/Arandas, Aug. 9, 1921.

33. Pope Pius X in 1912 had ordered the coordination of this sort of information between source and destination dioceses to avoid Protestant and socialist inroads among Italian migrants (Tessarolo 1962).

34. AAG, CEM, 1929.

35. Dolan and Hinojosa 1994.

36. *Firmissimam constantiam* (March 28, 1937), *Acta Apostolicae Sedis*, 29, 189–99.

37. AAG, CEM, 1939.

38. Dolan and Hinojosa 1994; Camp 1997; Espinosa 1998.

39. At least since 1921, Arandenses in the United States had returned for the fiesta, where they spent the savings they had earned after six months to a year working in the United States (*El Informador*, Jan. 22, 1921).

40. "Sección de Acción Católica: La Cuestión de los Emigrados," *Boletín Eclesiástico*, July 22, 1944.

41. *El Arandense*, n.d. 1947.

42. AAG, Gobierno/Parroquia/Arandas, May 10, 1951.

43. Reilly 1969. The bracero population is drawn from García y Griego 1988.

44. AAG, CEM, 1960. Based on interviews in Los Altos, Espinosa (1999) suggests that some priests even encouraged poor men to participate in the bracero program so they could help finance Church projects.

45. Internal migration to northern border regions to work in *maquiladoras* (inbond manufacturing plants created as a putative alternative to the bracero program) and related commuter migration across the border led to a renewed interest in a domestic migrant policy as well (AAG, CEM, 1968).

46. Zizzamia 1989; Espinosa 1999.

47. United States Conference of Catholic Bishops, www.nccbuscc.org/mrs/stranger.shtml#1.

48. AAG, CEM, 1968. The Vatican's 1969 "De Pastorali Migratorum Cura" also warned of the brain drain problem for underdeveloped countries.

49. *Migrantes* (25–29), June–Nov. 1985.

50. "Subsidios para una pastoral de migrantes," n.d., Pastoral Social, Departamento de Migrantes, Diócesis de San Juan de los Lagos, Jalisco.

51. The gender of *hijos ausentes* is ambiguous in Spanish and can refer to either absent children or absent sons.

52. "Carta de Mons. J. Trinidad Sepúlveda Ruíz Velasco a los Católicos de San Juan de los Lagos que viven y trabajan en los Estados Unidos," 1988 (letter in author's possession).

53. Independent studies have found that the few non-Catholics who live in Los Altos often converted to other faiths while they were working in the United States. Mormons founded their first church in Los Altos in Lagos de Moreno in 1977, though missionary work was initially suspended after two missionaries were found in a ditch shot dead. A Protestant convert who returned to the county of Unión de San Antonio was expelled violently when he began proselytizing. Despite this hostility to religious outsiders, by the mid-1990s there were 290 Jehovah's Witnesses in five congregations in Los Altos and other evangelical groups of roughly a dozen members each. There is evidence of small-scale Protestant conversion among returned migrants in the neighboring states of Michoacán and Zacatecas (Hernández Madrid 1999).

54. Camp 1997; Hernández Madrid 2003.

55. APSJL, *Boletín de Pastoral* (53) 1986.

56. "Los migrantes y el plan diocesano de pastoral," *Migrantes* (53), Apr. 1988.

57. APSJL, *Boletín de Pastoral* (42) 1986.

58. AAG, CEM, 1960; Espinosa 1998.

59. See Hagan and Ebaugh 2003 and Levitt 2003 on how migrants draw on religion to legitimate their migration decisions.

60. "Subsidios para una pastoral de migrantes," n.d., Pastoral Social, Departamento de Migrantes, Diócesis de San Juan de los Lagos, Jalisco.

61. Field Notes, Oct. 30, 2003.

62. See Massey, Durand, and Malone 2002.

63. AAG, CEM, 1968.

64. Durand (1994) reports other cases of priests crossing the border illegally when they were denied permission to go north by their bishop.

65. *El Mensajero Guadalupano*, Jan. 16, 2000; interview with club leaders, 2003.

66. Editorial, *Migrantes* (13), Apr. 1984. Douglass (1984) describes similar fund-raising by Italian parish priests visiting *paesani* in Canada.

67. In other circumstances, the Vatican has expressed concern that priests may emigrate to richer countries for economic motives, and it banned the practice in 1912 (Tessarolo 1962).

68. "Subsidios para una pastoral de migrantes," n.d., Pastoral Social, Departamento de Migrantes, Diócesis de San Juan de los Lagos, Jalisco.

69. Espinosa 1999.

70. One of the purposes of the Day of the Emigrant was a special collection to be sent to Rome for the global emigrant ministry (*Boletín Eclesiástico* 1961, 197). In later formulas, 70 percent of the collection was kept for the national emigrant ministry, and 30 percent was sent to the Vatican for redistribution to poorer regions. Mexican parishes participated in this universal collection (AAG, Gobierno/Parroquia/Arandas, Dec. 27, 1966). See also instructions on the Day of the Emigrant in APSJL, *Boletín de Pastoral* (53) 1986.

71. "Los migrantes y el plan diocesano de pastoral," *Migrantes* (53), Apr. 1988.

72. "Sección de Acción Católica: La Cuestión de los Emigrados," *Boletín Eclesiástico*, July 22, 1944.

73. AVAN, *Libro de Gobierno,* 1997.

74. Torpey 2000: 11.

75. Tessarolo 1962; Caliaro and Francesconi 1977.

76. Evidence from this paragraph is drawn from APA, Libros de Gobierno, June 28, 1933; AAG, CEM, 1939; APA, Libros de Gobierno, Oct. 15, 1951; APA, *Libro de Correspondencia,* Mar. 5, 1956; and AAG, Gobierno/Parroquia/Arandas, Jan. 3, 1954.

77. According to census takers, the vicariate also conducted the 2002 census to determine Agua Negra's eligibility to become a parish, which requires a minimum population of five thousand. Absent migrants were included in the total population because the vicariate considers them part of the local religious community, and Agua Negra became a quasi-parish in 2003. Counting absentees for the purposes of Church administration districts is strikingly similar to demands by a successful social movement in San Ignacio Cerro Gordo, in the *municipio* of Arandas, to secede based on the large numbers of Sanignacienses in the United States, as described in chapter 4.

78. Field Notes, Jan. 12, 2004.

79. Marcelli and Cornelius 2001.

80. Higham 1994.

81. Odem 2004.

82. Christiansen 1996; Hondagneu-Sotelo et al. 2004.

83. Programa Paisano, www.paisano.gob.mx.

84. U.S. Citizenship and Immigration Services, www.uscis.gov/graphics/shared/aboutus/statistics/msrsep03/SWBORD.HTM.

85. Castles and Miller 1998: 97–98.

86. United States Conference of Catholic Bishops, www.nccbuscc.org/mrs/stranger.shtml#1.

87. See Scott 1998: 79 and Loveman 2005: 1662 for other instances of state imitation of nonstate institutions in their administration of populations.

88. Ruggie 1993: 165.

89. Vallier 1971.

FOUR. COLONIES OF THE LITTLE
MOTHERLAND

1. The names of club leaders are pseudonyms.

2. Basch, Schiller, and Blanc 1994; Smith 1994; Levitt 2001; Portes and Landolt 2002; Smith 2006.

3. I use the term "transborder" rather than "transnational" HTA to emphasize that such associations are formed across the geographic and administrative borders of states, even if they include people who claim to belong to one imagined nation transcending the state border. For comparative examples of domestic HTAs, see Moch 2004 on France, Ottenberg 1955 on Cameroon, Jongkind 1974 on Peru, Abu-Lughod 1961 on Egypt, Armentrout Ma 1984 on China, and Skeldon 1980 on Papua New Guinea.

4. Taylor 1933; Winnie 1984. The account of the domestic HTAs is based on a review of three HTA newspapers published at various periods from the 1940s to the 1980s; interviews with former and current HTA members from Guadalajara, León, and Mexico City; Catholic Church archives in Arandas and Guadalajara; and participant observation of HTA-related events in Arandas and Guadalajara. The history of the transborder HTAs is drawn from interviews with current and former leaders in Arandas and southern California, three Arandense newspapers published during the 1990s, and participant observation of HTA-related events in Arandas. The account of relations between the government of Jalisco and Jalisciense HTAs in the United States is based on research in the archives of the Jalisco state Office of Attention to Jaliscienses Abroad from 1996 to 2004 and interviews with Jalisco state officials and HTA leaders in southern California.

5. Internal migration is defined here as a change in residence from one Mexican county to another.

6. AAG, Gobierno/Parroquia/Arandas, Apr. 14, 1945.

7. *El Arandense* 2(18), June 1947.

8. *El Arandense* 1(12), Dec. 1946.

9. Domestic migrants have been influential intermediaries between the national center and periphery in Oaxaca as well (Hirabayashi 1993).

10. *El Arandense* 1(10), 1946; *El Arandense*, n.d.

11. Díaz-Cayeros 1995: 82.

12. Taylor 1933: 41.

13. Lanly and Valenzuela 2004; *Migration News* 2006.

14. Suro 2005. The matrícula consular is an identification document issued by Mexican consulates to their nationals in the United States.

15. *Migration News* 2006.

16. Fitzgerald 2000; Goldring 2002; Smith 2006.

17. The PAN has been active in Arandas since the 1940s. It won six out of the seven elections for county president between 1988 and 2006.

18. Mexican Migration Project, 2003 MMP Los Altos Survey, http.//mmp.opr .princeton.edu.

19. The account of the secessionist movement is drawn from interviews with movement leaders, politicians, and journalists in Arandas and San Ignacio; government and secessionist committee publications; and a University of Guadalajara study (Valenzuela 2002).

20. *Periódico Oficial,* Estado de Jalisco, Dec. 30, 2003, No. 32, Section 9, pp. 20–22.

21. Massey, Durand, and Malone 2002.

22. Valenzuela 2002.

23. See Rodríguez 1997.

24. A similar process occurred in Peru, where the domestic HTAs that were once important liaisons between village governments and Lima lost their importance as the national government strengthened its provincial presence (Roberts 1974).

25. Smith 2006.

26. Deutsch, 1966: 94.

27. Moya 2005.

28. See Massey et al. 1987.

29. Appadurai 1991; Smith 1994; Basch, Schiller, and Blanc 1994.

30. *El Arandense,* vol. 5, February 1950.

31. Cf. Kearney and Besserer 2004 on indigenous villages in Oaxaca with transborder HTAs that are critical channels for local development.

32. Smith 2006.

33. Orellana and Carlos 1973; Hirabayashi 1986.

34. See Kane 2002 on Senegalese HTAs.

FIVE. THE STRANGER OR THE PRODIGAL SON?

1. See Orozco 1998.

2. Cf. Durkheim 1995 [1912]: 208.

3. Reese 2001: 464.

4. Jiménez and Fitzgerald, 2008.

5. Hobsbawm and Ranger 1992.

6. Zolberg (1981) identifies weighing the economic benefits and cultural costs of international migration as one of the main dilemmas for countries of immigration as well.

7. See Reese 2001.

8. Zogby and Rubio 2006.

9. Centeno 1997, 2002: 213; Knight 1992: 128.

10. Sacks 1992: 41; Rumelhart 1980: 34.

11. Secretaría del Trabajo 1946: 70.

12. "Se volcó por manejar borracho," 7 *Días*, May 17, 2003.

13. Sacks 1992.

14. See Sayad 2004 for a similar account of reckless returnee driving in Algeria.

15. Uribe Salas and Ochoa Serrano 1990.

16. On the other hand, several Arandense officials said in interviews that delinquency would be even greater were migration not available as a safety valve for the poor.

17. Secretaría del Trabajo 1946.

18. ADAI 2003.

19. *El Arandense* 1(1), Sept. 1986, p. 10.

20. ADAI 2003.

21. Intermittent community protests since the 1930s have prompted the government to close the brothels downtown.

22. The fear of American police intervention in family life and the sense that this unjustly gives power to children over their parents is common in the history of immigration to the United States across time, immigrant group, and destination cities (e.g., Thomas and Znaniecki 1927; Kibria 1993; Levitt 2001).

23. See Fitzgerald 2000 and Smith 2006: 11–12 for a discussion of the tension between efforts to exclude and include emigrants in the community.

24. 2003 Los Altos Household Head Survey (see appendix). The acceptance of migrants in these two historic source communities contrasts with the negative impression of migrants in a 1997 survey in Mexico City, in which 47 percent of respondents said they had a "negative or very negative" impression of Mexicans who go to work in the United States (González Gutiérrez 1998). The difference between Mexico City and Los Altos is probably due to much less personal exposure to U.S.-bound migration among residents of Mexico City and a political culture more generally suspicious of the United States.

25. A similar pattern is seen in views about whether migrants should have the right to vote in Mexican presidential elections by absentee ballot. Seventy-five percent of the sample supported the right to vote from abroad, including 71 percent of nonmigrants, but nonmigrants were three times more likely than migrants to oppose it.

26. Taylor 1933: 54.

27. Balistreri and Van Hook 2004: 121.

28. The historical fact of the customs' origins in Europe is irrelevant here, since from the perspective of Los Altos de Jalisco, they are national U.S. or Mexican customs.

29. "Santa Claus Debería Desaparecer," *El Arandense*, Dec. 25, 1993, p. 1; "Halloween," *Notiarandas*, Nov. 8, 1990, p. 4; *Notiarandas*, Nov. 14, 1990.

30. See N. Gutiérrez 1999: 149–51.

31. Paz 1961 [1950]: 14.

32. See Wimmer 2005 and Reese 2001. In popular usage, *norteamericano* refers to someone from the United States, not the entire continent of North America.

33. *Gabachos* is a pejorative term for "Anglos" in the United States.

34. Alba and Nee 2003.

35. PSTP, Series 2, Ctn. 1, Field Notes 1: 22, 1931–1932.

36. Field Notes, Jan. 11, 2004.

37. See also de la Garza et al. 2000: 62–63.

38. For similar accounts of class resentments among source community elites, see Douglass 1984 on Italy, Guarnizo 1997 on the Dominican Republic, Mahler 1995 on El Salvador, and Sayad 2004 on Algeria.

39. *El Mensajero Guadalupano,* May 27, 2001.

40. See Weber's (1978) classic account of schools as a nationalizing institution in France and Vázquez's (1975) analysis of Mexico.

41. Martínez de Alva 1934: 306–9.

42. Avila 2006. See also Brimelow 1996: 194.

43. The 4.5 million figure inflates the state government's usual statistic of approximately 3 million Jaliscienses in the United States.

44. See Clark 1908; Gamio 1930; Taylor 1933; and Gilbert 1934.

45. Secretaría del Trabajo 1946.

46. See Alarcón et al. 1990.

47. PSTP, Series 2, Ctn 1, Field Notes 1: 22, 1931–1932.

48. See Thompson 1989.

49. Clark 1908: 517.

50. Piore 1979.

51. Simmel 1971 [1908].

CONCLUSION

1. Buchanan 2006: 128.

2. Spiro 2005: 163. Between 1961 and 1965, five thousand people lost their U.S. citizenship as a result of foreign voting (Spiro 2005).

3. See Tilly 1975 for a classical account of critical domains of nation and state building.

4. Uribe Salas and Ochoa Serrano 1990; AMA P/July 1935, Aug. 1947, Aug. 1960.

5. Secretariat of Foreign Relations May 12, 2004, available at portal. sre.gob.mx/eua/pdf/ExtFactsheet.pdf.

6. Deflem 2000; Magaloni and Zepeda 2004: 181; López Portillo Vargas 2002: 123; Zepeda Lecuona 2004: 13.

7. See Arana 2005 on return migrant gangs, Smith 2006 on Puebla, and Magaloni and Zepeda 2004: 181 for a comparison of policing efficiency in Chiapas and the rest of Mexico.

8. Cornelius 2005: 780.

9. Cornelius 2001; McDonald 2002.

10. Genschel 2005.

11. Adelman and Taylor 1990.

12. Hancock 1959: 2; Banco de México, www.banxico.org.mx/SieInternet/consultarDirectorioInternetAction.do?accion=consultarCuadro&idCuadro=CE81&locale=es; Suro 2003.

13. Instituto Nacional de Estadística Geografía e Informática, www.inegi.gob.mx/est/contenidos/espanol/cuestionarios/censos/cgpyv2000basico.pdf.

14. SRE 2004. A 2005 survey of migrants soliciting the matrícula found that 75 to 80 percent were unauthorized (Suro 2005).

15. *Migration News* 2003, 2005.

16. Seif 2003; Fitzgerald 2005; *Migration News* 2005.

17. Verduzco and Unger 1998.

18. González Gutiérrez 1997: 60.

19. See Lozoya 1970 and Rath 2003 on the history of Mexican conscription.

20. This account is based on a review of Arandas municipal archives from 1942 to 1964.

21. ADAI, Apr. 2001.

22. Lozoya 1970; Camp 1992; IISS 2001; Centeno 2002: 225.

23. Zolberg 1999. See also Scott 1985: 245 on the relatively open borders of Southeast Asia as a deterrent to the extreme concentration of state power.

24. Fitzgerald 2004b.

25. See Martínez Saldaña and Ross Pineda 2002 on the history of changes in constitutional and election law relating to citizens abroad.

26. Fitzgerald 2004b.

27. IFE 2006.

28. Suro and Escobar 2006; IFE 2006.

29. Fábregas 1986.

30. De la Garza 1997: 82. The rest of this paragraph is drawn from de la Garza and Velasco's (1997) edited collection; Gómez-Quiñones 1983; Santamaría Gómez 1994; and Martínez Saldaña and Ross Pineda 2002.

31. Fitzgerald 2005.

32. De la Garza and DeSipio 1998.

33. Uhlaner 1996.
34. De la Garza 1997: 83.
35. De la Garza and DeSipio 1998.
36. González Gutiérrez 1995.
37. De la Garza and DeSipio 1998; Suro and Escobar 2006.
38. Brubaker 1992.
39. Basch, Schiller, and Blanc 1994: 7.
40. Sherman 1999: 869.
41. Brubaker 1998: 300.
42. See Turner 1968: 38–41.
43. For a sampling of this literature, see Østergaard-Nielsen's (2003) edited volume on India, Cyprus, Turkey, the Philippines, Armenia, and Eritrea; Cook-Martín 2006 on Spain and Italy; Itzigsohn 2000 on Haiti, the Dominican Republic, and El Salvador; Brand 2006 on Morocco, Tunisia, and Jordan; and Nyíri 2001 on China.
44. Schmitter Heisler 1985.
45. Østergaard-Nielsen 2003.
46. Itzigsohn et al. 1999.
47. Cook-Martín and Viladrich forthcoming.
48. Hugo 2006.
49. Cohen 1988: 909; Gold 2007.
50. See Heleniak 2004 on Russia, Cannistraro and Rosoli 1979 on Italy, and Joppke 2005 on Spain.
51. Anderson 1998; Fitzgerald 2004a.
52. See Barry 2006.
53. See Loveman's (2005) Bourdieu-inspired interpretation of the Brazilian state's imposition of the census as an exercise in symbolic power. When symbolic power is wielded successfully, citizens' cooperation with the state becomes part of their internalized dispositions, or habitus.
54. Mann 1993: 7–9.
55. Fitzgerald 2006b.
56. Barry 2006: 22.
57. Constitution of the Philippines (1987), Art. 13; Constitution of Spain, Art. 42 (1978).
58. Hannum 1987.
59. Hammar 1989.
60. Sandel 1998.
61. See Brand 2006 and Østergaard-Nielsen 2003.
62. Fitzgerald 2004a. On the "flexible citizenship" of ethnic Chinese elites who collect passports from multiple countries, see Ong 1999.
63. See Oishi 2005.

64.   The immigration figures are drawn from Passel 2004 and Davy 2006.

65.   Levitt 2001; Fitzgerald 2004a; Smith 2006.

66.   See Tsuda 2003 on Japan; Joppke 2005 on Germany; Segev 2005 on Israel; and Cook-Martín and Viladrich forthcoming on Argentina.

67.   An important exception to the pattern of decreasing interest in Mexican politics over time within the first generation is the fact that most Mexican civic hometown associations are led by long-time residents of the United States. Survey evidence from Salvadorans, Dominicans, and Colombians in the United States suggests the same holds true for a core of transborder activists in those cases. See de la Garza and DeSipio 1998 on Mexicans; Guarnizo, Portes, and Haller 2003 on Salvadorans, Dominicans, and Colombians; and Portes, Escobar, and Radford 2007 on Colombian, Dominican, and Mexican immigrant "transnational" associations.

Bibliography

NEWSPAPERS

Antorcha (Guadalajara, 1977–82)
Arandas (Arandas, 1971–72)
El Arandense (Arandas, 1986–2003)
El Arandense (Mexico City, 1946–51)
Boletín Eclesiástico (Guadalajara, 1951–86)
La Época (Guadalajara, 1918–21)
El Informador (Guadalajara, 1917–22)
El Mensajero Guadalupano (Arandas, 1992–2003)
Migrantes (Guadalajara, 1983–89)
Notiarandas (Arandas, 1992–2003)
Provincia (Mexico City, 1966–67)

ARCHIVES

AAG   Archivo de la Arquidiócesis de Guadalajara
ADAI   Archivo de la Direccíon de Asuntos Internacionales, Gobierno de Jalisco
AHJ   Archivo Histórico de Jalisco
AMA   Archivo Municipal de Arandas
APA   Archivo de la Parroquia de Santa María de Guadalupe, Arandas
APSJL   Archivo de la Parroquia de San Juan de los Lagos
AVAN   Archivo de la Vicaría de Agua Negra
PSTP   Paul Schuster Taylor Papers, University of California, Berkeley, Bancroft Library

SECONDARY SOURCES

Abu-Lughod, Janet.
 1961.   "Migrant Adjustment to City Life: The Egyptian Case." *American Journal of Sociology* 67(1): 22–32.
Adelman, Irma, and J. Edward Taylor.
 1990.   "Is Structural Adjustment with a Human Face Possible? The Case of Mexico." *Journal of Development Studies* 26(3): 387–407.
Aguila, Jaime R.
 2000.   "Protecting 'México de Afuera': Mexican Emigration Policy, 1876–1928." Unpublished PhD dissertation, Arizona State University.
Alanís Enciso, Fernando S.
 1999.   *El Primer Programa Bracero y el Gobierno de México, 1917–1918.* San Luis Potosí: Colegio de San Luis.
———.
 2003.   "No cuenten conmigo: La política de repatriación del gobierno mexicano y sus nacionales en Estados Unidos, 1910–1928." *Mexican Studies* 19(2): 401–61.
Alarcón, Rafael, Macrina Cárdenas, Germán Vega, and Rebeca Moreno.
 1990.   "Las debilidades del poder: Oligarquías y opciones políticas en Los Altos de Jalisco." Pp. 125–224 in *Política y Región: Los Altos de Jalisco,* edited by Jorge Alonso, Juan García de Quevedo, and Rafael Alarcón. Mexico City: Secretaría de Educación Pública.
Alba, Richard, and Victor Nee.
 2003.   *Remaking the American Mainstream: Assimilation and Contemporary Immigration.* Cambridge, MA: Harvard University Press.
Aleinikoff, Alexander, and Douglas Klusmeyer.
 2001.   "Plural Nationality: Facing the Future in a Migratory World." Pp. 63–88 in *Citizenship Today: Global Perspectives and Practices,* edited

by Alexander Aleinikoff and Douglas Klusmeyer. Washington, DC: Carnegie Endowment for International Peace.

Anderson, Benedict.

1998.   "Long-Distance Nationalism." Pp. 58–74 in *The Spectre of Comparisons: Nationalism, Southeast Asia, and the World,* edited by Benedict Anderson. London: Verso.

Andrews, George Reid.

1980.   *The Afro-Argentines of Buenos Aires, 1800–1900.* Madison: University of Wisconsin Press.

Appadurai, Arjun.

1991.   "Global Ethnoscapes: Notes and Queries for a Transnational Anthropology." Pp. 191–210 in *Recapturing Anthropology,* edited by R. Fox. Santa Fe, NM: School of American Research Press.

Arana, Ana.

2005.   "How the Street Gangs Took Central America." *Foreign Affairs* 84(3): 98.

Arias, Patricia, and Jorge Durand.

1997.   "De la ciudad al campo: La fabricación de esfera navideña de Los Altos de Jalisco." Pp. 177–94 in *Los Altos de Jalisco a fin de Siglo: Segundo Simposium,* compiled by Cándido González Pérez. Guadalajara: Centro Universitario de los Altos, Universidad de Guadalajara.

Armentrout Ma, L. E.

1984.   "Fellow-Regional Associations in the Ch'ing Dynasty: Organizations in Flux for Mobile People. A Preliminary Survey." *Modern Asian Studies* 18(2): 307–30.

Associated Press.

2001a.   "Mexican Government Says It Will Dissuade Migrants from Crossing Border." June 29.

———.

2001b.   "Mexican Migrant Unit Will Shift Focus from Enforcement to Rescue." August 7.

Avila, Rosemarie.

2006.   "Mexican Meddling in Our Schools." In *Orange County Register* (California), February 21.

Balistreri, Kelly S., and Jennifer Van Hook.

2004.   "The More Things Change the More They Stay the Same: Mexican Naturalization before and after Welfare Reform." *International Migration Review* 38(1): 113–30.

Barry, Kim.

2006.   "Home and Away: The Construction of Citizenship in an Emigration Context." *New York University Law Review* 81(1): 11–59.

Basch, Linda, Nina Glick Schiller, and Cristina Szanton Blanc.
　1994.　*Nations Unbound: Transnational Projects, Postcolonial Predicaments, and the Deterritorialized Nation State.* Langhorne, PA: Gordon and Breach.
Bean, Frank D., and Gillian Stevens.
　2003.　*America's Newcomers and the Dynamics of Diversity.* New York: Russell Sage Foundation.
Borjas, George J.
　1999.　*Heaven's Door: Immigration Policy and the American Economy.* Princeton, NJ: Princeton University Press.
Brand, Laurie A.
　2006.　*Citizens Abroad: Emigration and the State in the Middle East and North Africa.* Cambridge: Cambridge University Press.
Brenner, Neil.
　1994.　"Foucault's New Functionalism." *Theory and Society* 23(5): 679–709.
———.
　1999.　"Beyond State-Centrism? Space, Territoriality, and Geographical Scale in Globalization Studies." *Theory and Society* 28(1): 39–78.
Brimelow, Peter.
　1996.　*Alien Nation: Common Sense about America's Immigration Disaster.* New York: HarperPerennial.
Brown, Thomas N.
　1980.　*Irish-American Nationalism, 1870–1890.* Westport, CT: Greenwood Press.
Brubaker, Rogers.
　1992.　*Citizenship and Nationhood in France and Germany.* Cambridge, MA: Harvard University Press.
———.
　1998.　"Myths and Misconceptions in the Study of Nationalism." Pp. 272–306 in *The State of the Nation: Ernest Gellner and the Theory of Nationalism,* edited by John Hall. Cambridge: Cambridge University Press.
Buchanan, Patrick.
　2006.　*State of Emergency: The Third World Invasion and Conquest of America.* New York: Thomas Dunne Books.
Buchenau, Jürgen.
　2001.　"Small Numbers, Great Impact: Mexico and Its Immigrants, 1821–1973." *Journal of American Ethnic History* 20(3): 23–49.
Burawoy, Michael.
　2003.　"Revisits: An Outline of a Theory of Reflexive Ethnography." *American Sociological Review* 68(5): 645–79.
Calavita, Kitty.
　1992.　*Inside the State: The Bracero Program, Immigration, and the I.N.S.* New York: Routledge.

Caliaro, Marco, and Mario Francesconi.
 1977. *John Baptist Scalabrini, Apostle to Emigrants*. Staten Island, NY: Center for Migration Studies.
Calvo, Thomas, and Gustavo López Castro, eds.
 1988. *Movimientos de población en el occidente de México*. Zamora, Mexico: Colegio de Michoacán.
Camp, Roderic A.
 1992. *Generals in the Palacio: The Military in Modern Mexico*. New York: Oxford University Press.
———.
 1997. *Crossing Swords: Politics and Religion in Mexico*. New York: Oxford University Press.
Cannistraro, Philip V., and Gianfausto Rosoli.
 1979. "Fascist Emigration Policies in the 1920s: An Interpretive Framework." *International Migration Review* 13(4): 673–92.
Cárdenas, Lázaro.
 1934. *The Mexican Government's Six Year Plan, 1934–1940: Complete Textual Translation of the Revised Plan and General Lázaro Cárdenas' Nomination Address*. Mexico City: Trens Agency.
Cardoso, Lawrence A.
 1980. *Mexican Emigration to the United States, 1897–1931*. Tucson: University of Arizona Press.
Carreras de Velasco, Mercedes.
 1974. *Los Mexicanos que Devolvió la Crisis, 1929–1932*. Tlatelolco, Mexico: Secretaría de Relaciones Exteriores.
Castles, Stephen, and Alastair Davidson.
 2000. *Citizenship and Migration: Globalization and the Politics of Belonging*. New York: Routledge.
Castles, Stephen, and Mark J. Miller.
 1998. *The Age of Migration: International Population Movements in the Modern World*. New York: Guilford Press.
Centeno, Miguel A.
 1997. *Democracy within Reason: Technocratic Revolution in Mexico*. University Park: Pennsylvania State University Press.
———.
 2002. *Blood and Debt: War and the Nation-State in Latin America*. University Park: Pennsylvania State University Press.
Christiansen, Drew.
 1996. "Movement, Asylum, Borders: Christian Perspectives." *International Migration Review* 30(1): 7–17.

Cinel, Dino.

1991.   *The National Integration of Italian Return Migration, 1870–1929*. Cambridge: Cambridge University Press.

Clark, Victor S.

1908.   "Mexican Labor in the United States." *United States Bureau of Labor Bulletin* 78 (September): 466–522.

Cohen, Deborah.

2001.   "Caught in the Middle: The Mexican State's Relationship with the United States and Its Own Citizen-Workers, 1942–1954." *Journal of American Ethnic History* 20(3): 110–32.

Cohen, Yinon.

1988.   "War and Social Integration: The Effects of the Israeli-Arab Conflict on Jewish Emigration from Israel." *American Sociological Review* 53(6): 908–18.

CONAPO (Consejo Nacional de Población).

2000.   "Índice de intensidad migratoria México-Estados Unidos." Available at www.conapo.gob.mx.

———.

2006.   *La situación demográfica de México, 2006*. Mexico City: CONAPO.

Cook-Martín, David.

2006.   "Soldiers and Wayward Women: Gendered Citizenship and Migration Policy in Argentina, Italy and Spain Since 1850." *Citizenship Studies* 10(5): 571–90.

Cook-Martín, David, and Anahí Viladrich.

Forthcoming.
         "The Problem with Similarity: Ethnic Affinity Migrants in Spain." *Journal of Ethnic and Migration Studies.*

Corchado, Alfredo.

1995.   "Zedillo Seeking Closer Ties with Mexican-Americans." *Dallas Morning News*, April 8, A11.

Cornelius, Wayne A.

1976.   *Mexican Migration to the United States: The View from Rural Sending Communities*. Cambridge, MA: Cambridge Migration and Development Study Group, Center for International Studies, Massachusetts Institute of Technology.

———.

1998.   "Ejido Reform: Stimulus or Alternative to Migration?" Pp. 229–46 in *The Transformation of Rural Mexico: Reforming the Ejido Sector*, edited by Wayne A. Cornelius and David Myhre. La Jolla: Center for U.S.-Mexican Studies, University of California, San Diego.

———.
2001.   "Death at the Border: Efficacy and Unintended Consequences of U.S. Immigration Control Policy." *Population and Development Review* 27(4): 661–85.

———.
2005.   "Controlling 'Unwanted' Immigration: Lessons from the United States, 1993–2004." *Journal of Ethnic and Migration Studies* 31(4): 775–95.

Cornelius, Wayne A., David Fitzgerald, and Scott Borger, eds.
Forthcoming.
Four Generations of Norteños: New Research from the Cradle of Mexican Migration. La Jolla, CA: Center for Comparative Immigration Studies, University of California, San Diego.

Cornelius, Wayne A., Takeyuki Tsuda, Philip L. Martin, and James F. Hollifield, eds.
2004.   *Controlling Immigration: A Global Perspective.* 2nd ed. Stanford: Stanford University Press.

Corwin, Arthur F.
1978.   "Mexican Policy and Ambivalence toward Labor Emigration to the United States." Pp. 176–219 in *Immigrants—and Immigrants: Perspectives on Mexican Labor Migration to the United States,* edited by Arthur F. Corwin. Westport, CT: Greenwood Press.

Craig, Ann L.
1983.   *The First Agraristas: An Oral History of a Mexican Agrarian Reform Movement.* Berkeley: University of California Press.

Craig, Richard B.
1971.   *The Bracero Program: Interest Groups and Foreign Policy.* Austin: University of Texas Press.

Curso Social Agrícola Zapopano desarrollado en Guadalajara, con ocasión de la pontificia coronación de la imagen de Ntra. Sra. de Zapopan, en enero de 1921, bajo los auspicios del 50 Arzobispado de Guadalajara. Breve historia. Trabajos. Nómina de semaneros. Con licencia de la Autoridad Eclesiástica. 1921. Guadalajara: Renacimiento.

Davy, Megan.
2006.   "The Central American Foreign Born in the United States." Migration Policy Institute. Available at www.migrationinformation.org/USFocus/display.cfm?ID=385.

Deflem, Mathieu.
2000.   "Bureaucratization and Social Control: Historical Foundations of International Police Cooperation." *Law & Society Review* 34(3): 739–78.

de la Garza, Rodolfo O.
1997.   "Foreign Policy Comes Home: The Domestic Consequences of the Program for Mexican Communities Living in Foreign Countries."

Pp. 69–88 in *Bridging the Border: Transforming Mexico-U.S. Relations*, edited by Rodolfo O. de la Garza and Jesús Velasco. Lanham, MD: Rowman & Littlefield.

de la Garza, Rodolfo O., and Louis DeSipio.

1998.   "Interests Not Passions: Mexican-American Attitudes toward Mexico, Immigration from Mexico, and Other Issues Shaping U.S.-Mexico Relations." *International Migration Review* 32(2):401–22.

de la Garza, Rodolfo O., Harry Pachon, Manuel Orozco, and Adrián D. Pantoja.

2000.   "Family Ties and Ethnic Lobbies." Pp. 43–101 in *Latinos and U.S. Foreign Policy: Representing the "Homeland,"* edited by Rodolfo O. de la Garza and Harry Pachon. Lanham, MD: Rowman & Littlefield.

de la Garza, Rodolfo O., and Gabriel Szekely.

1997.   "Policy, Politics and Emigration." Pp. 201–25 in *At the Crossroads: Mexican Migration and U.S. Policy,* edited by Frank D. Bean, Rodolfo O. de la Garza, Bryan R. Roberts, and Sidney Weintraub. Lanham, MD: Rowman & Littlefield.

de la Garza, Rodolfo O., and Jesús Velasco, eds.

1997.   *Bridging the Border: Transforming Mexico-U.S. Relations.* Lanham, MD: Rowman & Littlefield.

del Castillo Vera, Gustavo.

1979.   *Crisis y Transformación de una Sociedad Tradicional.* Mexico City: Centro de Investigaciones Superiores del INAH.

DeSipio, Louis, and Rodolfo O. de la Garza.

1998.   *Making Americans, Remaking America: Immigration and Immigrant Policy.* Boulder, CO: Westview Press.

Deutsch, Karl W.

1966.   *Nationalism and Social Communication.* New York: MIT Press.

Díaz-Cayeros, Alberto.

1995.   *Desarrollo económico e inequidad regional: Hacia un nuevo pacto federal en México.* Mexico City: M.A. Porrúa Grupo Editorial.

Dib, George.

1988.   "Laws Governing Migration in Some Arab Countries." Pp. 168–879 in *International Migration Today,* Vol. 1: *Trends and Prospects,* edited by Reginald T. Appleyard. Perth: University of Western Australia for the United Nations Educational, Scientific, and Cultural Organization.

Docquier, Frédéric, and Abdeslam Marfouk.

2005.   "International Migration by Education Attainment, 1990–2005." In *Migration, Remittances and the Brain Drain,* edited by C. Ozden and M. Schiff. Washington, DC: World Bank.

Dolan, Jay P.
  1975.   *The Immigrant Church: New York's Irish and German Catholics, 1815–1865.*
          Baltimore: Johns Hopkins University Press.
Dolan, Jay P., and Gilberto M. Hinojosa.
  1994.   *Mexican Americans and the Catholic Church, 1900–1965.* Notre Dame,
          IN: University of Notre Dame Press.
Douglass, William A.
  1984.   *Emigration in a South Italian Town: An Anthropological History.* New
          Brunswick, NJ: Rutgers University Press.
Dowty, Alan.
  1987.   *Closed Borders: The Contemporary Assault on Freedom of Movement.* New
          Haven, CT: Yale University Press.
Durand, Jorge.
  1994.   *Más allá de la línea: Patrones migratorios entre México y Estados Unidos.*
          Mexico City: Consejo Nacional para la Cultura y las Artes.
Durand, Jorge, and Douglas S. Massey.
  1992.   "Mexican Migration to the United States: A Critical Review." *Latin
          American Research Review* 27(2): 3–42.

————.

  1995.   *Miracles on the Border: Retablos of Mexican Migrants to the United
          States.* Tucson: University of Arizona Press.
Durand, Jorge, Douglas S. Massey, and René M. Zenteno.
  2001.   "Mexican Immigration to the United States: Continuities and
          Changes." *Latin American Research Review* 36(1): 107–27.
Durkheim, Emile.
1995 [1912]. *The Elementary Forms of Religious Life.* Translated by Karen Fields.
          New York: Free Press.
Espinosa, Víctor M.
  1998.   *El dilema del retorno: Migración, género y pertenencia en un contexto
          transnacional.* Zamora, Mexico: El Colegio de Michoacán.

————.

  1999.   "El día del emigrante y el retorno del purgatorio: Iglesia, migración a
          los Estados Unidos y cambio sociocultural en un pueblo de Los Altos
          de Jalisco." *Estudios Sociológicos* 17(50): 375–418.
Fabila, Alfonso.
  1991.   "El problema de la emigración de obreros y campesinos mexicanos."
          Pp. 35–64 in *Migración México-Estados Unidos Años Veinte,* edited by
          Jorge Durand. Mexico City: Consejo Nacional para la Cultura y las
          Artes.
Fábregas, Andrés.

1986.   *La Formación Histórica de una Región: Los Altos de Jalisco.* Mexico City: Centro de Investigaciones y Estudios Superiores en Antropología Social.

Fitzgerald, David.

2000.   *Negotiating Extra-Territorial Citizenship: Mexican Migration and the Transnational Politics of Community.* La Jolla: Center for Comparative Immigration Studies, University of California, San Diego.

———.

2004a.   "Beyond 'Transnationalism': Mexican Hometown Politics at an American Labor Union." *Ethnic and Racial Studies* 27(2): 228–47.

———.

2004b.   " 'For 118 Million Mexicans': Emigrants and Chicanos in Mexican Politics." Pp. 523–48 in *Dilemmas of Political Change in Mexico,* edited by Kevin Middlebrook. London: Institute of Latin American Studies, University of London.

———.

2005.   "Nationality and Migration in Modern Mexico." *Journal of Ethnic and Migration Studies* 31(1): 171–91.

———.

2006a.   "Towards a Theoretical Ethnography of Migration." *Qualitative Sociology* 29(1): 1–24.

———.

2006b.   "Rethinking Emigrant Citizenship." *New York University Law Review* 81(1): 90–116.

Fitzgerald, Keith A.

1996.   *The Face of the Nation: Immigration, the State, and the National Identity.* Stanford: Stanford University Press.

Foucault, Michel.

1979.   *Discipline and Punish.* Translated by Alan Sheridan. New York: Vintage.

———.

2003 [1978]. "Governmentality." Pp. 229–45 in *The Essential Foucault,* edited by Paul Rabinow and Nikolas Rose. New York: New Press.

———.

2003 [1979]. " 'Omnes et Singulatim': Toward a Critique of Political Reason." Pp. 180–201 in *The Essential Foucault,* edited by Paul Rabinow and Nikolas Rose. New York: New Press.

———.

2003 [1982]. "The Subject and Power." Pp. 126–44 in *The Essential Foucault,* edited by Paul Rabinow and Nikolas Rose. New York: New Press.

Fox, Nick J.

1998.   "Foucault, Foucauldians, and Sociology." *British Journal of Sociology* 49(3): 415–33.

Gamio, Manuel.

    1930. *Mexican Immigration to the United States.* Chicago: University of Chicago Press.

García y Griego, Manuel.

    1983. "The Importation of Mexican Contract Laborers to the United States, 1942–1964: Antecedents, Operation, and Legacy." Pp. 49–98 in *The Border That Joins: Mexican Migrants and U.S. Responsibility,* edited by Peter G. Brown and Henry Shue. Totowa, NJ: Rowman & Littlefield.

———.

    1988. "The Bracero Policy Experiment: U.S.-Mexican Responses to Mexican Labor Migration, 1942–1955." Unpublished PhD dissertation, University of California, Los Angeles.

García y Griego, Manuel, and Fernando S. Alanís Enciso.

    2003. "The Illusion of Return: *Exiliados Mexicanos* in the United States during the Great Depression, 1929–1934." Paper presented at the 24th International Congress of the Latin American Studies Association, Dallas, TX, March 27–29.

Geddes, Andrew.

    2003. *The Politics of Migration and Immigration in Europe.* London: Sage.

Genschel, Phillip.

    2005. "Globalization and the Transformation of the Tax State." *European Review* 13(1): 53–71.

Giddens, Anthony.

    1985. *The Nation-State and Violence.* Berkeley: University of California Press.

Gilbert, James.

    1934. "A Field Study in Mexico of the Mexican Repatriation Movement." Unpublished MA thesis, University of Southern California, Los Angeles.

Glick Schiller, Nina, and Peggy Levitt.

    2006. "Haven't We Heard This Somewhere Before? A Substantive View of Transnational Migration Studies by Way of a Reply to Waldinger and Fitzgerald." CMD Working Paper 06–01. Center for Migration and Development, Princeton University.

Godines, Valeria.

    2004. "A Final, Familiar Resting Place." *Orange County Register* (California), November 14.

Godoy, S. Mara Pérez.

    1998. "Social Movements and International Migration: The Mexican Diaspora Seeks Inclusion in Mexico's Political Affairs, 1968–1998." Unpublished PhD dissertation, University of Chicago.

Gold, Steve.

2007.   "Israeli Emigration Policy." Pp. 283–304 in *Citizenship and Those Who Leave: The Politics of Emigration and Expatriation,* edited by Nancy L. Green and François Weil. Urbana. University of Illinois.

Goldring, Luin.

2002.   "The Mexican State and Transmigrant Organizations: Negotiating the Boundaries of Membership and Participation." *Latin American Research Review* 37(3): 55–99.

Gómez-Quiñones, Juan.

1983.   "Notes on an Interpretation of the Relations between the Mexican Community in the United States and Mexico." Pp. 417–39 in *Mexican-U.S. Relations: Conflict and Convergence,* edited by Carlos Vásquez and Manuel García y Griego. Los Angeles: UCLA Chicano Studies Research Center Publications.

González, Gilbert G.

1999.   *Mexican Consuls and Labor Organizing: Imperial Politics in the American Southwest.* Austin: University of Texas Press.

González Gutiérrez, Carlos.

1995.   "La organización de los inmigrantes mexicanos en Los Angeles: La lealtad de los oriundos." *Revista Mexicana de Política Exterior* 46 (spring): 59–101.

————.

1997.   "Decentralized Diplomacy: The Role of Consular Offices in Mexico's Relations with Its Diaspora." Pp. 49–67 in *Bridging the Border: Transforming Mexico-U.S. Relations,* edited by Rodolfo de la Garza and Jesús Velasco. Lanham, MD: Rowman & Littlefield.

————.

1998.   "Mexicans in the United States: An Incipient Diaspora." Paper presented at the workshop on Advancing the International Interests of African-Americans, Asian-Americans and Latinos, Pacific Council on International Policy, Los Angeles, March 20–21.

————.

1999.   "Fostering Identities: Mexico's Relations with Its Diaspora." *Journal of American History* 86(2): 545–67.

González Navarro, Moisés.

1994.   *Los Extranjeros en México y los Mexicanos en el Extranjero, 1821–1970.* Vol. 3. Mexico City: Colegio de México.

————.

2001.   *Cristeros y Agraristas en Jalisco.* Vol. 2. Mexico City: Colegio de México.

Green, Nancy, and François Weil, eds.

2007.   *Citizenship and Those Who Leave: The Politics of Emigration and Expatriation.* Urbana: University of Illinois Press.

Grindle, Merilee S.

1988.   *Searching for Rural Development: Labor Migration and Employment in Mexico.* Ithaca, NY: Cornell University Press.

Guarnizo, Luis E.

1997.   " 'Going Home': Class, Gender, and Household Transformation among Dominican Return Migrants." Pp. 13–60 in *Caribbean Circuits: New Directions in the Study of Caribbean Migration,* edited by Patricia R. Pessar. New York: Center for Migration Studies.

Guarnizo, Luis E., Alejandro Portes, and William J. Haller.

2003.   "Assimilation and Transnationalism: Determinants of Transnational Political Action among Contemporary Migrants." *American Journal of Sociology* 108(6): 1211–48.

Guiraudon, Virginie, and Christian Joppke, eds.

2001.   *Controlling a New Migration World.* New York: Routledge.

Gutiérrez, Natividad.

1999.   *Nationalist Myths and Ethnic Identities: Indigenous Intellectuals and the Mexican State.* Lincoln: University of Nebraska Press.

Hagan, Jacqueline, and Helen R. Ebaugh.

2003.   "Calling upon the Sacred: Migrants' Use of Religion in the Migration Process." *International Migration Review* 37(4): 1145–53.

Hammar, Tomas.

1985.   "Dual Citizenship and Political Integration." *International Migration Review* 19(3): 438–50.

———.

1989.   "State, Nation, and Dual Citizenship." Pp. 81–95 in *Immigration and the Politics of Citizenship in Europe and North America,* edited by William R. Brubaker. New York: University Press of America.

Hancock, Richard H.

1959.   *The Role of the Bracero in the Economic and Cultural Dynamics of Mexico: A Case Study of Chihuahua.* Stanford, CA: Hispanic American Society.

Hannum, Hurst.

1987.   *The Right to Leave and Return in International Law and Practice.* London: Martinus Nijhoff.

Hansen, Randall, and Patrick Weil, eds.

2001.   *Towards a European Nationality: Citizenship, Immigration, and Nationality Law in the EU.* New York: Palgrave.

Haydu, Jeffrey.

1998.   "Making Use of the Past: Time Periods as Cases to Compare and as Sequences of Problem Solving." *American Journal of Sociology* 104(2): 339–71.

Held, David, and Anthony G. McGrew, eds.
2000.   *The Global Transformations Reader: An Introduction to the Globalization Debate.* Malden, MA: Polity Press.

Heleniak, Timothy.
2004.   "Migration of the Russian Diaspora after the Breakup of the Soviet Union." *Journal of International Affairs* 57(2): 99–118.

Herberg, Will.
1960.   *Protestant-Catholic-Jew.* Revised ed. New York: Anchor.

Hernández Madrid, Miguel J.
1999.   "Iglesias sin fronteras. Migrantes y conversos religiosos: Cambios de identidad cultural en el noroeste de Michoacán." Pp. 393–404 in *Fronteras Fragmentadas,* edited by Gail Mummert. Zamora, Mexico: El Colegio de Michoacán.

———.
2003.   "Diversificación religiosa y migración en Michoacán." Pp. 165–92 in *Diáspora Michoacana,* edited by Gustavo López Castro. Zamora, Mexico: El Colegio de Michoacán.

Higham, John.
1994.   *Strangers in the Land: Patterns of American Nativism, 1860–1925.* New Brunswick, NJ: Rutgers University Press.

Hirabayashi, Lane Ryo.
1986.   "The Migrant Village Association in Latin America: A Comparative Analysis." *Latin American Research Review* 21(3): 7–29.

———.
1993.   *Cultural Capital: Mountain Zapotec Migrant Associations in Mexico City.* Tucson: University of Arizona Press.

Hobsbawm, Eric, and Terence Ranger, eds.
1992.   *The Invention of Tradition.* Cambridge: Cambridge University Press.

Hondagneu-Sotelo, Pierrette, Genelle Gaudinez, Hector Lara, and Billie C. Ortiz.
2004.   " 'There's a Spirit That Transcends the Border': Faith, Ritual, and Postnational Protest at the U.S.-Mexico Border." *Sociological Perspectives* 47(2): 133–59.

Hugo, Graeme.
2006.   "An Australian Diaspora?" *International Migration* 44(1): 105–33.

Huntington, Samuel P.
2004.   *Who Are We? The Challenges to America's Identity.* New York: Simon and Schuster.

IFE (Instituto Federal Electoral).
2006.   *Informe Final Sobre el Voto de los Mexicanos Residentes en el Extranjero.*

Available at http://mxvote06.ife.org.mx/libro_blanco/pdf/tomoI/
capituloI. pdf.

IISS (International Institute for Strategic Studies).

2001. *The Military Balance 2001–2002.* Oxford: Oxford University Press.

INEGI (Instituto Nacional de Estadística, Geografía e Informática).

2000. *XII Censo General de Población y Vivienda,* Available at www.inegi.gob
.mx.

International Bank for Reconstruction and Development.

2006. *Global Economic Prospects: Overview and Global Outlook.* Washington,
DC: World Bank.

Itzigsohn, José.

2000. "Immigration and the Boundaries of Citizenship: The Institutions of
Immigrants' Political Transnationalism." *International Migration Review* 34(4): 1126–54.

Itzigsohn, José, Carlos Dore Cabral, Esther Hernández Medina, and Obed
Vázquez.

1999. "Mapping Dominican Transnationalism: Narrow and Broad
Transnational Practices." *Ethnic and Racial Studies* 22(2): 316–39.

Jacobson, David.

1996. *Rights across Borders: Immigration and the Decline of Citizenship.* Balti-
more: Johns Hopkins University Press.

Jiménez, Tomás, and David Fitzgerald.

Forthcoming.
"Mexican Assimilation: A Temporal and Spatial Reorientation." *Du
Bois Review.*

Johnson, James.

2005. "Stopping Africa's Medical Brain Drain." *British Medical Journal*
331(7507): 2–3.

Johnston, Hugh J. M.

1972. *British Emigration Policy: "Shoveling Out Paupers."* Oxford: Clarendon
Press.

Jones-Correa, Michael.

2000. "Under Two Flags: Dual Nationality in Latin America and Its Consequences for the United States." Working Paper on Latin America
99/00–3. Cambridge: David Rockefeller Center for Latin American
Studies, Harvard University.

Jongkind, Fred.

1974. "A Reappraisal of the Role of Regional Associations of Lima, Peru."
Comparative Studies in Society and History 16(4): 471–82.

Joppke, Christian.

1998. "Immigration Challenges the Nation-State." Pp. 5–46 in *Challenge to the Nation-State: Immigration in Western Europe and the United States,* edited by Christian Joppke. Oxford: Oxford University Press.

————, ed.

1999. *Immigration and the Nation-State.* Oxford: Oxford University Press.

————.

2005. *Selecting by Origin: Ethnic Migration in the Liberal State.* Cambridge, MA: Harvard University Press.

Joseph, Gilbert, and Daniel Nugent, eds.

1994. *Everyday Forms of State Formation: Revolution and the Negotiation of Rule in Modern Mexico.* Durham, NC: Duke University Press.

Kane, Abdoulaye.

2002. "Senegal's Village Diaspora and the People Left Ahead." Pp. 245–63 in *The Transnational Family: New European Frontiers and Global Networks,* edited by D. Bryceson and U. Vuorela. Oxford, UK: Berg.

Kapur, Devesh, and John McHale.

2005. *Give Us Your Best and Brightest: The Global Hunt for Talent and Its Impact on the Developing World.* Washington, DC: Center for Global Development.

Kearney, Michael.

1991. "Borders and Boundaries of State and Self at the End of Empire." *Journal of Historical Sociology* 4(1): 52–74.

————.

1995. "The Local and the Global: The Anthropology of Globalization and Transnationalism." *Annual Review of Anthropology* 24(2): 547–65.

Kearney, Michael, and Federico Besserer.

2004. "Oaxacan Municipal Governance in Transnational Context." Pp. 449–66 in *Indigenous Mexican Migrants in the United States,* edited by Jonathan Fox and Gaspar Rivera-Salgado. La Jolla, CA: Center for U.S.-Mexican Studies and Center for Comparative Immigration Studies.

Keohane, Robert O., and Joseph S. Nye Jr.

1987. *"Power and Interdependence* Revisited." *International Organization* 41(4): 725–53.

Kibria, Nazli.

1993. *Family Tightrope: The Changing Lives of Vietnamese Americans.* Princeton, NJ: Princeton University Press.

Knight, Alan.

1987. *U.S.-Mexican Relations, 1910–1940: An Interpretation.* La Jolla: Center for U.S.-Mexican Studies, University of California, San Diego.

————.

1992. "The Peculiarities of Mexican History: Mexico Compared to Latin

America, 1821–1992." *Journal of Latin American Studies* 24 (quincentenary suppl.): 99–144.

———.

2001.   "The Modern Mexican State: Theory and Practice." Pp. 177–218 in *The Other Mirror: Grand Theory through the Lens of Latin America*, edited by Miguel A. Centeno and Fernando López-Alves. Princeton, NJ: Princeton University Press.

Koslowski, Rey.

2000.   *Migrants and Citizens: Demographic Change in the European State System.* Ithaca, NY: Cornell University Press.

Krasner, Stephen D.

1995.   "Compromising Westphalia." *International Security* 20(3): 115–51.

Kratochwil, Friedrich.

1986.   "Of Systems, Boundaries, and Territoriality: An Inquiry into the Formation of the State System." *World Politics* 39(1): 27–52.

Krauze, Enrique.

1997.   *Mexico: Biography of Power.* New York: HarperCollins.

Laguerre, Michel S.

1998.   *Diasporic Citizenship: Haitians in Transnational America.* New York: St. Martin's Press.

Landa y Piña, Andrés.

1930.   *El Servicio de Migración en México.* Mexico City: Talleres Gráficas de la Nación.

Lanly, Guillaume, and Volker Hamann.

2004.   "Solidaridades transfronterizas y la emergencia de una sociedad civil transnacional: La participación de los clubes de migrantes en el desarrollo local del occidente de México." Pp. 127–74 in *Clubes de migrantes oriundos mexicanos en los Estados Unidos: La política transnacional de la nueva sociedad civil migrante*, edited by Guillaume Lanly and M. Basilia Valenzuela. Guadalajara: Universidad de Guadalajara.

Lanly, Guillaume, and M. Basilia Valenzuela.

2004.   "Introducción." Pp. 11–36 in *Clubes de migrantes oriundos mexicanos en los Estados Unidos: La política transnacional de la nueva sociedad civil migrante*, edited by Guillaume Lanly and M. Basilia Valenzuela. Guadalajara: Universidad de Guadalajara.

Lázaro Salinas, José.

1955.   *La Emigración de Braceros: Visión Objetiva de un Problema Mexicano.* León: Imprenta Cuauhtémoc.

Lesser, Jeffrey.

1999.   *Negotiating National Identity: Immigrants, Minorities, and the Struggle for Ethnicity in Brazil.* Durham, NC: Duke University Press.

Levitt, Peggy.

2001.   "Transnational Migration: Taking Stock and Future Directions." *Global Networks* 1(3): 195–216.

————.

2003.   " 'You Know, Abraham Was Really the First Immigrant': Religion and Transnational Migration." *International Migration Review* 37(3): 847–74.

Levitt, Peggy, and Rafael de la Dehesa.

2003.   "Transnational Migration and the Redefinition of the State: Variations and Explanations." *Ethnic and Racial Studies* 26(4): 587–611.

Licea de Arenas, Judith, Emma Santillán-Rivero, Miguel Arenas, and Javier Valles.

2003.   "Desempeño de becarios mexicanos en la producción de conocimiento científico ¿de la bibliometría a la política científica?" Paper no. 147. *Information Research* 8(2). Available at http://InformationR.net/ir/8–2/paper147.html.

Lindstrom, David P.

1996.   "Economic Opportunity in Mexico and Return Migration from the United States." *Demography* 33(3): 357–74.

López Castro, Gustavo, ed.

1988.   *Migración en el occidente de México.* Zamora, Mexico: Colegio de Michoacán.

————, ed.

2003.   *Diáspora michoacana.* Zamora, Mexico: Colegio de Michoacán.

López Portillo Vargas, Ernesto.

2002.   "The Police in Mexico: Political Functions and Needed Reforms." Pp. 109–135 in *Transnational Crime and Public Security: Challenges to Mexico and the United States,* edited by John Bailey and Jorge Chabat. La Jolla: Center for U.S.-Mexican Studies, University of California, San Diego.

Louie, Miriam Ching Yoon.

2001.   *Sweatshop Warriors: Immigrant Women Workers Take on the Global Factory.* Cambridge, MA: South End Press.

Loveman, Mara.

2005.   "The Modern State and the Primitive Accumulation of Symbolic Power." *American Journal of Sociology* 110(6): 1651–83.

Lowell, B. Lindsay, and Allan M. Findlay.

2001.   "Migration of Highly Skilled Persons from Developing Countries:

Impact and Policy Responses." Report prepared for the International Labour Office, Geneva.

Loyo, Gilberto.
1935. *La Política Demográfica de México.* Mexico City: La Impresora.

Lozoya, Jorge A.
1970. *El Ejército Mexicano (1911–1965).* Mexico City: Colegio de México.

Luna Zamora, Rogelio.
1990. "La agroindustria del tequila y sus empresarios en Los Altos de Jalisco." Pp. 91–124 in *Política y Región: Los Altos de Jalisco,* edited by Jorge Alonso, Juan García de Quevedo, and Rafael Alarcón. Mexico City: Secretaría de Educación Pública.

Magaloni, Beatriz, and Guillermo Zepeda.
2004. "Democratization, Judicial and Law Enforcement Institutions, and the Rule of Law in Mexico." Pp. 523–48 in *Dilemmas of Political Change in Mexico,* edited by Kevin J. Middlebrook. London: Institute of Latin American Studies, University of London.

Mahler, Sarah. J.
1995. *American Dreaming: Immigrant Life on the Margins.* Princeton, NJ: Princeton University Press.

Mann, Michael.
1993. *The Sources of Social Power.* Vol. 2. Cambridge: Cambridge University Press.

Marcelli, Enrico A., and Wayne A. Cornelius.
2001. "The Changing Profile of Mexican Migrants to the United States: New Evidence from California and Mexico." *Latin American Research Review* 36(3): 105–31.

Martin, David A.
2002. "New Rules for Dual Nationality." Pp. 34–60 in *Dual Nationality, Social Rights and Federal Citizenship in the U.S. and Europe: The Reinvention of Citizenship,* edited by Randall Hansen and Patrick Weil. New York: Berghahn Books.

Martínez, John.
1972 [1957]. *Mexican Emigration to the U.S., 1910–1930.* San Francisco: R. and E. Research Associates.

Martínez de Alva, Ernesto.
1934. *Vida Rural: Los Campesinos de México.* Mexico City: Talleres Gráficas de la Nación.

Martínez Saldaña, Jesús.
1993. "At the Periphery of Democracy: The Binational Politics of Mexican

Immigrants in Silicon Valley." Unpublished PhD dissertation, University of California, Berkeley.

Martínez Saldaña, Jesús, and Raúl Ross Pineda.

2002.   "Suffrage for Mexicans Residing Abroad." Pp. 275–92. In *Cross-Border Dialogues: US-Mexico Social Movement Networking*, edited by David Brooks and Jonathan Fox. La Jolla: Center for US-Mexican Studies, University of California, San Diego.

Martínez Saldaña, Tomás.

1976.   "Formación y transformación de una oligarquía: El caso de Arandas, Jalisco." Pp. 17–147 in *Política y Sociedad en México: El Caso de Los Altos de Jalisco*, edited by Tomás Martínez Saldaña and Leticia Gándara Mendoza. Tlalpan, Mexico: Centro de Investigaciones Superiores, Instituto Nacional de Antropología e Historia.

———.

1985.   "Los impactos políticos y económicos de los emigrados en Jalisco: El caso de Arandas, Jalisco." Pp. 123–34 in *Desarrollo Rural en Jalisco: Contradicciones y Perspectivas*, edited by Sergio Alcántara Ferrer and Enrique E. Sánchez Ruiz. Guadalajara: Colegio de Jalisco.

Massey, Douglas S., Rafael Alarcón, Jorge Durand, and Humberto González.

1987.   *Return to Aztlán: The Social Process of International Migration from Western Mexico*. Berkeley: University of California Press.

Massey, Douglas S., Joaquín Arango, Graeme Hugo, Ali Kouaouci, Adela Pellegrino, and J. Edward Taylor.

1998.   *Worlds in Motion: Understanding International Migration at the End of the Millennium*. Oxford, UK: Clarendon Press.

Massey, Douglas S., and Chiara Capoferro.

2004.   "Measuring Undocumented Migration." *International Migration Review* 38(3): 1075–102.

Massey, Douglas S., Jorge Durand, and Nolan J. Malone.

2002.   *Beyond Smoke and Mirrors: Mexican Immigration in an Era of Free Trade*. New York: Russell Sage Foundation.

Massey, Douglas S., and Kristin E. Espinosa.

1997.   "What's Driving Mexico-U.S. Migration? A Theoretical, Empirical, and Policy Analysis." *American Journal of Sociology* 102(4): 939–99.

McDonald, William F.

2002.   "Mexico, the United States, and the Migration-Crime Nexus." in *Transnational Crime and Public Security: Challenges to Mexico and the United States*, edited by John Bailey and Jorge Chabat. La Jolla: Center for U.S.-Mexican Studies, University of California, San Diego.

Meyer, Jean.

1976. *The Cristero Rebellion: The Mexican People between Church and State, 1926–1929.* Cambridge: Cambridge University Press.

Meyer, John W., John Boli, George M. Thomas, and Francisco O. Ramirez.
1997. "World Society and the Nation State." *American Journal of Sociology* 103(1): 144–81.

Migration News.
2001a. Fox Visits Bush." 8(4). Available at http://migration.ucdavis.edu/mn.

———. 2001b. "INS: Border Deaths, Trafficking." 8(7). Available at http://migration.ucdavis.edu/mn.

———. 2003. "Mexico: Legalization, Elections, IDs." 10(4). Available at http://migration.ucdavis.edu/mn.

———. 2005. "Mexico: Migrants, Mexicans in U.S., Economy." 12(2). Available at http://migration.ucdavis.edu/mn.

———. 2006. "Mexico: HTAs, Fertility, Labor." 13(4). Available at http://migration.ucdavis.edu/mn.

———. 2007. "EU at 50: East-West, Services." 14(2). Available at http://migration.ucdavis.edu/mn.

Moch, Leslie P.
2004. "Migration and the Nation: The View from Paris." *Social Science History* 28(1): 1–18.

Moctezuma Langoria, Miguel.
2003. "La voz de los actores sobre la ley migrante y Zacatecas." *Migración y Desarrollo* 1(October): 100–103.

Monroy, Douglas.
1999. *Rebirth: Mexican Los Angeles from the Great Migration to the Great Depression.* Berkeley: University of California Press.

Morales, Patricia.
1989. *Indocumentados Mexicanos: Causas y razones de la migración laboral.* 2nd ed. Mexico City: Grijalbo.

Morgenthau, Hans. J.
1967. *Politics among Nations: The Struggle for Power and Peace.* New York: Knopf.

Moya, Jose C.
1998. *Cousins and Strangers: Spanish Immigrants in Buenos Aires, 1850–1930.* Berkeley: University of California Press.

———.

2005. "Immigrants and Associations: A Global and Historical Perspective." *Journal of Ethnic and Migration Studies* 31(5): 833–64.

Nyíri, Pál.

2001. "Expatriating Is Patriotic? The Discourse on 'New Migrants' in the People's Republic of China and Identity Construction among Recent Migrants from the PRC." *Journal of Ethnic and Migration Studies* 27(4): 635–53.

Odem, Mary E.

2004. "Our Lady of Guadalupe in the New South: Latino Immigrants and the Politics of Integration in the Catholic Church." *Journal of American Ethnic History* 21(4): 26–57.

Oishi, Nana.

2005. *Women in Motion: Globalization, State Policies, and Labor Migration in Asia.* Stanford: Stanford University Press.

Olesen, Henrik.

2002. "Migration, Return, and Development: An Institutional Perspective." *International Migration* 40(5): 125–50.

Ong, Aihwa.

1999. *Flexible Citizenship: The Cultural Logics of Transnationality.* Durham, NC: Duke University Press.

Orellana, S., and L. Carlos.

1973. "Mixtec Migrants in Mexico City: A Case Study of Urbanization." *Human Organization* 32(3): 273–83.

Orozco, José.

1998. "Esos Altos de Jalisco: Race and Immigration in the Construction of Mexican Nationalism, 1926–1950." Unpublished PhD dissertation, Harvard University.

Orozco, Juan L.

1992. *El Negocio de los Ilegales: Ganancias para Quién.* Guadalajara: Instituto Libre de Filosofía.

Østergaard-Nielsen, Eva, ed.

2003. *International Migration and Sending Countries: Perception, Policies, and Transnational Relations.* London: Palgrave.

Ottenberg, Simon O.

1955. "Improvement Associations among the Afikpo Ibo." *Africa* 25 (1): 3–27.

Passel, Jeffrey.

2004. "Mexican Immigration to the U.S.: The Latest Estimates." Migration Information Source. Available at www.migrationinformation.org/feature/display.cfm?ID=208.

Pastore, Ferruccio.

2001.   "Nationality Law and International Migration: The Italian Case."
Pp. 95–117 in *Towards a European Nationality: Citizenship, Immigration,
and Nationality Law in the EU*, edited by Randall Hansen and Patrick
Weil. New York: Palgrave.

Paz, Octavio.
1961 [1950]. *The Labyrinth of Solitude: Life and Thought in Mexico*. New York: Grove
Press.

Perotti, Antonio.
1997.   *L'église et les migrations. Un précurseur: Giovanni Battista Scalabrini*.
Paris: CIEMI.

Petras, Elizabeth.
1981.   "The Global Labor Market in the Modern World-Economy." Pp. 44–63
in *Global Trends in Migration: Theory and Research on International Population Movements*, edited by Mary M. Kritz, Charles B. Keely, and Silvano M. Tomasi. Staten Island, NY: Center for Migration Studies.

Piore, Michael J.
1979.   *Birds of Passage: Migrant Labor and Industrial Societies*. Cambridge:
Cambridge University Press.

Plan Nacional de Desarrollo 1995–2000.
1995.   Mexico City: Talleres Gráficos de México.

Portes, Alejandro.
2003.   "Conclusion: Theoretical Convergences and Empirical Evidence in
the Study of Immigrant Transnationalism." *International Migration
Review* 37(3): 874–93.

Portes, Alejandro, Christina Escobar, and Alexandria Walton Radford.
2007.   "Immigrant Transnational Organizations and Development: A Comparative Study." *International Migration Review* 41(1): 242–81.

Portes, Alejandro, and Patricia Landolt.
2002.   "Social Capital: Promise and Pitfalls of Its Role in Development." *Journal of Latin American Studies* 32(2): 529–47.

Quirk, Robert E.
1973.   *The Mexican Revolution and the Catholic Church, 1910–1929*. Blooming-
ton: University of Indiana Press.

Rath, Thomas.
2003.   " 'Que el cielo un soldado en cada hijo te dio . . .'; Conscription, Re-
calcitrance and Resistance in Mexico in the 1940s." Unpublished
MPhil thesis, Latin American Centre, University of Oxford.

Reese, Leslie.
2001.   "Morality and Identity in Mexican Immigrant Parents' Visions of the
Future." *Journal of Ethnic and Migration Studies* 27(3): 455–72.

Reilly, de Prague.
    1969.   "The Role of the Churches in the Bracero Program in California."
             Unpublished MA thesis, University of Southern California, Los An-
             geles.
Reisler, Mark.
    1976.   *By the Sweat of Their Brow: Mexican Immigrant Labor in the United
             States, 1900–1940.* Westport, CT: Greenwood Press.
Renshon, Stanley.
July 2000.   "Dual Citizens in America: An Issue of Vast Proportions and Broad
             Significance." Policy paper. Washington, DC: Center for Immigration
             Studies.
Rico, Carlos.
    1992.   "Migration and U.S.-Mexican Relations, 1966–1986." Pp. 221–83
             in *Western Hemisphere Immigration and United States Foreign Policy,* ed-
             ited by Christopher Mitchell. University Park: Pennsylvania State
             University Press.
Roberts, Bryan R.
    1974.   "The Interrelationships of City and Provinces in Peru and
             Guatemala." *Anthropological Perspectives on Latin American Urbaniza-
             tion,* edited by Wayne A. Cornelius and Felicity M. Trueblood. Spe-
             cial issue of *Latin American Urban Research* 4: 207–35.
Rodríguez, Victoria E.
    1997.   *Decentralization in Mexico: From Reforma Municipal to Solidaridad to
             Nuevo Federalismo.* Boulder, CO: Westview Press.
Rosenblum, Marc R.
    2004.   "Moving beyond the Policy of No Policy: Emigration from Mexico
             and Central America." *Latin American Politics and Society* 46(4):
             91–126.
Ruggie, John Gerard.
    1993.   "Territoriality and Beyond: Problematizing Modernity in Interna-
             tional Relations." *International Organization* 47(1): 139–74.
Rumelhart, David E.
    1980.   "Schemata: The Building Blocks of Cognition." Pp. 38–58 in *Theoretical
             Issues in Reading Comprehension: Perspectives from Cognitive Psychology,
             Linguistics, Artificial Intelligence, and Education,* edited by Rand J. Spiro,
             Bertram C. Bruce, and William F. Brewer. Hillsdale, NJ: Erlbaum.
Sacks, Harvey.
    1992.   *Lectures on Conversation.* Edited by Gail Jefferson. Oxford: Blackwell.
Sadiq, Kamal.
    2005.   "When States Prefer Non-Citizens over Citizens: Conflict over Illegal

Immigration into Malaysia." *International Studies Quarterly* 49(1): 101–22.

Sandel, Michael J.
    1998.   *Liberalism and the Limits of Justice.* Cambridge: Cambridge University Press.

Santamaría Gómez, Arturo.
    1994.   *La Política entre México y Aztlán.* Culiacán: Universidad Autónoma de Sinaloa.

Santibáñez, Enrique.
    1991.   "Ensayo acerca de la inmigración mexicana en los Estados Unidos." Pp. 65–129 in *Migración México-Estados Unidos. Años Veinte,* edited by Jorge Durand. Mexico City: Consejo Nacional para la Cultura y las Artes.

Sassen, Saskia.
    1998.   *Globalization and Its Discontents.* New York: New Press.

Sayad, Abdelmalek.
    2004.   *The Suffering of the Immigrant.* Translated by David Macey. Cambridge, UK: Polity Press.

Schmitter Heisler, Barbara.
    1985.   "Sending Countries and the Politics of Emigration and Destination." *International Migration Review* 19(3): 469–84.

Scott, James C.
    1985.   *Weapons of the Weak: Everyday Forms of Peasant Resistance.* New Haven, CT: Yale University Press.

———.
    1998.   *Seeing Like a State.* New Haven, CT: Yale University Press.

Secretaría de Gobernación.
    1996.   *Compilación Histórica de la Legislación Migratoria en México, 1909–1996.* Mexico City: Secretaría de Gobernación.

Secretaría del Trabajo.
    1946.   *Los Braceros.* Mexico City: Secretaría del Trabajo, Dirección de Previsión Social.

Secretaría de Relaciones Exteriores (SRE).
    2004.   "Matrícula Consular de Alta Seguridad (MCAS)." *Mexicanos en el Exterior* 1(10): 1.

Segev, Tom.
    2005.   "Twists on the Law of Return." *Los Angeles Times,* January 21, B11.

Seif, Hinda.
    2003.   " 'Estado de Oro' o 'Jaula de Oro'? Undocumented Mexican Immigrant Workers, the Driver's License, and Subnational Illegalization in

California." Working Paper 86. La Jolla: Center for Comparative Immigration Studies, University of California, San Diego.

Shain, Yossi.

1999.   *Marketing the American Creed Abroad: Diasporas in the U.S. and Their Homelands.* New York: Cambridge University Press.

Sheffer, Gabriel.

2003.   *Diaspora Politics: At Home Abroad.* Cambridge: Cambridge University Press.

Sherman, Rachel.

1999.   "From State Introversion to State Extension in Mexico: Modes of Emigrant Incorporation, 1900–1997." *Theory and Society* 28(6): 835–78.

Simmel, Georg.

1971 [1908].   "The Stranger." Pp. 143–49 in *On Individuality and Social Forms,* edited by Donald N. Levine. Chicago: University of Chicago Press.

Skeldon, Ronald.

1980.   "Regional Associations among Urban Migrants in Papua New Guinea." *Oceania* 50: 248–72.

Smith, Anthony D.

1990.   "The Supersession of Nationalism?" *International Journal of Comparative Sociology* 31(1): 1–31.

Smith, James P., and Barry Edmonston, eds.

1997.   *The New Americans: Economic, Demographic, and Fiscal Effects of Immigration.* Washington, DC: National Research Council.

Smith, Michael P.

1994.   "Can You Imagine? Transnational Migration and the Globalization of Grassroots Politics." *Social Text* 39 (summer): 15–33.

Smith, Robert C.

2006.   *Mexican New York: The Transnational Lives of New Immigrants.* Berkeley: University of California Press.

Soysal, Yasemin Nuhoglu.

1994.   *Limits of Citizenship: Migrants and Postnational Membership in Europe.* Chicago: University of Chicago Press.

Spener, David.

2005.   "Mexican Migration to the United States, 1882–1992: A Long Twentieth Century of Coyotaje." Working Paper 124. La Jolla: Center for Comparative Immigration Studies, University of California, San Diego.

Spiro, Peter J.

2002.   "Embracing Dual Nationality." Pp. 19–33 in *Dual Nationality, Social Rights, and Federal Citizenship in the U.S. and Europe: The Reinvention of*

Citizenship, edited by Randall Hansen and Patrick Weil. New York: Berghahn Books.

———.

2005. *"Afroyim:* Vaunting Citizenship, Presaging Transnationality" Pp. 147–68 in *Immigration Stories,* edited by David A. Martin and Peter H. Schuck. New York: Foundation Press.

Suro, Roberto.

2003. "Remittance Senders and Receivers: Tracking the Transnational Channels." Washington, DC: Pew Hispanic Center.

———.

2005. "Attitudes about Voting in Mexican Elections and Ties to Mexico." Washington, DC: Pew Hispanic Center.

Suro, Roberto, and Gabriel Escobar.

2006. "Survey of Mexicans Living in the U.S. on Absentee Voting in Mexican Elections." Washington, DC: Pew Hispanic Center.

Sutherland, Howard.

2001. "Mexico Has a Plan for the U.S. Guess What It Is." Available at www .vdare.com/sutherland/mexico_plan.htm.

Taylor, Paul S.

1928–34. *Mexican Labor in the United States.* 12 vols. Berkeley: University of California Press.

———.

1933. *A Spanish-Mexican Peasant Community: Arandas in Jalisco, Mexico.* Berkeley: University of California Press.

Tessarolo, Giulivo, ed.

1962. *Exsul Familia: The Church's Magna Charta for Migrants.* Staten Island, NY: St. Charles Seminary.

Thomas, William I., and Florian Znaniecki.

1927. *The Polish Peasant in Europe and America.* New York: Knopf.

Thompson, Paul B.

1989. *The Nature of Work: An Introduction to Debates on the Labour Process.* London: Palgrave Macmillan.

Thunø, Mette, and Frank N. Pieke.

2005. "Institutionalizing Recent Rural Emigration from China to Europe: New Transnational Villages in Fujian." *International Migration Review* 39(2): 485–514.

Tilly, Charles.

1975. "Reflections on the History of European State-Making." Pp. 84–163 in *The Formation of National States in Western Europe,* edited by Charles Tilly. Princeton, NJ: Princeton University Press.

Torpey, John C.

2000.   *The Invention of the Passport: Surveillance, Citizenship, and the State.* Cambridge: Cambridge University Press.

Tsuda, Takeyuki.

2003.   *Strangers in the Ethnic Homeland: Japanese Brazilian Return Migration in Transnational Perspective.* New York: Columbia University Press.

Turner, Frederick C.

1967.   "The Compatibility of Church and State in Mexico." *Journal of Inter-American Studies* 9(4): 591–602.

———.

1968.   *The Dynamic of Mexican Nationalism.* Chapel Hill: University of North Carolina Press.

Uhlaner, Carole J.

1996.   "Latinos and Ethnic Politics in California: Participation and Preference." Pp. 33–72 in *Latino Politics in California,* edited by Aníbal Yáñez-Chávez. La Jolla: Center for U.S.-Mexican Studies, University of California, San Diego.

United Nations.

2000.   *Replacement Migration: Is It a Solution to Declining and Aging Populations?* New York: UN Population Division, Department of Economic and Social Affairs.

———.

2003.   *World Population Policies.* New York: UN Population Division, Department of Economic and Social Affairs.

———.

2007.   *Trends in Total Migrant Stock: The 2005 Revision.* New York: UN Population Division, Department of Economic and Social Affairs.

Uribe Salas, José A., and Álvaro Ochoa Serrano.

1990.   *Emigrantes del Oeste.* Mexico City: Consejo Nacional para la Cultura y las Artes.

Urry, John.

2000.   "Mobile Sociology." *British Journal of Sociology* 51(1): 185–203.

Valenzuela, M. Basilia.

2002.   "Municipalización, ciudadanía y migración en Los Altos de Jalisco." In *Experiencias Municipales de Cambio Institucional,* edited by Antonio Sánchez Bernal. Guadalajara: Universidad de Guadalajara.

Vallier, Ivan.

1971.   "The Roman Catholic Church: A Transnational Actor." *International Organization* 25(3): 479–502.

Vanderwood, Paul J.
  2004.   *Juan Soldado: Rapist, Murderer, Martyr, Saint.* Durham, NC: Duke University Press.
Vázquez, Josefina.
  1975.   *Nacionalismo y educación en México.* Mexico City: Colegio de México.
Verduzco, Gustavo, and Kurt Unger.
  1998.   "Impacts of Migration in Mexico." Pp. 395–435 in *Migration between Mexico and the United States: Binational Study.* Mexico City and Washington, DC: Mexican Ministry of Foreign Affairs and U.S. Commission on Immigration Reform.
Waldinger, Roger, and David Fitzgerald.
  2004.   "Transnationalism in Question." *American Journal of Sociology* 109(5): 1177–95.
Wallerstein, Immanuel M.
  1974.   *The Modern World-System; Capitalist Agriculture and the Origins of the European World-Economy in the Sixteenth Century.* New York: Academic Press.
Warner, R. Stephen.
  1993.   "Work in Progress toward a New Paradigm for the Sociological Study of Religion in the United States." *American Journal of Sociology* 98(5): 1044–93.
Weber, Eugen.
  1976.   *Peasants into Frenchmen: The Modernization of Rural France, 1870–1914.* Stanford: Stanford University Press.
Weber, Max.
  1946.   *From Max Weber: Essays in Sociology.* London: Routledge.
  ———.
  1978.   *Economy and Society.* Edited by Guenther Roth and Claus Wittich. Berkeley: University of California Press.
Weiner, Myron.
  1992.   "Security, Stability, and International Migration." *International Security* 17(3): 91–126.
Wimmer, Andreas.
  2002.   *Nationalist Exclusion and Ethnic Conflict: Shadows of Modernity.* Cambridge: Cambridge University Press.
  ———.
  2005.   "Elementary Forms of Ethnic Boundary Making: A Processual and Interactionist Approach." Paper no. 33, Theory and Research in Comparative Social Analysis, UCLA Department of Sociology.
Wimmer, Andreas, Richard J. Goldstone, Donald L. Horowitz, Ulrike Joras, and Conrad Schetter, eds.

2004.   *Facing Ethnic Conflicts: Toward a New Realism.* Lanham, MD: Rowman & Littlefield.

Winnie, William W.

1984.   *La Movilidad Demográfica.* Guadalajara: Universidad de Guadalajara.

Zepeda Lecuona, Guillermo.

2004.   *Crimen sin castigo: Procuración de justicia penal y Ministerio Público en México.* Mexico City: Centro de Investigación para el Desarrollo, A.C., Fondo de la Cultura Económica.

Zizzamia, Alba.

1989.   *A Vision Unfolding: The Scalabrinians in North America (1888–1988).* Staten Island, NY: Center for Migration Studies.

Zogby, John, and Luis Rubio.

2006.   "How We See Each Other: The CIDAC-Zogby International Survey of Attitudes in Mexico and the United States of America." Available at www.zogby.com/cidacfinalreport.pdf.

Zolberg, Aristide.

1981.   "International Migrations in Political Perspective." Pp. 3–27 in *Global Trends in Migration: Theory and Research on International Population Movements,* edited by Mary M. Kritz, Charles B. Keel, and Silvano M. Tomasi. Staten Island, NY: Center for Migration Studies.

———.

1997.   "The Great Wall against China." Pp. 111–121 in *Migration, Migration History, and History: New Perspectives,* edited by Jan Lucassen and Leo Lucassen. New York: Peter Lang.

———.

1999.   "Matters of State: Theorizing Immigration Policy." Pp. 71–93 in *The Handbook of International Migration: The American Experience,* edited by Charles Hirschman, Philip Kasinitz, and Josh DeWind. New York: Russell Sage Foundation.

———.

2006.   *A Nation by Design: Immigration Policy in the Fashioning of America.* New York: Russell Sage Foundation.

———.

2007.   "The Exit Revolution." In *Citizenship and Those Who Leave: The Politics of Emigration and Expatriation,* edited by Nancy Green and François Weil. Urbana: University of Illinois Press.

Zolberg, Aristide R., Astri Suhrke, and Sergio Aguayo.

1989.   *Escape from Violence: Conflict and the Refugee Crisis in the Developing World.* New York: Oxford University Press.

Index

Israel: immigrant policy, 17, 173
Israelis, 178
Italians, 73, 178–79, 194n33
Italy, 17, 31, 34, 173

Jalisciense Federation in Los Angeles,
103, 112
Jaliscienses, 42, 200n43; as internal migrants,
106–8; mexicanidad of, 126–27
Jalisco, 48, 49, 142, 143; bracero program, 50,
51; fund-raising for, 103–4; home commu-
nity projects, 64–65; labor shortages in,
40, 42–43; migration from, 6, 7; substance
abuse, 132–33
Jamaica, 22
Janos, 51
Japan, Japanese, 17, 178
Jiang Zemin, 24
job creation, 56
jobs hotlines, 59
Joppke, Christian, 17
Juárez, Benito, 165, 167
Juárez Clubs, 167

Khomeini, Ayatollah, 21

labor, 9, 18, 22, 24, 155, 191n35; agricultural,
1, 48–50, 66, 146–47, 152; contract, 41, 61,
67, 190n11; internal migrant, 53, 54–55,
148–51; shortages, 40, 42–43, 50–51; work
ethic and, 147–48
Labor Exchange Office, 53
labor markets, 152; internal, 53–54
labor unions, 50, 192n66
land reform, 45, 142
language: of migrants, 138–39, 162
La Ordeña, Rancho, 8–9
Latin America, 17, 26; dual nationality,
33–34; nationality and nationhood in,
29–30
Latino National Political Survey, 168
law enforcement, 19
Law of Migration (1930), 45
Law of Population (1947), 55
laws: international, 176; Mexican, 7
legislation: 1926 migration, 44
Léon, 105, 106, 110, 141
liberalism: Mexican, 38; political, 37, 69
loans: small business, 108
lobbying: Mexican, 167, 172; migrant, 26,
103, 123
London, 30
Los Altos de Jalisco, 106, 114, 127, 128, 130,
138, 199n24; Catholicism in, 76, 86, 91,

195n53; Cristero War, 43–44; migration
from, 6–7, 86, 105
Los Altos Household Head Survey,
182
Los Angeles, 6, 58, 91, 94, 103, 112, 117, 138;
Arandese migrants in, 10, 111
Los Angeles Police Department, 19
lotteries: bracero contracts, 51, 53

Madero, Francisco, 165
Magón, Flores, 165
malinchismo, 137
Mann, Michael, 34, 175
"Manual for Braceros," 83, 88
Manuel Doblado, 131
market economies, 22
marriage, 94
martial law, 44
Martinez, John, 43
Massey, Douglas, 28
mass media, 143
matrícula consulares, 160–61, 197n14
Maximillian, Emperor, 75
McGrew, Anthony, 27
medical care, 22
Medina Ascencio, Francisco, 107
membership categories, 129–30
mental health, 132
mercantilism, 21–22, 37, 79
Mexican Americans, 33, 167
Mexican Apostolic Catholic Church, 75
Mexican Catholic Union, 82, 106
Mexican Episcopal Conference, 88
mexicanidad, 33, 126–27, 178; maintaining,
80–81, 145
Mexican Migration Project (MMP), 7, 10(fig.),
111; methodology of, 181–84
Mexican Revolution, 39, 40; migration
during, 9, 41, 165, 166–67
Mexicans, 63(fig.); migration of, 22–23; PRD
and, 57–58
Mexican Unity Group, 56
Mexican War, 39
Mexico, 18, 24, 26, 68, 155, 191n61; Catholic
Church in, 34, 74–81, 175; dual national-
ism, 32–33; emigration from, 2–3; emigra-
tion policy, 68–69, 154; and international
border, 1–2; levels of migration, 5–6; and
U.S. sovereignty, 3–4
Mexico City, 108; hometown associations in,
104, 106, 122; migration to, 105–6
Michigan, 143
Michoacán, 6, 40, 43, 87, 89, 131, 156; bracero
program, 50, 51

Migrantes (weekly), 85, 87; on fund-raising, 90, 91, 92

migrante, 19, 21, 149, 178, 177, 199n41; Catholic Church administration of, 93–95; returning, 125–27; transnational, 16–17

migration, 22, 198n6; European Union, 27–28; internal, 42, 44, 53, 105–10, 194n45, 197n5; levels of, 5–6; negative impacts of, 128–29; permanent, 118–19; undocumented, 9–10

migration policy, 67–68

military, 22; conscription, 163–64

Missionaries of St. Charles (Scalabrinians), 73, 84, 85

MMP. *See* Mexican Migration Project

mobility, 21, 22, 175, 188n16

modernization, 122, 144; in agriculture, 145–46; Arandas, 106–8, 120–21

Monterrey, 52, 54

Montezuma (N.M.), 82

morals, 134, 143, 145

Morocco, 24

multiculturalism, 18, 96

Mussolini, Benito, 173

mutual aid societies, 108

NAFTA. *See* North American Free Trade Agreement

National Action Party (PAN), 59, 75, 112, 114, 166, 198n17

National Coordination of State Offices of Attention to Migrants, 64

National Council of La Raza, 167

National Development Plan, 58

National Guard, 2

National Hispanic Chamber of Commerce, 167

nationalism, 17, 22, 23, 40, 48, 77, 96, 128, 170, 171; cultural, 35, 162–63; dual, 32–33, 174

nationality, 29; cultural, 142–43; dual, 32–34, 58, 135–36, 161, 177, 179; multiple, 30–31, 178; self-identification, 159–60

nationalization, 23–24, 96; cultural, 162–63

National Latino Immigrant Survey, 168

National Migration Institute, 60

National Repatriation Committee, 47

National Research Council, 18–19

National Science and Technology Council, 59–60

National Solidarity Program, 119

National Survey of Democratic Dynamics (ENADID), 182

nationhood, 29–30

nation-states, 15, 18, 154; building, 3, 17, 19, 27, 162, 165, 175, 179; and Catholic Church, 14, 17; defining, 170–77; deterritorialization, 3, 4–5, 16, 29–30

naturalization: U.S., 31, 58, 87, 135–36, 163

Netherlands, 18

New York: Dominican candidates in, 172–73

Nogales, 42

norteños, 129, 130, 151–52; disorderly behavior of, 131–32, 133–34; negative views of, 125–27; substance abuse by, 132–33

North Africans, 18

North American Development Bank, 167

North American Free Trade Agreement (NAFTA), 63, 128, 167–68

Nuevo León, 52

Oaxaca, Oaxacans, 51, 124

obligations: and rights, 176–77

OECD. *See* Organization for Economic Cooperation and Development

Office of Attention to Jaliscienses Abroad (OFAJE), 99, 104, 112, 116

OMD. *See* Organization of Mexicans for Democracy

Orange County, 7, 103, 111, 114, 181

Organization for Economic Cooperation and Development (OECD), 22, 60, 192n68

Organization of Mexicans for Democracy (OMD), 56, 57

Ortiz Rubio, Pascual, 165

pachucos, 138

Paisano program, 58

Palestine, 173

PAN. *See* National Action Party

Paquete Paisano, 116

parishes, 196n77; migrants and, 73–74, 80; U.S., 80–81

Party of the Democratic Revolution (PRD), 56–57, 165; territorial issues, 57–58

passports, 44, 65–66

Pastorali Migratorum Cura, De (Paul VI), 74

patriotism, 143, 162

Paul VI, Pope: *De Pastorali Migratorum Cura,* 74

Paz, Octavio, 137–38

PCME. *See* Program for Mexican Communities Abroad

peasants, 51, 80

peasant unions, 50

Perez v. Brownell, 154

Persian Gulf, 18, 177

Pew Hispanic Center survey, 166

Philippines, 24, 176, 192n68

Text:	10/14 Palatino
Display:	Univers Condensed Light, Bauer Bodoni
Compositor:	Binghamton Valley Composition, LLC
Cartographer:	Bill Nelson
Printer and binder:	Maple-Vail Manufacturing Group